# Bioarchaeology and Social Theory

**Series editor**

Debra L. Martin
Professor of Anthropology
University of Nevada, Las Vegas
Las Vegas, NV, USA

More information about this series at http://www.springer.com/series/11976

Krista E. Latham • Alyson J. O'Daniel
Editors

# Sociopolitics of Migrant Death and Repatriation

## Perspectives from Forensic Science

Springer

*Editors*
Krista E. Latham
Biology & Anthropology Departments
University of Indianapolis
Indianapolis, IN, USA

Alyson J. O'Daniel
Anthropology Department
University of Indianapolis
Indianapolis, IN, USA

Bioarchaeology and Social Theory
ISBN 978-3-319-61865-4 ISBN 978-3-319-61866-1 (eBook)
DOI 10.1007/978-3-319-61866-1

Library of Congress Control Number: 2017951280



Printed on acid-free paper

This Springer imprint is published by Springer Nature
The registered company is Springer International Publishing AG
The registered company address is: Gewerbestrasse 11, 6330 Cham, Switzerland

# Foreword

In 2010, the director of the award-winning documentary, *Who Is Dayani Cristal?*, was retracing the footsteps of a man who had died while trying to cross the US-Mexico border and following the body through the process of identification and repatriation. Marc Silver, the director, had accompanied the sheriff's office to the scene on the day the man's body had been found in the desert, just 20 min from Tucson. He then spent weeks in the Pima County Office of the Medical Examiner, following every step of the identification process. When the remains of the Honduran man, Dilcy, were positively identified at the medical examiner's office, Marc accompanied the body to the funeral home, and then onto the same flight itinerary from Tucson to Atlanta, and then to Tegucigalpa, the capital of Honduras. Upon arrival in Tegucigalpa, Marc greeted Dilcy's family, who had driven 8 h from the countryside in order to pick up Dilcy's body from the airport. After waiting for the passengers and cargo to exit the plane, an airline representative told the family that the casket containing Dilcy's remains had not made it onto the flight from Atlanta to Tegucigalpa. Apparently, luggage took priority over caskets, and with a full flight, Dilcy's body had stayed on the tarmac overnight in Atlanta.

In the current global economy, some bodies can move across borders with relative ease, while other bodies face numerous obstacles, walls, and blockages, even when they are no longer living. The British filmmaker recording the story of the man who had died arrived in Honduras unimpeded. The filmmaker's luggage, and the luggage of the other passengers on the plane, arrived without complication. But a dead body, something traditionally guarded, respected, and treated with care, had been left to wait on the tarmac alone, not even making the cut to be treated as cargo. Dilcy's family made the long drive back home that night, returning a few days later to retrieve his body and take him home where they could finally care for him, months after he had disappeared in the desert.

Much as migrants, refugees, and immigrants face various obstacles to mobility during life, they also face impediments to movement after death. Undocumented Americans often avoid major highways, state borders, or government offices for fear of deportation. Refugees struggle to get a meeting with an asylum officer, and immigrants spend years longing to see the faces of close family members who live outside the country due to travel restrictions on their visas. These blockages to movement, exclusions from access to services, and walls between families continue in the world of the dead.

This powerful anthology offers a timely conversation on the work done by families, forensic scientists, and human rights advocates to care for the dead in a context that makes such caregiving political. The remains of at least 7,000 people have been discovered in the desert borderlands over the past 20 years. The true number of dead is unknown, not only because of the vast and remote nature of the geography of the border where many remains will never be found, but also because, in essence, no one is counting. The only annual numbers that address migrant deaths for the entire border, rather than one state or county, are released by the Border Patrol. Border Patrol has admitted that the agency does not collect these numbers systematically but rather compiles them based on at-will reporting from local counties. In turn, many of these counties, especially in southern Texas, do not differentiate between cases of deceased migrants and any other medicolegal case managed by officials overseeing autopsy and investigation. Many have not kept paper records, let alone digital records, of decedent cases for years past. The unidentified dead have been buried in unmarked graves in dozens of cemeteries in counties from California to Texas. The data regarding the dead has been scattered like ashes along the entire US-Mexico border.

The lack of an organized effort to even count the dead indicates intentional ignorance and the maintenance of certain blind spots on the part of the state. It was, after all, US federal border policies that caused the massive increase in migrant deaths in the early 2000s that never decreased, despite substantial decreases in the estimated number of migrants attempting the crossing. It is inconvenient for the state when these bodies are visible. Many of the chapters in this edition discuss the various challenges faced by those wishing to find the missing or name the dead. The work of connecting the dead back to their names, identities, families, and homes in this context has become complicated and challenging because such a project works against the grain of an increasingly organized system that produces disappearance, erasure, and silence. By naming the border's dead, forensic scientists declare that these dead, too, can take up space in the public sphere and historical record. Evidence is not just produced for the legal courts, but also for the court of public discourse, memory, and history. The word "evidence" derived from the Latin, "videre," to see, means "to make visible." The work of forensic scientists along the border makes these dead visible, and in the current sociopolitical context where the bodies of Latin American workers are often exploited in life and left to be nameless in death, this is uniquely powerful.

In addition to engaging in a highly political project of visibility and care, forensic scientists and the family advocacy organizations and human rights defenders working with them are also revealing the various forms of violence that flourish and are condensed at the US-Mexico border. From the exploitation of Latin American workers and the lack of access migrants have to legal mechanisms for working in the United States, to the structural violence of malnutrition and poverty, to the denial of information to the families of the disappeared and the lack of funding for identification efforts, the authors in this volume are using the science and technology of forensics to reveal evidence of crimes that have taken place in the darkness and obscurity created by time, distance, historical amnesia, and alternate facts backed by the power of the state. The authors in this volume are practicing a counter-hegemonic forensics that reappropriates techniques such as exhumation, evidence collection, and witness interviewing to monitor and record violence perpetrated by the state.

This project of course is not the first to turn the powerful lens of forensics on the state. Indeed, the international human rights movement defined by war crimes tribunals would not have been nearly as successful in holding genocidal regimes accountable without the science and technology of forensics, especially forensic anthropology. However, the authors in this volume are at the cutting edge of using forensics to reveal as violent those actions and inactions of the powerful which often fail to be recognized as such. By applying tools developed in contexts seen as legitimately violent, forensic experts recast the border landscape as a space where something has gone terribly wrong. Their work in this space is producing new publics, new forums, and new possibilities for justice.

This volume comes at a critical historical moment. Once again, during the 2016 election and the inauguration of Donald Trump, the geographical space of the border has been thrust into the national spotlight as a space to be feared, monitored, and dominated. The border has historically been used as a nationalism factory, relied upon to violently demarcate those legitimate members of the nation-state from those seen as external and threatening to the increasingly xenophobic definition of America. In the neoliberal version of state violence, acts of intimidation, brutality, and terror are outsourced. In the case of the border, this violence is outsourced to the desert, to the sea, to narcotraffickers, to border bandits, to citizen militia groups like the Minutemen, and to smugglers. At the border, one of the most heavily surveilled landscapes in the world, all forms of violence flourish. The victims of such violence are then left without official avenues for recourse to justice or services of care. In the absence of the welfare state, citizen groups, nonprofits, academics, students, and volunteer forensic scientists step in to provide relief, care, and justice where it is being demanded. In many cases, the victims tend to themselves, finding support and resilience within their own families and communities. Several decedents brought to the Pima County Office of the Medical Examiner were recovered with handmade stretchers that had been crafted by the traveling companions of the deceased in desperate attempts to save their lives and preserve the dead body. *Aguilas del Desierto*, an organization in California that does search and rescue on the border, was founded by the brother of a man who died crossing the border. A group of families of some of the thousands of missing in Mexico hired a forensic archeologist to train them how to find and exhume graves and have taken it upon themselves to unearth the bodies of their children.

Whether done by forensic scientist volunteers or by families of the dead and missing themselves, the work to care for, identify, and repatriate the dead in the context of the US-Mexico border is predominantly done by women. This labor is often invisible, dismissed, or devalued. It is life-saving work. It is life-saving in the sense that it declares the dead to be fully human. To identify a nameless dead body is to reconnect that person to an individual name, a memory, and a person. To refuse to give up the search for someone who has disappeared is to claim that they existed.

This book is important and rare. Students, scholars, and practitioners alike have the opportunity in this volume to hear from writers who have each not only done the labor of research and writing but have also shared food with the families of the missing, held the bones of the dead in their hands, stood in the graves of the unidentified removing shovel after shovel of dirt, organized countless meetings with officials to demand humane policies, made phone call after phone call to authorities to seek information, and searched for justice in countless visible and invisible ways. The authors in this volume are both witnesses and experts. They offer their testimonies with the confidence that both the legal courts and the courts of public opinion not open to them now will be open in the future. That can only happen with the support of more witnesses to the violence occurring along the US-Mexico border.

Colibri Center for Human Rights
Tucson, AZ, USA

Robin Reineke

# Preface

This collection of studies on the *Sociopolitics of Migrant Death and Repatriation: Perspectives from Forensic Science* is the first in this series to address current events as they are playing out along the borderlands of the United States and Mexico. As Dr. Robin Reineke, executive director of the Colibri Center for Human Rights, says in her foreword, "... this book is important and rare." I could not agree more! The chapters are focused on the twin (and entwined) themes of practicing forensic science within a global historical and political context and reflections about what the production of forensic knowledge on this topic means for human rights and social justice. This is not just a book about case studies and how the work of forensic anthropology is carried out, but it offers a critical reflection of how forensic science is situated within broader interacting spheres of influence. The chapters and case studies shared in this volume are powerful and moving, and they demonstrate the multiple roles that forensic anthropologists must play today in the complex borderscape that runs hundreds of miles in all directions. In these chapters we learn that the border is shaped by dynamic forces that are constantly being transgressed and redefined based on who is doing the crossing and at what point in the series of events this crossing happens. Thus, the editors have encouraged their authors to take an intersectionality approach where they simultaneously consider history, power, and scientific practice as they bear on identification and (when possible) repatriation. While everyone knows that people die crossing the border, virtually no one knows (except those involved in the numerous nonprofit and other organizations that do this work) how the science of exhuming, identifying, and repatriating these people back to their families is carried out.

Every chapter presents a devastating yet engaging eyewitness set of accounts about the nature of the crisis at the border and the challenges of remaining a so-called neutral scientist in the midst of emotion-laden interactions on numerous levels with players from many different spheres of power and influence. Many of these chapters engage with the concept of humanitarian science as a heuristic to demonstrate the ways that in applying their scientific knowledge, workers hope to help alleviate suffering and pain in their effort to do their jobs. Other chapters focus on how working at the border permits participation in the larger social justice movements that ebb and flow depending on a myriad of influences.

The first seven chapters in this volume provide a valuable primer on the complexities of border deaths and the attempt to return those who died to their families. All of these early chapters connect what is happening at local levels and specific places along the border with the broader context of global politics and history. The economic push-pull of emigration out of many different countries in Latin America into Mexico and over the border is addressed through multiple lenses in these early chapters. Some authors present vivid accounts of the almost unthinkable dangers that migrating people encounter, and almost all of the first seven chapters highlight how border policies directly shape who lives and who dies.

The second half of the book invites authors to reflect on their work as scientists and the ways that the bureaucracy and legal frameworks stymie their efforts. In these chapters we see that only some bodies are identified and repatriated, while others are more difficult to do so. In these chapters the reader will appreciate the ways that authors attempt to overcome their frustrations with various agencies, policies, and the public in order to be able to collaborate and work toward common goals.

If the reader only reads the inspiring and haunting preface followed by the introductory and concluding chapters by the coeditors, they would have a good working knowledge about the challenges and complexities of doing work at the border as forensic scientists. The case studies however are so richly detailed and nuanced, so carefully laid out, and so engagingly presented, it is doubtful that any reader will stop reading once they start. Each section of the book and the chapters within sections all reflect upon different aspects of the challenges posed by this work, and many offer points of light where there is movement toward affirming and carrying out social justice and creating new ways to work toward universal human rights, especially in the final concluding chapter. My guess is that this volume will inspire the next generation of forensic anthropologists/bioarchaeologists to continue where this generation leaves off.

This volume is quite unlike any edited volume on forensic anthropology and border work currently available. The collective body of theories and self-reflection is what sets this volume apart from all others. Methodologically, being able to provide an identity for those who have died is but the tip of the iceberg, and these methods are applied with respect and professionalism. It is clear in the writing of these chapters that this is a dedicated group of scholars for whom the work is neither easy nor simple.

Forensic anthropology and bioarchaeology both have similar goals in wanting to be of use in the contemporary world by identifying the dead and then working within a rich context of additional information to be able to tell a full and empirically based story or to provide a history of individuals who died. Forensic anthropologists such as those who authored the chapters in this book are producing a body of scholarship that demonstrates the relevance of this kind of work for not only the unknown ancient past but also for, in this case, the present crisis at the border. The empirical data combined with other lines of evidence are producing a far more accurate, nuanced, and variable narrative of not only why and how people emigrate from their places of origin to the United States but also documenting and "witnessing" for those who didn't survive the crossing.

Las Vegas, NV, USA Debra L. Martin

# Acknowledgments

The editors would like to thank the contributors for their chapters and dedication to issues of social justice. It has been a pleasure working with you over the last year to create this volume. We would like to extend our gratitude to Helen Brandt, Erica Cantor, Jessica Miller, Leann Rizor, and Haley Rock for reviewing the material and formatting the chapters. We would like to acknowledge Dr. Debra Martin for inviting us to contribute to her new book series on Bioarchaeology and Social Theory and express our gratitude to everyone at Springer for their support and patience throughout this process.

# Contents

# Contributors

## Authors

**Eric J. Bartelink** California State University, Chico, CA, USA

**Jared S. Beatrice** Department of Sociology and Anthropology, The College of New Jersey, Ewing, NJ, USA

**Cate E. Bird** Forensic National Advisor, International Committee of the Red Cross, Republic of Georgia, Tampa, FL, USA

**Timothy P. Gocha** University of Nevada, Las Vegas, NV, USA

**Christine Kovic** University of Houston-Clear Lake, Houston, TX, USA

**Krista E. Latham** Biology and Anthropology Departments, University of Indianapolis, Indianapolis, IN, USA

**Justin Maiers** Human Identification Center, University of Indianapolis, Indianapolis, IN, USA

**Daniel E. Martínez** School of Sociology, University of Arizona, Tucson, AZ, USA

**Alyson J. O'Daniel** Anthropology Department, University of Indianapolis, Indianapolis, IN, USA

**Dawn Paley** Meritorious Autonomous University of Puebla, Puebla, Mexico

**Adriana Paramo** Low Residency MFA Program, Fairfield University, Fairfield, CT, USA

**Angela Soler** Office of Chief Medical Examiner, New York, NY, USA

**Gabriella Soto** School of Anthropology, University of Arizona, Tucson, AZ, USA

**Ryan Strand** South Texas Human Rights Center, Falfurrias, TX, USA

**M. Katherine Spradley** Texas State University, San Marcos, TX, USA

**Wendy A. Vogt** Department of Anthropology, Indiana University-Purdue University Indianapolis, Indianapolis, IN, USA

# About the Editors

**Dr. Krista E. Latham** is an associate professor of biology and anthropology at the University of Indianapolis, where she has taught since 2007. She is also the director of the University of Indianapolis Human Identification Center. She received her B.S. in biology and chemistry from the University of North Texas in 2000, her M.S. in human biology from the University of Indianapolis in 2003, and her M.A. and Ph.D. in anthropology from Temple University in 2006 and 2008. Dr. Latham is a board-certified forensic anthropologist (D-ABFA) and a fellow of the American Academy of Forensic Sciences. Her research investigates different aspects of human biological variation, skeletal biology, population genetics, and skeletal DNA, and she has produced numerous scientific publications. She currently serves as a consulting forensic anthropologist for police, coroners, and pathologists in the Midwestern United States and has delivered numerous lectures for state and local agencies around the country. Dr. Latham also serves as a DNA expert in the US Federal Court System.

**Dr. Alyson J. O'Daniel** is an assistant professor of medical and cultural anthropology at the University of Indianapolis in Indianapolis, Indiana. Her scholarship and teaching explore intersections of state power, policy, and practice, social and bodily vulnerability, and health-care inequality in United States. She has worked for 14 years on discerning racial, class, and gendered dimensions of HIV-related health inequalities and the relationships between federal public health-care policy and the structure and content of local initiatives for the health care and support of HIV–positive women. During this time, she has conducted extensive ethnographic research among HIV-positive women and their service providers in Denver, Colorado, "Midway," North Carolina, and Indianapolis, Indiana. Her HIV/AIDS–related work has been published in journals such as *Medical Anthropology*, *Human Organization*, and *Transforming Anthropology*. Her recent book-length ethnography, *Holding On: African American Women Surviving HIV/AIDS*, was published by University of Nebraska Press in 2016. More recently, Dr. O'Daniel's research program has expanded to include examining response to the migrant death crisis in South Texas. In partnership with the humanitarian forensic science team from the University of Indianapolis, the project explores volunteer forensic science as a crucial, yet politically fraught, part of the human migration story.

# Part I
# Beyond Local Jurisdictions: Science in a Global Web of Relations

# Chapter 1
# Introduction

**Alyson J. O'Daniel and Krista E. Latham**

## Responding to Death at the Border

Since 1998, more than 6,500 migrants have died along the US-Mexico border (Wexler 2016). Historically, undocumented border crossers have entered the US by traveling the border terrains nearest California (Rose 2012). Changes in border policy and practice in the early 2000s, however, funneled would-be border crossers into more treacherous landscapes of Arizona and, more recently, Texas borderlands. This shift has been catastrophic for migrants who find themselves in the far reaches of the desert with little, if any, resort to help when they are lost, dehydrated, injured, or otherwise endangered (De León 2015). As a result, known migrant deaths in these states have steadily risen.

Arizona has now had more than 15 years to develop the infrastructure necessary to address the large number of forensic investigations associated with this mass death scenario. The Medical examiner's system provides resources, such as centralized locations to conduct scientific investigations into identity, the equipment necessary for autopsies, skeletal examinations or sampling for DNA profiling, and personnel that are trained and qualified to perform these examinations. The medico-legal authorities have best practices in place that enable high identification rates of migrant deaths due to collaborations between the scientists, law enforcement entities, and humanitarian organizations (Anderson and Spradley 2016).

The crisis in Texas, however, only recently garnered significant public attention when, in 2012, Texas surpassed Arizona for the number of undocumented migrant

A.J. O'Daniel (✉)
Anthropology Department, University of Indianapolis, Indianapolis, IN, USA
e-mail: odaniela@uindy.edu

K.E. Latham
Biology and Anthropology Departments, University of Indianapolis, Indianapolis, IN, USA
e-mail: lathamke@uindy.edu



K.E. Latham, A.J. O'Daniel (eds.), *Sociopolitics of Migrant Death and Repatriation*, Bioarchaeology and Social Theory,
DOI 10.1007/978-3-319-61866-1_1

deaths. As a result, an institutionalized notion of migrant death as a crisis is still relatively new in the state and is therefore largely underfunded and under-addressed. Brooks County bore a particular burden with 130 recovered sets of presumed migrant remains in 2012 alone. In response, forensic volunteers from a variety of organizations and institutions have been donating their time, materials, and expertise to aid in the recovery, identification, and repatriation of perished migrants found along migrant routes in Texas. The attention and awareness raised by these efforts and by vocal nongovernmental organizations helped in securing some funds from the state for autopsies and DNA sampling of unidentified migrant remains discovered in Brooks County. However, no funding was provided to cover the exhumation and analysis of migrants discovered prior to 2013 and buried in the Sacred Heart Cemetery located in Falfurrias, the county seat (Anderson and Spradley 2016).

As case studies in migrant identification and repatriation, Arizona and Texas both make clear that the challenging work of exhumation, identification, and repatriation requires cooperation and communication among various and differently situated entities. Cooperative efforts may include volunteer exhumation teams, local authorities, federal agents, university laboratories, human rights organizations, family members in Mexico and Central and South America, and various Latin American Consulates (Fleishman et al. 2017; Hinkes 2008). The work of migrant identification and repatriation thus entails communication, information sharing, and resource coordination among various local and national governmental and nongovernmental groups, as well as between volunteers and those whose job involves border issues on a regular basis. While all are working toward a common goal, differences in organizational structure, missions, goals, motivations, and access to resources complicate the effort. The migrant death crisis is in this way simultaneously a local, transnational, and supranational phenomenon that is as much about conditions producing migrant death as it is about conditions structuring the response. The enormity and dynamism of the task at hand have presented several challenges for all involved, including in the realms of communication, organization, accountability, funding, and dissemination of information.

In this volume, we use the interconnected lenses of history, power, and scientific practice as our vantage point from which to examine the migrant identification and repatriation process. In relation to broader social, political, and economic contexts, we illuminate how the daily work of forensic scientists in this setting may reproduce familiar forms of sociality and knowledge-power hierarchies at the same time that they raise new political, moral, social, and cultural imperatives in response to the values and practices of differently situated actors, entities, and organizations. Seen in this light, the work of forensic science in the US border crisis is perhaps socially and politically fraught as a crucial nexus wherein social relations and institutions of knowledge production and dissemination meet other kinds of state and non-state actors. Our dominant interest is in spotlighting how sociopolitical conditions and processes, broadly conceived, shape the work of forensic scientists and then in how forensic scientists themselves navigate and transform social relationships and power dynamics circumscribing their work. This volume thus takes as its central task the creation of pause suspension of familiar and perhaps normalizing ways of thinking and writing about migrant death from vantage points of forensic science in favor of critical reflection and an expanded view of the forms of engagement engendered by death at the border.

## Global History as Strategy of Critical Reflection

At the heart of this book is the recognition that forensic science applied to the US border region crisis operates within a broader political economic context. That is to say that the science of migrant identification unfolds within and as part of local and global histories, realities, and relationships. In order to understand the crisis of migrant death and the complexities of crisis response at the US-Mexico border, we must locate and map where and how the local work of migrant identification connects with global systems and history. It is through this historical context of "the global" that we come to understand forensic scientists as specifically situated social actors who may at times wield a great deal of power as it relates to the creation and circulation of knowledge and discourses of migration and migrant death. Challenging ourselves to locate the work of migrant identification within global frames of history has sharpened our focus on the role of social, political, and economic factors in structuring the conditions under which science is applied in this context.

While forensic scientists often find comfort in the neutrality of the scientific method, the politically and emotionally charged environment associated with practice in a humanitarian crisis context requires them to balance neutrality and engagement in novel ways. This shifting balance between neutrality and engagement provides a window onto forensic science as operating within and shaped by processes of global capitalism, at times itself influencing and (re)producing those processes through the work. At a basic level, forensic attention to migrant death responds to changing parameters of US border policy and shifting sociopolitical conditions in Latin America. Yet, as scientists navigate complexities of the work, they come to shape the meanings and realities of local ideological and material landscapes in sometimes surprising ways.

## A Preliminary Note on Terms and Labels

As authors in this volume underscore, the work of migrant identification takes place at the well-traversed and entangled intersections of biological and cultural inquiry (Birkby et al. 2008; Goodman and Leatherman 2001) and humanitarianism and human rights (Fassin 2012; Bornstein and Redfield 2008), as well as at the intersections of scientific neutrality and politics of engagement (Low and Merry 2010; Rylko-Bauer et al. 2006; Marks 2000). No doubt, the conceptual and reflective work of forensic scientists here follows the deep footsteps of anthropologists from across the subdisciplinary divides. It is our aim that, in this moment of pause, the reflections and conceptual and contextual work represented in the chapters to come will expand the field of vision currently used to make sense of forensic science practiced in the border region. Seeking to move beyond the common methodological filters predominating the forensic science record of migrant identification, we conceptualize the forensic science of migrant death as socially productive, politically fraught, and power laden within global contexts of neoliberal capitalist expansion (see Chaps. 3 and 4 in this volume) and structural violence (see Chap. 5 in this volume) and the concomitant ascendance of volunteerism as the preferred response to social crises (see Chap. 7 in this volume). We seek to open dialogue for a politics of engagement among forensic anthropologists working in the charged terrains of humanitarian science. By politics of engagement, we refer to various forms of advocacy, collaboration, and activism that consciously position us within public dialogue and practice for purposes of making a political impact (Mullins 2011).

Yet, within our self-conscious attempt to construct a broadened perspective, we are cognizant that some of the categorical distinctions and definitional lines authors use in this volume to talk about the work of migrant identification remain murky. This is in part because the motivations of individual scientists and practical realities of humanitarian forensic identification are themselves varied and negotiated in their institutionally specific contexts (Rosenblatt 2015). Some of our authors, for example, are employed within human rights organizations, while others approach their work from settings of academia. Each context may entail different constraining and facilitating factors for the work, conditions which no doubt shape how we think and talk about the forensic science of migrant identification. We therefore see this volume as an opportunity to illuminate, rather than resolve, these kinds of conceptual variations within forensic science as applied to migrant death in the US border region. It is our contention that, whatever the language used, forensic science as applied to migrant death is a kind of sociopolitical undertaking.

Our readers may notice, for example, that for some of our contributing authors, the phrase *humanitarian science* provides a predominant framework and set of discourses through which they imagine and narrate the motivations and patterns of forensic science in the border region. They perhaps implicitly depoliticize the work and position the forensic science of migrant death within the range of a number of scientific activities and methodologies carried out in service of improving the human condition. Fields as diverse as mathematics, biomedicine, genetics, chemistry, engineering, and botany have all been practiced as efforts to alleviate pressing and persistent problems of health, hunger, disaster, poverty, and underdevelopment. Forensic science in the US border region thus articulates with a longer history and tradition of easing the physical, psychological, and social suffering of populations suffering misfortune (Redfield and Bornstein 2008). The application of forensic science is for some practitioners a project fundamentally concerned with alleviating the suffering of families for whom the grief process is suspended by lack of concrete knowledge concerning the fate of their loved ones (see Chap. 5 in this volume). Migrant identification is thus literally focused on identity as a moral and "compassionate response" to the misery presumably endured by family members who are missing their loved ones.

Even so, as Fassin (2012) points out, humanitarianism is an inherently political undertaking. Highlighting humanitarianism as a particular form of contemporary governance whereby politics of rights and justice have been replaced by politics of compassion, Fassin's work challenges us to consider how possibilities and practices of forensic science in the border region reflect and inform a wider global moral economy that is itself rooted in a particular political economic reality. Our stance is that we must begin to think critically about places and practices of migrant death, identification, and repatriation as important modes of enacting or resisting administrative and hierarchical rationalities of governance (Das and Poole 2004). How might the forensic science of migrant identification reproduce and/or challenge modes of governance? Is it possible that by positioning this work as "humanitarian," we eclipse the state violence that produced its need? Alternatively, to what extent can we envision a forensic science ethics of compassion? And, how might such an ethics cultivate new affects, language, methodologies, relationships, and material conditions in service of addressing on-the-ground realities of migrant death?

For other scholars in this volume, the forensic science of migrant death is explicitly articulated as part of a broader project for *social justice* and *human rights*. Those working in this vein seek to name and confront policy-driven wrongdoings and tend to frame their work as contending with inhumane effects of capitalist expansion and border policy (see Chaps. 4 and 6 in this volume). In these cases, practitioners may well position their work within the more specific history and trajectory of forensic investigation practiced in fields of global activism (Rosenblatt 2015). For example, Dr. Clyde Snow, a prominent US forensic anthropologist, began training anthropology students in Argentina to locate, recover, and identify the bodies of thousands of individuals that "disappeared" in the 1970s and 1980s. The formation of the Equipo Argentino Antropologia Forense/Argentine Forensic Anthropology Team (EAAF) signaled an important milestone in the history of forensic anthropology: the recognition that proper forensic science technique in combination with respect for the wishes of victims' relatives and communities was the best approach to death investigations in a humanitarian crisis context. This combined scientific and cultural approach involved the stakeholders in all aspects of the investigation and worked to advocate on behalf of the victims (Fondebrider and Scheinsohn 2015; Fondebrider 2009; Doretti and Snow 2003).

Such an approach explicitly recognizes that forensic scientists are uniquely positioned as cultural brokers who inhabit political frontiers of inequality and, in so doing, may well represent a new pathway for imagining social justice and human rights. In assuming such a stance, forensic scientists may find themselves working from both within and *outside* familiar positions relative to law. In what ways do processes and ideologies of migrant death and repatriation reflect an ethics of solidarity and/or care that transcends national borders? What are the relationships between forensic science practitioners in this setting and human rights advocates and the various organizations with which they affiliate? In what ways and through what various forms does the forensic science of migrant death articulate with rights claims and the documentation of rights violations? How might the scientific authority of forensic science provide a site where new kinds of political claims and challenges be articulated?

Still for other practitioners, the politically and morally charged languages of humanitarianism and human rights don't always map onto the local immediacy of the work or the ethical imperative of scientific objectivity that is embedded more generally within forensic science. As some in this volume have articulated, maintaining a language of scientific neutrality protects the integrity of the work and reduces the capacity for media sensationalism and public misunderstanding (see Chap. 8 in this volume). It also, however, may assist in bringing together diverse stakeholders with varied levels of interest in supporting diverse migrant identification activities. In some instances then, our colleagues describe the work they do as *civic duty.* In this vein, migrant identification is a form of volunteerism aimed at alleviating the resource-related stresses and strains that the crisis poses for local medicolegal systems. In this sense, the work is enabled by construing forensic scientific investigation as having capacity to transcend political subjectivities, economic interests, and social dynamics characterizing migrant death and identification initiatives.

As the practice of forensic science in the US border region crisis continues to evolve, so too will the language and concepts used to describe it. Our hope with this volume is to perhaps open up a new set of conversations that explores the forensic science of migrant identification as acting within and on a broader sociopolitical context. In undertaking this task, practitioners of forensic science in this setting have an incredible opportunity to deepen our abilities to build collaborative knowledge and action that is cognizant of our position within the human migration story.

## Scope and Organization of the Book

Our approach to forensic science perspectives on migrant death and repatriation grapples in fine detail with the politically charged and sometimes conflicting terrains of scientific inquiry, state intelligence and border control, humanitarian effort, international relations, and supranational rights. The volume is based on deeply and critically reflective analyses, submitted by individual scholars, wherein they navigate and position themselves as social actors embedded within and perhaps partially constituted by relations of power, cultural ideologies, and the social structures characterizing this moment in history. As stand-alone chapters, each contribution addresses a different variation on themes of power relations, production of knowledge, and reflexivity in practice. In sum, however, the chapters of this book trace relationships between institutions, entities, and individuals comprising the landscapes of migrant death and repatriation and consider their articulation with sociopolitical dynamics of the state. For purposes of flow and analytical clarity, the book is organized into two sections.

In the first sequence of chapter "Beyond local jurisdictions: Forensic Science in a Global Web of Relations," readers are introduced to the transnational phenomenon of migrant death and repatriation. The section begins with a general discussion of migrant death and repatriation within a global context (Paramo) and moves to discuss these issues within the context of Latin America more specifically. The readers get an introduction to the economic, social and political circumstances that structure migration from Latin America and shape the social lives of undocumented border crossers who perish along their journeys. Paley's chapter traces a long history of conquest and capitalist expansion, inviting our readers to consider the usefulness of a "long-range view" for teasing out complexities of migrant flows. She is followed by Kovic and Vogt's respective discussions of often unrecognized aspects of migration, the violence of the journey and lasting effects on and strategies of the families of the missing. Both authors carefully situate their analyses within current logics and realities of global capitalism outlined by Paley. Soto and Martinez further invite readers to thicken their understanding of undocumented migration with respect to changing US border policy and practice over the last two decades. Carefully tracing the dangers inherent to current border policy, the authors illuminate how policy shapes migrant death via strategic use of harsh desert terrain. The final chapter in this section contextualizes forensic scientists themselves within the global contexts outlined in previous chapters. O'Daniel traces the rise of community disinvestment and volunteerism alongside anti-immigrant sentiment in order to highlight the conditions under which forensic volunteers in the US engage with migrant identification via varied forms of social obligation. These macro-level processes shape the everyday circumstances of resources and social relationships described by the scientists in local settings in the following section.

This second section of chapter "Producing and Situating Forensic Science Knowledge" focuses on exploring systems and processes of knowledge production characterizing a forensic science of migrant death and repatriation. Through in-depth elaboration of and reflection on the bureaucratic and methodological processes and challenges of their work, forensic investigators contributing to this section grapple with the social implications of their scientific practice and how forensic knowledge is constituted through relationships between various forms of data and inquiry. Additionally many reflect on the personal and political motivations, ethical concerns, professional constraints, and/or facilitating factors they experience as forensic scientists working under conditions of international humanitarian crisis. Latham and Strand begin this section by situating forensic archeologists conducting the exhumations in a complex role where they function as both the forensic scientists that are uniquely trained to unearth the migrant burials and as humanitarian volunteers that act to bring awareness and resources to the identification initiatives by telling the narratives of migrant death. Solar and Beatrice then introduce readers to the expanded role of forensic anthropologists beyond their traditional scientific obligations while operating in a humanitarian crisis, which they call the biosocial approach. This approach includes the traditional tools of identification in additional to documenting indicators of physiological stress and poor oral health that suggest an embodied structural violence experienced by this migrant population. They are followed by Bartelink and Gocha and colleague's discussions of the complexities of identification and why some bodies may have a greater chance of being identified than others. These authors discuss circumstances ranging from preconceived notions of the value of the life in question, to recovery efforts in the field and at the cemetery, to laboratory techniques that may impact the amount of time until or chances of identification. Bird and Maiers then explore ethical concerns and considerations regarding how forensic science in the context of a humanitarian crisis may differ from forensic science practiced in more traditional contexts. They discuss the difficulty of navigating complex relationships with multiple agencies and stakeholders and emphasize that personal interests and concerns must be put aside in order to collaborate for the common goal of identification.

From start to finish, the texts gathered here allow for study of migrant identification and repatriation as social practice that is firmly entrenched within and responsive to global and local sociopolitical processes. The point of examining forensic science in this context is to invite new ways of thinking about the work as it unfolds at intersections not commonly explored through the lens of identification. In the process, we come to differently see and understand the nature of forensic science as it is conceptualized, enacted, and applied in contexts of crisis. Our hope is that this volume represents an entry point for focused and sustained attention to a broadened conceptualization of the sociopolitics of migrant death that include ways in which remains of perished migrants may animate novel forms of sociality in forensic science and beyond.

## References


Anderson, B. E., & Spradley, K. (2016). The role of the anthropologist in the identification of migrant remains in the American Southwest. *Academic Forensic Pathology, 6*(3), 432–438.

Birkby, W. H., Fenton, T. W., & Anderson, B. E. (2008). Identifying Southwest Hispanics using nonmetric traits and the cultural profile. *Journal of Forensic Science, 53*(1), 29–33.

Das, V., & Poole, D. (2004). *Anthropology in the margins of the state*. Santa Fe: School of American Research.

De León, J. (2015). *The land of open graves: Living and dying on the migrant trail*. Berkeley: University of California Press.

Doretti, M., & Snow, C. C. (2003). Forensic anthropology and human rights: The Argentine experience. In D. W. Steadman (Ed.), *Hard evidence, case studies in forensic anthropology* (pp. 290–310). Upper Saddle River: Prentice Hall.

Fassin, D. (2012). *Humanitarian reason: A moral history of the present*. Berkeley: University of California Press.

Fleishman, J. M., Kendell, A. E., Eggers, C. C., & Fulginiti, L. C. (2017). Undocumented border crosser deaths in Arizona: Expanding intrastate collaborative efforts in identification. *Journal of Forensic Sciences*. doi:10.1111/1556-4029.13368.

Fondebrider, L. (2009). The application of forensic anthropology to the investigation of political violence: Perspectives from South America. In S. Blau & D. H. Ubelaker (Eds.), *Handbook of forensic anthropology and archaeology* (pp. 65–74). Walnut Creek: Left Coast Press.

Fondebrider, L., & Scheinsohn, V. (2015). Forensic archaeology: The Argentinian way. In W. J. M. Groen, N. Marquez-Grant, & R. Janaway (Eds.), *Forensic archaeology: A global perspective*. Chichester: Wiley-Blackwell.

Goodman, A. H., & Leatherman, T. L. (2001). *Building a new biocultural synthesis: Political-economic perspectives on human biology*. Ann Arbor: University of Michigan Press.

Hinkes, M. J. (2008). Migrant deaths along the California–Mexico border: An anthropological perspective. *Journal of Forensic Science, 53*(1), 16–20.

Low, S. M., & Merry, S. E. (2010). Engaged anthropology: Diversity and dilemmas: An introduction to supplement 2. *Current Anthropology, 51*(S2), S203–S226.

Marks, J. (2000). Human biodiversity as a central theme of biological anthropology: Then and now. *Kroeber Anthropological Society Papers, 84*, 1–10.

Mullins, P. R. (2011). Practicing anthropology and the politics of engagement: 2010 year in review. *American Anthropologist, 113*(2), 235–245.

Redfield, P., & Bornstein, E. (2008). An introduction to the anthropology of humanitarianism. In E. Bornstein & P. Redfield (Eds.), *Forces of compassion: Humanitarianism between ethics and politics* (pp. 3–30). Santa Fe: School for Advanced Research Press.

Rose, A. (2012). *Showdown in the Sonoran Desert: Religion, law, and the immigration controversy*. New York: Oxford University Press.

Rosenblatt, A. (2015). *Digging for the disappeared: Forensic science after atrocity*. Stanford: Stanford University Press.

Rylko-Bauer, B., Singer, M., & Van Willigen, J. (2006). Reclaiming applied anthropology: Its past, present, and future. *American Anthropologist, 108*(1), 178–190.

Wexler, C. (2016). Introduction. In *Responding to migrant deaths along the Southwest Border: Lessons from the field,* 5. Washington, DC: Police Executive Research Forum.

# Chapter 2
# All That Remains

**Adriana Paramo**

## All That Remains of an Afghan Girl

According to The International Organization for Migration, IOM (2016a), approximately 239,923 migrants and refugees have arrived in Europe by sea as of June 2016. The organization reports 2,933 deaths in 2016–1095 more than in 2015. In April alone, a trawler sank off the Libyan coast on its way to Italy. The same analysis reports that the human cost of this failed sea crossing was 458 bodies found inside the vessel, the remains of 169 victims found on or around the wreck, and 48 more bodies recovered and brought to shore by Italian divers, for a tragic total of 675 confirmed victims. There are only 28 known survivors of the shipwreck. Who initiates the repatriation process of these human remains? Without an official passengers' list, who are the remains given back to? Who can identify a body that has been in the water for days, weeks, and months and maybe even eaten by sea animals? Who pays, or is in a position to pay, for coffins, transportation of the body, air tickets, and funeral expenses?

In the last few years the world has seen an unprecedented exodus of peoples fleeing violence and hunger in their homelands. Europe has been flooded with waves of Turks, Afghans, and Syrians escaping years of civil war and violence. Thousands of refugees pay smugglers for passage into Europe and thousands of them perish in the attempt. What happens to those who die at sea while trying to sail derelict boats to the Mediterranean shores?

According to Rahimi (2016), Mohammed Nowroz Noori, a husband and father of three, tried to make the trip with his family from Afghanistan to Greece. His trip was cut short when their boat capsized after leaving the port of Ayvacik, Turkey. Thirty-nine refugees looking for hope died that night. Sixty were rescued,

A. Paramo (✉)
Low Residency MFA Program, Fairfield University, Fairfield, CT, USA
e-mail: adriana@paramoadriana.com



K.E. Latham, A.J. O'Daniel (eds.), *Sociopolitics of Migrant Death and Repatriation*, Bioarchaeology and Social Theory,
DOI 10.1007/978-3-319-61866-1_2

Mohammed among them. By the time he was taken ashore, his wife and three children had disappeared in the water. It took him 13 days to find his wife and two of the children, whom he identified in pictures. In mourning, stunned by the loss, and unable to repatriate the remains of his family on his own, Mohammed traveled 275 miles to Istanbul to ask the Afghan consulate for help. What he found was that the consulate does not offer financial help in these cases and that Mohammed will have to pay for the coffins, transportation, ambulance, and plane tickets to repatriate this family's remains. He had to borrow US$8,500 to bring the bodies of his two children and wife back to Afghanistan. Considering that the highest average monthly income in Afghanistan is approximately US$250, this loan would chain Mohammed to a life of debt and hunger. Ariana Afghan Airlines is a silent witness of this tragedy. The airline has at any point between two and seven bodies on each flight; at the peak of the tragedy, the cargo area is almost full with the bodies of those who failed in their attempt to sea cross to Europe.

Within hours of Mohammed's harrowing homecoming, his family had been buried in a patch of desert, with their names scribbled in Arabic on rudimentary tombstones. And his daughter, the one he couldn't find in Ayvacik, was later found, but by then, Mohammed had run out of resources and couldn't afford going back to Turkey to repatriate her remains. She is buried somewhere far away from home, alone, most likely in an unmarked grave. She will never go home.

## All That Remains of Cambodian and Myanmar Migrants in Thailand

While it might be true that we are all born equal, death and the way the dead are treated seem to exacerbate class, sociopolitical, and religious differences. This is particularly true when the dead is a migrant worker from an underprivileged country. Let us examine a Southeast Asian country like Thailand, where the treatment given to the dead varies immensely according to their status.

Usually, when a tourist or an expatriate dies in Thailand, their embassy in Bangkok will assist the family in returning the body back to their home country (International Labour Organization 2015) . This is rather costly, and most people opt for having their loved ones cremated in Thailand and take the ashes back home for a formal funeral. Should a relative of yours die while in Thailand, you will have to follow the Immigration Bureau's protocol for repatriation of human remains. Normally your embassy would do most of the work: obtain a death certificate for the person, contact and notify the next of kin, and do other paper works that fall under what's called "consular assistance." In order to initiate the repatriation of human remains, the following documents are required:

- Death certificate
- Letter from the police
- Passport of the deceased

In order to avoid having to navigate their internal bureaucracy, hand the documents to your embassy. Let the embassy manage the reporting to immigration and obtain all the needed certificates as required. As stated above, the embassy will likely advise you to cremate in Thailand in order to save costs as it is very expensive to transfer a body out of Thailand to your home country.

It is easy enough and painful but easy, unless the dead migrant is one of the tens of thousands of undocumented Rohingya from western Myanmar. According to Chuensuksawadi and Boonchote (2015), most Rohingya are Muslim asylum seekers who fled western Myanmar since religious violence erupted there in 2012. Their initial destination was Malaysia, but many were tricked by their smugglers and ended up either arrested by the authorities or held in trafficking jungle camps on the Thai border, from where the smugglers extorted money from their families. When their families couldn't produce the $2,000 the smugglers charged, 2015 rates, for their passage to Malaysia, they were held, tortured, raped, killed, and buried in mass graves, hundreds of them.

Most Rohingya are stateless and unrecognized by the two countries—Bangladesh and Myanmar—they call home, (Chuensuksawadi and Boonchote 2015), which means they don't have a passport. If the Rohingya is a migrant worker, his/her inability to produce a passport and the absence of consular assistance lead to lengthy repatriation processes that violate the 24-h period granted in Islam for the ablution and burial of the deceased. If the Rohingya dies in a jungle camp and is subsequently thrown into a mass grave, there is no hope of a forensic identification process and therefore no repatriation for their mortal remains. They die the same way they arrive in Thailand: voiceless and afraid.

According to Chang (2015), if the dead migrant is a Cambodian worker, he is repatriated through the Poipet International Border Checkpoint. Tens of thousands of Cambodians looking for jobs or already employed by Thai companies cross this checkpoint every year. Migrant death in their workplace, by law, awards the family monetary compensation. The compensation is paid after an autopsy is performed, and the cause of death is found to be work related. However, 90% of the surviving kin are not compensated because the Thai government tends to issue death certificates which state natural causes, heart attack, and other nonwork-related morbidities as the ultimate causes of death. Hence, no compensation is required. If the surviving relatives wish to contest this report, they need to pay for yet another autopsy in Cambodia and initiate a process demanding compensation from the Thai employer. This is highly unlikely, given the socioeconomic status of the mostly uneducated Cambodian migrant force in Thailand. Those Cambodians who die in Thailand but can't be identified and therefore repatriated are cremated at a pagoda, unceremoniously. A basic cremation is attended only by the man lighting the pyre.

Do all migrant workers who die in Thailand get the same treatment? The short, simplified answer is no, the longer more complex answer is: it depends on the industry. Migrant workers from Myanmar and Cambodia make up the backbone of the Thai fishing industry, one which is plagued with stories of forced labor, human trafficking, violence, and death. One of the most popular destinations for Thai fishing boats is a remote group of East Indonesian islands whose abundant slave-caught fish supply networks of American supermarket chains, restaurants, and pet shops. The islands of Benjina and Ambon (Chang 2015), where fishing vessels dock and unload their catch, are the most notorious among them.

Many workers from Cambodia and Myanmar who have escaped boats have settled on these two small islands. Those who died at sea are buried there. Their remains will not be sent home for a myriad of reasons, the most obvious being the prohibitive cost of repatriating the deceased from a remote place and the fact that fishing vessels usually spend years at sea before returning to Thailand.

According to the law (Chang 2015), fishing vessels docking in Benjina are required to release the bodies of those crew members who have died at sea. Local authorities transport each body in an ambulance and bury it at the local cemetery, which is divided into three separate areas for Muslims, Buddhists, and Christians. On their graves go the information recorded in the seaman's book of the deceased, which is largely fake, as the Thai industry is notorious for hiring undocumented migrants who possess neither passport nor official identification. It might look like a cemetery, but cemeteries created with wrong or no information about the buried are, for all intents and purposes, mass graves of unidentified remains. Those at home will be waiting forever and will never know the fate of those who, 1 day, left in search of good fortune.

## All That Remains of an Indian Migrant in Dubai

The process involving the repatriation of migrant workers' remains can be, in some cases, a true test to the surviving family's fortitude, resourcefulness, and knowledge of the host country's culture. Let's say you are an immigrant working in the emirate of Dubai. And because the repatriation of human remains changes according to the cause of death (natural, crime, accident, illness, etc.), religion, and country of provenance, let's assume you are a non-Muslim Indian who died of natural causes. Should your relatives want to have your body repatriated, these are the steps they need to follow, according to de León (2015):

1. The death needs to be reported to the police by calling 999.
2. Get the police to fill the initial death report and transfer your body to the mortuary.
3. If you died in a hospital, your family will need a death certificate issued by the hospital. Then they need to register your death at the nearest police station to your place of residence.
4. In order to move forward, your family needs to gather the following: the death report issued by the police, your passport, your work visa (original and copy), and Dh60 (approximately US$17). If you were an undocumented migrant worker, your family can forget about having your remains repatriated. Failing to produce a visa stops the process dead in its tracks.

5. In order to confirm your death, the Rashid Mortuary determines the cause of your death and issues a report. This report now needs to be stamped by the police at the hospital.
6. Now your family needs to gather all these documents and go back to the police station again. There, they will have to ask for an NOC—a no objection certificate—a document declaring no objection to the process of repatriation.
7. Your family will have to be well informed about the protocol, because at this point they must request that NOCs are addressed to each of the following:

   - Al Baraha Hospital, Ministry of Health, so that they can issue an unofficial death certificate. Here, they will need to pay another Dh60 (US$17).
   - The airport for repatriation of the human remains.
   - The mortuary for embalming.
   - The hospital for release of your body (if you died in the hospital).

8. Now with all NOCs and reports and stamped pieces of paper in a language that's completely alien to your family, they need to go to the Preventive Medicine Department of Al Baraha Hospital where the official death certificate will be issued.
9. Because you are/were from India—a non-Arabic speaking country—your family will need to have the certificates translated into the official language of your country (most likely Hindi).
10. If your family members are not too overwhelmed by now and considering that to give up on the process, they now need to go to the Ministry of Labor and Immigration to have your work visa canceled. This process may or may not require your sponsor's signature.
11. Your family now needs to go to your embassy or consulate and have the mission cancel your passport and register your death in your home country. The embassy will have to issue yet another NOC so that your body can be repatriated.
12. If your relative is accompanying your remains in the flight, she/he needs to book a ticket and cargo. Different airlines have different formalities, so your family will have to submit the proper paper work accordingly.
13. Now, they need to go back to the mortuary and formally identify your body.
14. They need to take your body to the Medical Fitness Centre to book the embalming. They will be required to pay Dh100 (US$28) for the embalming charges, a minimum of Dh1,750 (US$480) for a standard coffin, and Dh210 (US$55) for the ambulance to transport the body to the airport.
15. Assuming your family can meet the expense and that you don't have any contagious diseases, the embalming will take place, and later, the Medical Fitness Centre will issue the embalming certificate.
16. As an Indian, the embalming certificate has to be attested at the Indian embassy/consulate.
17. The DNATA, Dubai National Air Travel Agency, will transport the body to the Cargo Village and process the required documentation.
18. At the DNATA export office, your family needs to produce the NOC from the embassy, a minimum of eight copies of every document including the plane

ticket, all of which will need to be translated into your country's language. At the same time, your family will have to request the original NOC from police and another NOC from the Cargo Village police station.
19. After all the shipping costs are paid, your body will be finally labeled as human remains, scanned, and then shipped to India.
20. Your family will have to have made previous arrangements for a funeral service company at your country of destination to receive your body.

According to de León (2015), throughout this harrowing process, your family needs to know the ins and outs, not only of the repatriation process but also the local bureaucratic culture. For instance, government offices close at 2 pm; the offices are not in the same building, so unless your family members have their own transportation, they will need money to pay taxis from one point to the next. If they didn't know before you died, they will learn, as they try to take your dead body back home, that in the United Arab Emirates, everyone has to contend with history: The Buraimi Oasis (Pearce 2014), once home to an important slave market, provides a present-day reminder of the UAE's key role in a slave trade lasting well into the twentieth century. The legacies of the slave trade are manifest today as a part of the collective psyche. The right to own people is a deeply ingrained tradition, albeit frowned upon, and as result, Indian workers are not considered first-class citizens in the Gulf region. Your family needs to cope with the reality of belonging to a minority, desperately needed in Dubai but grossly despised.

## All That Remains Somewhere in the Sonoran Desert

According to the Missing Migrant Project (The Washington Office on Latin America 2016), between 1990 and 2000, the average death rate of presumed migrants in Southern Arizona alone was 12 every year. Between 2000 and 2014, the number spiked to 170 deaths per year. The US Border Patrol, according to Miller (2013), has logged more than 6,330 deaths of presumed migrants along the border from 1998 to 2014 and an average of 395 deaths per year. The real numbers are higher. The Washington Office on Latin America (2016) has records of more than 2,500 migrants missing last seen crossing the border. And these are only the written, verifiable reports of the dead and the missing while crossing.

Bomberger and Swing (2016) found "The United States-Mexico border has become a war zone. It is also a transfer station for sophisticated military technology and weapons. As our country's foreign wars have begun to wind down, defense contractors look here, on the southern border, to make money." The undesirable byproduct of this border vigilance is a subculture of trigger-happy xenophobes who might shoot unsuspected migrants trying to make it into the USA. What about those deaths that are not recorded anywhere? What about those who died far away from the border and whose bodies are either devoured by animals or destroyed by nature? What about those who died and were buried in unmarked graves in places that nobody could retrace? What about a 4-year-old girl named Esperanza?

According to Páramo (2012), in 2001, a Mexican woman named Esperanza Vazquez and her four children, Maura, Yohari, Gabriel, and Esperanza, paid a coyote to walk the five of them across the Sonoran Desert into the USA, their promised land. A few years after she arrived in this country, I read her story in a Florida newspaper and took it upon myself to look for her. Eighteen months later, when I finally found her, I interviewed her and shared with her food, rides, and anecdotes. I tiptoed lightly around her ordeal because I knew what the crossing had cost her. I knew she had the kind of scar that many migrant workers carry, a silent, but open, wound that never heals.

A chain of events led to the moment I knocked on her door in 2003. She had decided to cross the border because NAFTA, North Atlantic Free Trade Agreement, had robbed her father of his ability to compete in the market and feed his family with the proceedings of his rice crops. Esperanza left Mexico because her father gave her away in marriage in exchange for the food and shelter he could no longer provide under the new free trade agreement with the USA. She crossed because her father married her to an older, violent man. She crossed because he beat her constantly and because he had kicked her and her four children out of the house he now shared with a mistress. Esperanza crossed because she was out of options. She followed other Mexican women's example and hired a coyote—a smuggler— who promised her a swift passage. So swift she only needed 1 L of water per person, an easy jump over an imaginary line. She carried 5 L and just a little bit of food in a pink bag, and put her five lives in the coyote's hands. The following are excerpts from my interviews with Esperanza which were compiled in the book *Looking for Esperanza: The Story of a Mother, a Child Lost and Why they Matter to us.*

On day 1, they walked all night. Four-year-old Esperanza wrapped her arms around her mother's neck and whispered, "Mami tengo frio, Mommy, I'm cold." She did this many times throughout the first night. The desert wind blew in their faces, harder and colder with each passing hour. Little Esperanza's lips began to chap. At around 4 or 5 in the morning, the coyote and his human cargo stopped to rest. The following day they walked longer hours. The coyote seemed nervous and uncomfortable, as if the landscape was unfamiliar to him. The pollos—16 men and Esperanza's family— walked for three nights without asking too many questions, afraid of being abandoned if they complained. Little Esperanza's body started to cramp up, first one leg and then the other. Her eyes began to sink as though they were retreating inside her body looking for water. They ran out of food. There was no water left for anyone. On the fourth night, the coyote gathered the group. He took off his hat, scratched his head, and announced that the wind had blown the tracks he was familiar with and he needed to go solo and look for a better route. The 20 migrants waited for another day and another night, their fifth night in the desert. The coyote never came back.

Esperanza doesn't remember who made the decision to head back to Mexico or who guided the group from then on. What she remembers is how restless her little girl grew. "Imagine your baby dying in your arms. Imagine your baby telling you 'Mami, hug me tight.'"

They had been walking back to Mexico for 2 days when little Esperanza's skin turned a hue of blue. She felt cold and dry. Her lower jaw hung in the air exposing a jumble of sticky mucous inside her tiny mouth. "Mommy I'm so cold," the little girl kept saying with cracked lips caked with dry blood. Esperanza covered her with a pair of jeans one of the men lent her and made another layer with her own sweater and then another one with a beach towel. Maura fastened the towel on Esperanza's back with a knot, her little sister's body strapped to her mother's. Esperanza bargained with God, with the Virgen de Guadalupe, and with San Toribio Romo. She asked for water, for food, and for warmth. She asked for Mexico to appear on the horizon, for another day, and for life. Esperanza cradled her daughter's head with her right hand. Then she asked God for a merciful death for the five of them. She kept walking with little Esperanza strapped to her body. "Give me the longest hug ever, mami," the girl whispered. There was no denying. Esperanza knew that her little girl was dying.

Ay, Virgencita! Mi niña, mi niña!

Esperanza breaks into a long sob. I stop taking notes and hug her. I cry with her. I bear witness to her suffering, and the arc of her loss includes other women and other mothers. The arc of her loss includes me: a woman, a mother, and an immigrant, just like her.

One more long exhalation and the girl's body went limp. Little Esperanza died with her almond-shaped eyes open, looking straight into her mother's and straight through her mangled body and her dashed dreams. She pulled the towel up to cover little Esperanza's head and kept walking determined to cross into the USA with her dead baby. The other migrants would have asked her to leave her daughter behind if they knew she was dead. Esperanza couldn't bring herself to leave her little niña behind. She kept walking.

She doesn't know how long she walked with the dead body strapped to her chest; 1 day, maybe 2. She doesn't remember. They were lost in the desert, walking in circles and hungrily looking at the horizon for a glimpse of anything resembling Mexico or a border patrol, a gang of desert bandits, and anything but the barren desert. Whenever the group stopped to rest, Esperanza would sit away from them with her little girl. She asked her to forgive her for not having water, for running out of beans, for not having packed warmer clothes, and for failing her. Had anyone looked over, they would've just seen a mother talking to her little girl. But her plan didn't work for too long, and eventually Esperanza's secret was no longer kept. Maura tried to take her little sister away from Esperanza's arms, but they were encircled around her dead body with such fury, with such zeal, that Maura needed help from two of the men to pry open Esperanza's arms. By the time Esperanza surrendered the dead body, her arms had adopted a permanent cradle-like position. The inner edge of her left hand—where little Esperanza had sat—rested on her belly, face up, and her right hand suspended in the air facing Esperanza and cradled an invisible head. She looked demented with her body holding an imaginary child, like a dancer without a partner, Madonna without Jesus. They stuffed her body in the same pink bag they had used to carry their food. One of the men tightened a knot over little Esperanza's head with his belt. Esperanza knelt on the sand and watched the men dig a shallow hole with bare hands. Someone found a piece of cardboard, someone else slivers of wood. The men lowered the pink bag into the hole and covered it with sand. A cross topped the small mound.

Esperanza hits her forehead with one fist. “I looked around trying to memorize the place so I could go back for her and give her a proper burial, but the desert is all the same. I don’t know where I left her, mi niña.” Esperanza stayed in the same spot for a long time. She tried to cry but couldn’t. She was too dehydrated to cry. She knelt by the grave unable to move, her arms still in cradling position, looking at the mound, the cross, thinking that in order to save her other three children, she would have to leave her little girl behind. “Imagine that, only four years. Just four years.” Esperanza wipes her tears with the sleeve of her sweater. She shows me four right fingers.

Imagine that a 4-year-old immigrant dying in pursuit of her mother’s dream.

Esperanza still dreams of finding her daughter’s grave. If she were to find it, she would give her a proper burial. It would be preceded by the most splendid funeral anyone had ever seen. There would be flowers and music. The coffin would be tiny, white, and filled with stuffed animals and toys. In it, little Esperanza would lie and have a faint smile on her lips and a splash of color on her tiny cheeks, and her hair would be luscious and her skin soft to touch.

I listen to Esperanza and nod, but I don’t tell her the truth. I don’t tell her that the jackals can devour a whole body overnight and that whatever they don’t eat would be consumed by bobcats, javelinas, and a squadron of vultures, leaving a heap of bones scratched with the fury of their fangs and beaks. I don’t tell her that when the flesh is gone, the sun bleaches the skeletons into splinters of bone and teeth. I don’t tell her that if her baby girl’s body is ever recovered and brought to the border, it would most likely be thrown into a mass grave, a pit of human remains without names. I don’t tell her that in the off chance that a group of forensic scientists identify her daughter’s remains and a process of repatriation is set forth, there would be no real closure or funeral or burial, for she would be expecting the dead body of her daughter, not a phalange, not a piece of her jaw, and not one of her baby teeth. She would be making arrangements to bury a whole body but instead would be getting a code made out of four chemical bases, a molecule shaped like a twisted ladder, and a speck heavy with her DNA.

The International Organization for Migration (Brian and Laczko 2016) reports that in 2015 at least 5,417 migrants died or went missing during migration, and according to Willgress (2016), some 26,000 child migrants arrived in Europe last year without any family, and Europol reports that more than 10,000 of them may have disappeared after arriving in Europe. The numbers are staggering. The IOM (2016b) estimates that in the last 20 years, more than 60,000 migrants all over the world have died trying to reach their destinations. This is the official number of deaths for which there is some record. The unofficial and more realistic number is higher when we combine this figure with the unknown number of deaths that go unrecorded, plus those who die but are never identified. The unofficial number, whatever it might be, is staggering: the testimony of a worldwide social tragedy of catastrophic proportions.

According to HM Queen Noor (2016), each unidentified migrant represents a missing member of a family. Without knowing what ever happened to their loved one, families spend years or lifetimes going through what is known, according to Chuensuksawadi and Boonchote (2015), as "ambiguous loss": a type of unresolved and self-consuming mourning; an extraordinary grieving process complicated by ambiguous feelings of hope that the missing are alive, mixed with those that the missing are dead; and thus a search for a body ensues. A dead body, a wake, a funeral, a cremation, a set of parting rituals, and a gathering of friends and family to bid the body farewell are the things the grieving party needs to bring closure, to fully be able to grieve their loss.

Forensic science is being put to the service of families looking for missing migrants. Mass graves might be identified, human remains exhumed, DNA tests run, matches found, and families contacted with the news. But between "we found your son/daughter," and the delivery of DNA paperwork and a strand of hair, or a tooth, or a bone fragment, there is an unfathomable abyss separating not only cultures but also expectations from reality.

In an ideal world, there wouldn't be a need for forensic anthropologists to exhume human remains along geographical borders. In an ideal world, there wouldn't be mass graves filled with John, Jane, Johnnie, or Janie Doe, and the governments would guarantee the safety and well-being of their citizens so that they wouldn't have to make the hard choice of leaving everything behind and walk deserts and cross oceans to escape hunger and violence. In an ideal world, there wouldn't be Mohammeds and Esperanzas dreaming of their dead children's bodies or the need to come up with words like "ambiguous loss," and the common trait between a migrant worker dying on the US-Mexico border and Thailand or Dubai would be the dignity and expedition of his repatriation process. But our world, marvelous as it might be, is far from ideal. All we can do is hope that through the collective will of the people who crave peace and believe in justice and equality, the missing will be found, identified, and reunited with their loved ones, at home, at last.

## References

Bomberger, K., & Swing, W.L. (2016). Counting the missing migrants. *Wall Street Journal*. http://www.wsj.com/articles/counting-the-missing-migrants-1455562806.

Brian, T., & Laczko, F. (Eds.). (2016). *Fatal journeys volume 2: Identification and tracking of dead and missing migrants*. Geneva: International Organization for Migration.

Chang, C. (2015). Rohingya refugees buried in mass graves in Thailand. *News.com.au*. http://www.news.com.au/world/asia/rohingya-refugees-buried-in-mass-graves-in-thailand/news-story/5e5f454179a89e55dc85a83eb77e7ab1.

Chuensuksawadi, P., & Boonchote, W. (2015). Gangs abandon migrants. *Bangkok Post*. http://www.bangkokpost.com/archive/gangs-abandon-migrants/554727.

De León, J. P. (2015). Death in the family: Repatriation of expatriates' remains. *The Gulf News*, pp. 4A.

HM Queen Noor. (2016). Missing persons: From trauma to effective action. *International Commission on Missing Persons.* https://www.icmp.int/news/missing-persons-from-trauma-to-effective-action/.
International Labour Organization. (2015). Establishing migrant welfare funds in Cambodia, Lao PDR and Myanmar (Policy Brief 3). http://www.ilo.org/asia/WCMS_421193/lang--en/index.html.
International Organization for Migration. (2016a). Global migrations trends factsheet 2015. http://publications.iom.int/system/files/global_migration_trends_2015_factsheet.pdf.
International Organization for Migration. (2016b). Migration flows Europe: Arrivals and fatalities. https://missingmigrants.iom.int/sites/default/files/Mediterranean_Update_22_July_2016.pdf.
Miller, T. (2013). War on the border. *The New York Times*. http://www.nytimes.com/2013/08/18/opinion/sunday/war-on-the-border.html.
Páramo, A. (2012). *Looking for Esperanza: The story of a mother, a child lost, and why they matter to us*. Hopkins: Benu Press.
Pearce, C. (2014). Sandscapes of memory; A different history of the UAE. *The Gazelle*, (41). https://www.thegazelle.org/issue/41/features/history-2.
Rahimi, F. (2016). Afghanistan struggling to repatriate migrant workers. *The BBC.* http://www.bbc.com/news/world-asia-36202843.
The Washington Office on Latin America. (Producer). (2016). *Missing migrants: Families' search for answers and justice [video]*. Washington, DC: WOLA.
Willgress, L. (2016). More than 10,000 children missing. *The Daily Mail.* http://www.dailymail.co.uk/news/article-3425073/At-10-000-refugee-children-vanished-sex-work-slavery-trade-arriving-Europe.html.

# Chapter 3
# Capitalism and Crisis in Central America

**Dawn Paley**

## The Roots of Crisis in Central America

Each year, tens of thousands of Central Americans risk their lives crossing deserts, jungles, and mountains to get through Mexico in order to reach the USA. The routes they take are policed by migration officials, Mexican armed forces and police, as well as members of organized criminal groups who work closely with local officials. Regardless of the danger, people continue to migrate, and today millions of Central Americans live and work in the USA; the remittances they send home keep their families, and their countries, from starving. Many of those who manage to establish themselves in the USA are undocumented, facing precarious, exploitative labor and living conditions, cut off from their families, and unable to return home for a visit. While conditions of migrant labor in the USA have seemingly become mundane realities scarcely reported in the media, recent transformations in migration patterns have garnered popular interest and attention. Specifically, a significant increase in unaccompanied children making the journey north in 2014 captured the media's attention, and what is now called the crisis of unaccompanied minors took center stage.

Mexico continues to be the largest home country for migrants to the USA: 27.7% of all immigrants in the USA in 2014 were Mexican born (Brown and Stepler 2016). Historically, the vast majority of the unaccompanied minors apprehended at the US border were Mexican citizens. However, in 2014, 75% of the nearly 70,000 unaccompanied minors apprehended at the US border were from Honduras, Guatemala, and El Salvador. These three Central American nations make up the so-called Northern Triangle; media attention has focused on this region in particular since the increase in youth arriving at the US border in 2014.

D. Paley (✉)
Meritorious Autonomous University of Puebla, Puebla, Mexico
e-mail: dawnpaley@gmail.com



K.E. Latham, A.J. O'Daniel (eds.), *Sociopolitics of Migrant Death and Repatriation*, Bioarchaeology and Social Theory,
DOI 10.1007/978-3-319-61866-1_3

According to World Bank data, in 2011 nearly a quarter of Guatemalans lived on US$3.10 or less a day, as do currently a third of Hondurans and one in ten Salvadorans (2016). These three countries are also among the most violent on earth, with staggering homicide rates and high levels of extortion (Renwick 2016). But the difficult reality in Central America today isn't the product of local corruption or mismanagement: it can best be understood within a much longer history that dates back through centuries of institutionalized racism and violence. Current patterns of migration in and from Central America are intimately tied to colonial and authoritarian political systems, which favor large landowners and the wealthy at the expense of a poor majority. "The rural poor have been forced to live an uprooted life, migrating from rural area to rural area in search of temporary work, to urban areas where they join the ranks of the un- or underemployed, or to the outside, usually to the United States, from which they send remittances" (Schneider 2012: 90). In fact, 2014 was a record year for remittances sent back from the USA to Central America, totaling US$15.8 billion (Maldonado and Hayem 2015: 9).

But when news of unaccompanied children arriving at the USA-Mexico border broke in 2014, many news outlets reported that child migration had been propelled by rumors in Central America saying any child arriving at the US border would be granted papers allowing them to stay (Quinones 2014). I contend, however, that the sharp increase in child migration and the well-trodden migration routes from Central America to the USA cannot be attributed to rumor and misunderstanding. Rather, in order to understand this latest crisis, we must consider a much longer history of violence and displacement in the region.

This chapter takes a long view of the overlapping crises of economic and coercive violence in Central America, which have been activated through colonization, nation-state formation, and the wars of the twentieth century. A historical panorama helps establish a baseline of understanding that allows us to better interpret present-day events in the region. Such an approach avoids falling into a shallow and self-serving reading of the current crisis that would suggest that the reasons for mass out-migration are based on local mismanagement of politics and the economy or on rumors and misinformation. Within this historical overview of events, I integrate a series of journalistic interviews carried out in Guatemala in the spring of 2016. The combination of up-to-date information from activists, lawyers, and journalists on the ground with a historical overview of Central America aims to provide readers with a nuanced examination of issues often brushed over in mainstream media and buried in difficult to access academic literature on the region. Theoretically, this chapter shares Ana Patricia Rodríguez's view that "the same devastating effects produced in the South by the North come to represent Central America as a natural(ized) site of decomposition and underdevelopment, which requires regeneration by outside forces. Regeneration from the North comes to Central America in the form of imperialism, (neo)colonialism and now neoliberalism" (2009: 200). Put another way, a careful, if concise, read of history in the region teaches us that often it is foreign invasion and intervention imposed under the guises of development, security, and prosperity that create the very crises they claim to be solving.

## Colonization and Independence as Elite Lockstep

Spanish colonization in Central America pushed Indigenous people throughout the region into smaller and more remote areas with less access to trading routes, coastlines, and fertile lands. Military tactics including colonial war and massacres, the introduction of repressive colonial bureaucracies, the spread of fatal diseases, and a "near genocidal enslavement of natives" formed the basis of colonial governance, re-spatialization, and control (Smith 1996: 5). Argentine political ecologist Horacio Machado Aráoz describes the violence of colonialism and its characteristic dispossession as a dynamic of expropriation that "implies the systematic and long term exercise of productive violence, which is at the same time semiotic, economic, juridico-political; a violence through which the consecutive colonial production of 'subjectivities', 'natures', and 'territorialities' takes place, adapted and subjected to colonial rules of endless accumulation and accumulation as an end in itself" (2013: 24). The violence of colonialism destroyed communal worlds and, as suggested by Machado Aráoz, decimated diverse systems of language, social, economic, and political organization, attempting to replace them with rules in the service of kingdoms and capital accumulation. The multiple violences of colonialism are important today because they laid the groundwork for the formation of modern nation states and capitalist expansion in the hemisphere.

Threads of economic inequality, exclusion, and violence in these nations can be traced back to colonization, and these same threads were woven through the fabric of independence and the formation of modern nation states. Independence movements in Central America were essentially power disputes between "*criollos*, colonists of Spanish ancestry born in Central America, and *peninsulares*, who were born in Spain and favoured with official positions in the colonial empire" (Acker 1988: 36). In all three countries, formal independence was an end result of conflict between elite groups. The criollos gained autonomy from Spain in 1821 and formed the Kingdom of Guatemala, which split in 1823 to become the United Provinces of Central America, splitting again the following year into five states. By 1830 Central America was comprised of five independent nations: Guatemala, Honduras, El Salvador, Nicaragua, and Costa Rica. From the first moments of independence, newly empowered criollo elites implemented political systems based on exclusionary racism and despotism.

Independence from Spain meant further pressure on collective land rights, as did liberal reforms, which promoted coffee growing at the expense of traditional lifeways and small-scale farming in Guatemala and El Salvador in particular. "In summary, by the time of independence, Spanish colonial policy had established the basic conditions of underdevelopment in Guatemala: mono-crop export production, extreme concentration of wealth in the hands of elites, juxtaposed with extreme poverty, decapitalization (channeling of the economic surplus abroad or to a tiny local minority that was tied to overseas interests), lack of infrastructure, an impoverished state, a polarized class structure, and systematic oppression of the indigenous population" (Jonas 1991: 16). During a recent interview in Guatemala City,

Mayan lawyer Juan Jeremías Castro Simon explained that the first wave of dispossession of Indigenous peoples from their lands was during colonization, as people were pushed off the most fertile lands. At that time, however, their communal property and communal structures were recognized. "When independence happened, there was a break there. But the Indigenous communities who were well organized managed to survive and keep their communal lands," said Castro. "But when policies shifted to favor investment in coffee, those who didn't plant coffee were not considered as contributing to development and they were removed from their lands, which were granted to other people."

In all three Northern Triangle countries, erasure of communal governance, traditional lifeways, and local forms of autonomy have been inherent to nation-building since independence. According to Guatemala's Commission for Historical Clarification, which was formed in 1994 after the internal conflict, from its inception, the state of Guatemala benefited a minority of ruling elites with interests counter to those of the vast majority of the population. A small, light-skinned minority controlled the land and the means of production and established a political tradition in their own image, using dehumanizing violence against Indigenous and African peoples. "The State gradually evolved as an instrument for the protection of this structure, guaranteeing the continuation of exclusion and injustice" (Rothenburg 2012: 17). Likewise, in El Salvador, politics "was indeed defined by a longstanding system of non-democratic authoritarianism that dates to the earliest days of the republic" (Ching 2014: 2). Though many participated in the movement toward independence in El Salvador, "The popular push that led to independence was quickly channeled by economically powerful sectors of criollos and ladinos," according to Salvadoran writer and political activist Roque Dalton (1984). Regarding the period shortly after independence, Dalton wrote "the Indigenous masses soon realized that the only thing that had changed were the people who were their masters" (1984). Instead of Spanish-born masters, independence meant that it would be locally born criollos who ruled over an Indigenous majority.

Lack of access to fertile land and resources continues to be a key factor in inequality in Central America today and, as we have seen, is linked to the forced displacement of Indigenous peoples made in the name of development since colonization. The violence connected with these displacements cannot be separated from the political traditions in each country. In *Armies Without Nations*, Robert Holden writes that a readiness to kill one's opponents and demonize one's enemies and a contempt for the masses were salient features of governance throughout Latin America and that these features were brought into especially sharp relief in Central America (2004: 33). "What stands out in the history of the isthmus is both the frequency and the persistence over time (in comparison to the rest of Latin America) with which contenders in the field of state power resorted to violence" (Holden 2004: 32). Newly independent nation states in Central America shared features with the colonial model: with independence, decision-making in the former colonies was decentralized, but the continuity of overarching political structures was ensured, and wealthy elites and their economic interests were protected through the deployment of violence against majority populations. The connection between elites and the colonial project remains intact to this day. "We live in a colonial nation state, so the logic of colonialism is confabulated with the structures of the state such that there is a continuous reproduction… of an oligarchy," according to Lorena Cabnal, a Maya-Xinca communitarian feminist and traditional healer based in Guatemala City.

The twentieth century saw continued expansion of industrial agriculture in Central America, first through coffee plantations and later through banana, sugar, and cotton farms owned by families connected to trading circuits dependent on the USA. Conditions of poverty, racism, and landlessness carried over from the previous century contribute to escalating social conflicts and eventually all-out wars in the region.

## Total War as Foundation for Neoliberalism

Most scholars agree that the root causes of Central American wars in the latter half of the twentieth century include inequitable land distribution, the use of repressive violence by elites aimed ensuring their continued rule, the amplification of misery and protest that had been ushered in via modernization, and the increase of avenues of protest with the spread of democratic ideals (Smith 1996: 6). The social and economic upheaval was extreme: "the number of landless peasants tripled between 1960 and 1980, such that the average rural poverty rate in the early 1980s grew to 60 per cent" (Smith 1996: 9). Heavily militarized state responses to collective resistance and protest, carried out under Washington's watch and often with its support, fueled fiery wars that began in 1960 in Guatemala and in the late 1970s in El Salvador and Honduras and blazed through to the 1990s.

The wars in each of El Salvador, Guatemala, and Honduras had distinct characteristics, of which there is no space to examine it in depth in this chapter.[1] There are, however, three key similarities which connect the practices and outcomes of the wars in the three countries to the crises being lived in the region today. First, the vast majority of acts of terror, killings, disappearance, and torture were carried out by state forces or associated death squads. Second, the US government denied involvement and avoided acknowledgment of Washington's role in the violence. Third, the recommendations of the truth commissions in all three nations were virtually ignored.

State sponsored violence was the motor of the internal conflicts in Central America, and its impact cannot be underestimated. The role of armies and police forces in the violence in Central America through the second half of the twentieth century becomes evident through a cursory overview of what we know about these conflicts. The key role of government forces in carrying out acts of terror against the people of Honduras, Guatemala, and El Salvador during these conflicts represents a

[1] For further reading on the history and violence of the twentieth century in Central America: Booth et al. (2009) and LaFeber (1993).

form of continuity with the authoritarianism and violent exclusion that have been practiced by these states since independence.

In Guatemala, the 36-year internal conflict led to 200,000 people being killed or disappeared. Over 80% of the victims were of Mayan descent. Four hundred villages were destroyed completely, during scorched-earth military offensives which aimed to eliminate entire populations which were considered guerrilla supporters. In addition, 150,000 Guatemalans sought asylum in other countries, and 1.5 million people were internally displaced (Steinberg et al. 2006). It is estimated that state forces and paramilitary groups were responsible for 93% of all violations documented in the truth commission report (United States Institute of Peace 1997) . In 2013, Efrain Rios Montt, Guatemala's military dictator during the apex of scorched earth tactics, was convicted of genocide and crimes against humanity in a historic trial in Guatemala City. Shortly thereafter, his conviction was overturned on procedural grounds (Open Society Justice Initiative 2013) .

In El Salvador, the official truth commission documented 22,000 complaints related to extra-judicial killings, disappearances, and torture; 85% of those violations were carried out by state forces (United States Institute of Peace 1992) . According to the report of El Salvador's truth commission, "Violence was a fire which swept over the fields of El Salvador; it burst into villages, cut off roads and destroyed highways and bridges, energy sources and transmission lines; it reached the cities and entered families, sacred areas and educational centres; it struck at justice and filled the public administration with victims; and it singled out as an enemy anyone who was not on the list of friends," (Betancur et al. 1993: 3). At the funeral of murdered Archbishop Óscar Arnulfo Romero y Galdámez on March 30, 1980, the military attacked mourners with bombs, machine guns, and bazookas. "The main target wasn't the revolutionary organizations, which walked under protection from the self-defense militias. It was the great unarmed mass, in a deliberate attempt to use terror to paralyze any future initiative of struggle," (Gilly 1981). In El Salvador, as in Guatemala, state terror sought to quash social movements and grassroots organization. Despite this, many thousands continued to organize for autonomy, positive change, and self-defense in their communities.

Finally, in Honduras, the truth commission's preliminary report includes 179 documented cases of disappearance carried out by state forces and a US trained death squad between 1979 and 1990 (United States Institute of Peace 2012). The country was militarized by the USA throughout the 1980s, as US soldiers patrolled and trained local soldiers and funded Contra activity at bases and camps throughout the country, giving Honduras the nickname "Pentagon Republic" (Latin American Bureau 1985). It is worth noting that many of those fleeing violence in Northern Triangle countries in the 1970s and 1980s escaped to the USA, laying the groundwork for the arrival of a second generation of people who would be displaced under newly structured regimes of violence from the mid-1990s on.

There are persistent modes of denial regarding US participation in the wars in the Northern Triangle that continue to this day. While current literature about the ongoing crises in Central America generally acknowledges these wars were crucial in shaping modern day events, they are often presented as the result of disagreements between local law-and-order strongmen and armed peasant populations, which obfuscates US involvement. In fact, "intense collaboration between military and police authorities of the United States and the five Central American governments" began during World War II (Holden 2004: 119). The USA played a key role in funding and propping up dictatorial regimes in the lead up to and during the internal conflicts in Central America. Closer examination illuminates the unfolding of these conflicts under the mantle of a US-promoted discourse of anti-communism: democratic movements, Indigenous organizations, popular uprisings, and armed insurgencies alike were quashed by state forces armed and trained by the USA.[2] The US government armed and trained army units in El Salvador that were responsible for tens of thousands of killings and abuses, and yet US officials claim they set the stage for peace (Gibb 2002). Though the USA and Honduras denied it at the time, a CIA- and FBI-trained death squad was responsible for a systematic pattern of disappearances, as well as extra-judicial execution and torture there throughout the 1980s (Center for Justice & International Law and Human Rights Watch – Americas 1994) . In the case of Guatemala, following the release of the Commission for Historical Clarification report, "The U.S. government reacted coolly to allegations of its role in the Guatemalan civil war that were strongly condemned by the report," (United States Institute of Peace 1997). The USA's silent role in Central America, following the country's public defeat in Vietnam, makes it more difficult to connect that today's troubles in the region to US policy and not to domestic disagreements that led to conflict.

Finally, in El Salvador, Honduras, and Guatemala, truth commissions set up as part of the transition to peace produced reports that were largely ignored. As a consequence, to this day in each country, democracy and reconciliation are promises that ring hollow. According to the US Institute of Peace, in Guatemala "Without announcing any follow-up measures, Guatemala's President Arzu apologized for the role of the government in past abuses when he received the commission's report" (1997). In El Salvador "The civilian government and the armed forces rejected the commission's report and no follow-up organization was established" (US Institute of Peace 1992). Lastly, in Honduras, "Most recommendations of [Ombudsman] Dr. Valladares were not implemented" (US Institute of Peace 2012) . Under the close eye of Washington and the United Nations, war criminals were given amnesty, military officials lived large off of the profits of pillage, and to this day those responsible for enabling terror remain active in politics, public life, and economic affairs. Tens of thousands of people remain disappeared, and reparations for victims have been few and far between. In the words of William I. Robinson, "The very conditions that gave rise to the conflict are still present and, in fact, have been aggravated in recent years. These conditions are the extreme concentration of economic resources, of wealth, and of political power, in the hands of elite minorities, side by side with the pauperization and powerlessness of a dispossessed majority" (2003: 319).

The depth and intensity of the wars in Central America stagger the imagination, and the all too brief sketch provided here is meant to provoke a reflection on how

[2] See, for example, Kinzer and Schlesinger (2005), and Rabe (2015).

these wars effectively set the stage for the imposition of neoliberal governance and the expansion of capital into the region. Neoliberalism is a political and economic system that favors globalized capital expansion and foreign direct investment at the expense of local economies. It undermines social and environmental protections, of which there were few to begin with, because as established here, Northern Triangle governments have exercised structural violence on people and on the land since independence. But as the formal transition to peace took hold in Central America, state forces and especially the military formally withdrew from some aspects of public and political life. According to Geoff Mann, "The most obvious [role of the state in capitalism] is sometimes referred to as the state's 'police' or 'night-watchman' function: the guarantee of the sanctity of private property rights, the fundamental precondition of all market exchange" (2013: 15). After peace was signed in the Northern Triangle countries, democratic rhetoric and lofty promises floated over destroyed social and physical landscapes. With international support, Guatemala, Honduras, and El Salvador transitioned their repressive forces from war machines to something closer to a deeply corrupt and proactive version of the police and night watchmen role described by Mann. This was a necessary step in order to usher in renewed capital expansion in the region.

## From Tanks to Night Watchmen: Neoliberalism and the Continuum of Violence

The period during and immediately following the peace accords is now acknowledged to have been a key moment in the restructuring of Central American economies. Neoliberalism has generally unfolded in the region through a triumvirate of increasing foreign direct investment, opening new commercial markets, and increased promotion of exports (Machado Araóz 2013: 14). Indeed, "the sectors most attractive to U.S. markets have been tourism, final assembly manufacture (called *maquilas* in Spanish), nontraditional agriculture, and remittances" (Schneider 2012: 83). The extractive industries, understood as "activities that remove large volumes of natural resources, which are not processed (or are processed in a limited way), and are then exported," particularly in the mining and petroleum sectors but also in industrial agriculture, like palm oil plantations, have gained importance in this period (Gudynas 2009: 188). Privatization of government assets has also been key to economic restructuring in Central America; sectors ranging from ports to pensions and from sugar refining to phone companies to water, electricity, and gas provision were privatized in the region beginning in the 1980s and continuing today (Robinson 2003: 235). Financial sectors have also expanded as transnational capital increasingly penetrates the region. "High interest rates and high levels of public debt offer easy returns to boost financial sector profits, and alliances with global capital have provoked a process of consolidation that has left only a few actors in each market" (Schneider 2012: 86). With the economic plans that were launched upon the signing of peace agreements in Central America, a new era of displacement and attack on communities began.

Mayan lawyer Castro Simon explained that after the Peace Accords were signed in Guatemala, "A platform was created to guarantee security for foreign investment, that is promoted starting in 1996, but it really starts in the year 2000 and after, a series of licenses are given out without previous consultation with Indigenous peoples, and there is this wave of people believing the only way to save the Guatemalan economy is extractivism." Supporters of the extractivist model posit that the extraction of nonrenewable resources (including mono-crops) for export can provide a tax base that allows for states to develop better public infrastructure and devote new funds to health, education, and other social programs. Critics, however, liken contemporary extractivism to a continuation of colonialism: in both cases, foreign powers arrive to strip local people of their lands and resources, leaving destruction in their wake (Machado Aráoz 2013).

A long view of the political economy of Central America highlights how neoliberalism has been enabled by historically driven wars, racism, class conflict, and genocide. Formal peace has not translated into meaningful peace with dignity for the people of the region, and periodic elections do not signify a democratic society. As during the previous centuries, racism against Indigenous communities and communities of African descent remains a crucial barrier to equality. "Racism is the main obstacle in all of the systems, in the economic system and in the justice system as well," said Jovita Tzul Tzul, a young Maya K'iche' lawyer who has successfully litigated cases for the restoration of communal title in Guatemala. Tzul Tzul says racism in Guatemala is manifested in the failure to recognize community self-governance and community organizations and leaders, as well as in the refusal to recognize a popular desire for alternative education or a different economy.

Far removed from the towns and cities where the poor majority live and work, members of elite families eat at fancy restaurants ensconced in malls with bodyguards in tow, live behind enormous walls in closed off compounds, and do their weekend shopping in Houston or Miami. There are broad similarities, but elite classes in each of the three countries have different characteristics, which are reflections of their distinct national histories and geographies. Schneider typifies the Salvadoran elite as essentially cohesive and coherent around the right-wing ARENA party, the Honduran elite as brokers and intermediaries that are largely subordinated to transnational firms, and the Guatemalan elite as fractured and still dominated by a traditional export class (2012: 109, 137, 171). The elites of these nations have little interest in the health and well-being of the poor majorities, and remittances sent by migrants working abroad have long served as a crucial lifeline for families devastated by environmental degradation, armed conflict, and extreme poverty.

Today, the region is experiencing the reentry of national armies into political life, despite that they were forced to take a less visible role in national politics following the peace accords. "Militarization continues, with massive risks of a major setback," said Iduvina Hernández Batres of Guatemala City-based NGO Security and Democracy (SEDEM). Links between retired army officials responsible for serious violations and active duty army structures have strengthened in recent years in

Guatemala, as the army occupies an increasingly potent social and political role. "The current head of the army has presented, in his own name, a motion of unconstitutionality against one of the articles of the Law of Reconciliation, which defines which crimes are covered by amnesty, and which are not," said Hernández in an interview in 2016. The 2009 coup d'etat in Honduras also represented a clear reentry into political affairs of the army; following the coup, levels of violence and inequality in the country have skyrocketed. According to a report by the Centre on Economic Policy Research, "In the two years after the coup, Honduras had the most rapid rise in inequality in Latin America and now stands as the country with the most unequal distribution of income in the region" (Johnston and Lefebvre 2013).

In addition, in the post-Cold War context, state violence and militarization in Guatemala, El Salvador, and Honduras have been renewed and justified as in the interest of preventing movement of illegal narcotics into the USA. Homicide rates in the Northern Triangle have been on the rise, and according to a 2015 report by the Congressional Research Service, "In 2013, the homicide rate per 100,000 people in Mexico stood at 18.9, a rate exceeded by those of El Salvador (39.8), Honduras (84.3), and—according to local sources—Guatemala (39.3)" (Meyer and Seelke 2015). Similar to patterns set in Colombia and Mexico, Central America has received increased funding from the US government (first under the Merida Initiative and then under the Central America Regional Security Initiative [CARSI]) in order to bolster police and military activity and participate in the so-called war on drugs. There is little available information about how CARSI money is spent, and available data provides no evidence that CARSI funding has made Central America safer (Rosnick et al. 2016). The US government earmarked $750 million for the Alliance for Prosperity in 2016, and though it is not clear exactly how the money is being spent, approximately half of the funds are destined for policing, military, and counter-narcotics (The White House 2016).

Proponents of the Alliance for Prosperity in Washington, including Vice-President Joe Biden, have claimed the plan will reduce migration by stimulating economic growth and increasing security in the Northern Triangle. But a close examination of the Alliance for Prosperity and CARSI indicates that they promote the same types of policies that tie neoliberal economic reforms to militarized citizen security initiatives, which have pushed the region to experience crises like that of unaccompanied minors in 2014. In a joint communiqué last year, the Presidents of El Salvador, Honduras, and Guatemala committed their countries to six specific points as part of the Alliance for Prosperity. Out of the six points advanced by the three presidents, three involved promoting trade and facilitating the movement of goods, two involved gas and electricity markets and infrastructure, and one promised private sector oversight. The Alliance for Prosperity is a proposal worth $22 billion over the next 5 years, with additional funding from host governments and the Inter-American Development Bank, the European Union, and others. It proposes deeper economic integration on the basis of the Central America-Dominican Republic-USA Free trade agreement. It eliminates border crossings (between El Salvador, Honduras, and Guatemala) and promotes a closer customs union between the three countries. An integrated energy market is a key pillar of the Alliance for

Prosperity. Instead of the railways of old, owned, and operated by United Fruit, Central America is promised a new gas pipeline along the Pacific Coast connecting Oaxaca, Mexico, to Guatemala. This will create a new export market for the surplus of fracked gas that has shaken US energy producers. Critics of the Alliance for Prosperity like Fernando Solís, editor of the independent monthly *El Observador* in Guatemala City, see it as a plan that is about social control and the containment of social movements, on the one hand, and on the other, "an investment plan, an economic plan, that fundamentally guarantees stability for US investments."

Nontraditional agriculture, extractivism, and large-scale tourism projects tend toward displacing people from their traditional lands and lifeways into urban centers, where the primary employment options are in the *maquila* sector. Transnationalized *maquila* circuits (e.g., of garments and car parts) are concentrated in urban areas, and their very existence is predicated on the low cost of labor. For those formally employed in the maquila sector, as for those who are economically active in the informal sector and for the many unemployed, extortion and the constant threat of violence are often the final straw which led many to seek opportunities in the USA. In sum, it is the structure of "peacetime" economic development in Central America that drives these cycles of displacement and poverty, at the same time as national security programs and the militarized enforcement of prohibition contribute to the formation of armed groups that further degrade quality of life for millions in the region.

Elsewhere I have explored how the war on drugs has served as a vehicle for increased social control and control over resources, including in Central America, something I have called drug war capitalism (Paley 2014). The US operates various military bases in the region, most notably in Honduras, and has deployed US Marines to Guatemala to combat narco-trafficking on at least one occasion. The Honduran city of San Pedro Sula has occupied the number one position on lists of the world's murder capital of late, while the Northern Triangle is generally understood to be among the most violent places in the world. Extortion is a common feature in experiences of violence and whether the collection of "war tax" is carried out directly by state forces, by local paramilitaries, or by so-called street gangs and impunity reigns.

Border areas in Central America have also become key areas of military activity, even as neoliberal policymaking pushes for increased border coordination for the movement of goods. Plan Frontera Sur in Mexico promises to militarize the Mexico-Guatemala border, while the drug war in Mexico under the Merida Initiative has created a context in which the policing of migration has effectively been privatized, with important enforcement areas once policed by Mexican migration agents now being controlled and run by state-linked criminal groups (or paramilitary organizations) like Los Zetas. Central American migrants transiting through Mexico today are disciplined through the use of formal means including capture, incarceration, and deportation, as well as through informal means based on terror, extortion, kidnapping, and massacre.

Programs like the Alliance for Prosperity formally tie the militarization of the region with transnational capitalist expansion in Central America. In turn, these programs reproduce conditions of state-directed violence and exclusion that have plagued the region since colonization and independence. In this context Ana Patricia Rodríguez's call to interpret calls for Central American "regeneration" as a form of continuing imperialist, neocolonial, and neoliberal rule is especially apt. As outward migration remains one of few options for Northern Triangle residents, the already existing border wall along the southern border of the USA, the nationwide prison-for-profit system that cages Central American migrants, and the xenophobic racism increasingly present in US political discourse are of concern. The drug war fueled para-policing of migration, and the use of Mexico as a barrier to prevent Central Americans from accessing one of their only chances at achieving a dignified life for their families is also deserving of awareness and action by people in the USA.

## References

Acker, A. (1988). *Honduras: The making of a Banana Republic*. Toronto: Between the Lines.

Betancur, B., Figueredo Planchart, R., & Buergenthal, T. (1993). *From madness to hope: The 12-year war in El Salvador: Report on the Commission for Truth in El Salvador*. San Salvador: The Commission on the Truth for El Salvador.

Booth, J., Wade, C., & Walker, T. (2009). *Understanding Central America: Global forces, rebellion and change* (5th ed.). Boulder: Westview Press.

Brown, A., & Stepler, R. (2016). *Statistical portrait of the foreign-born population in the United States|Pew Research Center*. Pew Research Center. http://www.pewhispanic.org/2016/04/19/statistical-portrait-of-the-foreign-born-population-in-the-united-states-key-charts/.

Center for Justice & International Law, & Human Rights Watch – Americas. (1994). *The facts speak for themselves* (The Preliminary Report on Disappearances of the National Commissioner for the Protection of Human Rights in Honduras). USA. https://books.google.de/books?id=GDl-bUb 4KIC&lpg=PP1&dq=facts%20speak%20for%20themselves&hl=de&pg=PP3#v=onepage&q=facts%20speak%20for%20themselves&f=false.

Ching, E. (2014). *Authoritarian El Salvador: Politics and the origins of the military regimes, 1880–1940*. Notre Dame: University of Notre Dame Press. http://site.ebrary.com/lib/ubc/reader.action?docID=10824135.

Dalton, R. (1984). *El Salvador (monografía) (First)*. Puebla: Autonomous University of Puebla.

Gibb, T. (2002). US role in Salvador's brutal war. *BBC News*. http://news.bbc.co.uk/2/hi/1891145.stm.

Gilly, A. (1981). *Guerra y política en El Salvador (First)*. Mexico: Editorial Nueva Imagen.

Gudynas, E. (2009). Diez tesis urgentes sobre el nuevo extractivismo. *Extractivismo, Política Y Sociedad*.

Holden, R. H. (2004). *Armies without nations: Public violence and state formation in central America, 1821–1960*. New York: Oxford University Press.

Johnston, J., & Lefebvre, S. (2013). *Honduras since the coup: Economic and social outcomes*. Washington, DC: Center for Economic and Policy Research.

Jonas, S. (1991). *The battle for Guatemala: Rebels, death squads, and U.S. power*. Boulder: Westview Press.

Kinzer, S., & Schlesinger, S. (2005). *Bitter fruit: The story of the American coup in Guatemala*. Cambridge, MA: Harvard University Press.

LaFeber, W. (1993). *Inevitable revolutions: The US in Central America* (2nd ed.). New York: W. W. Norton & Company.

Latin America Bureau. (1985). *Honduras: State for sale*. Birmingham: Latin America Bureau.
Machado Aráoz, H. (2013). Orden neocolonial, extractivismo y ecología política de las emociones. *Revista Brasileira de Sociologia Da Emoção, 12*(34), 11–43.
Maldonado, R., & Hayem, M. (2015). *Remittances to Latin America and the Caribbean set a new record high in 2014*. Washington, DC: Multilateral Investment Fund, Interamerican Development Bank. http://idbdocs.iadb.org/wsdocs/getDocument.aspx?DOCNUM=39619143.
Mann, G. (2013). *Disassembly required*. Oakland: AK Press. http://www.akpress.org/disas semblyrequired.html.
Meyer, P. J., & Seelke, C. R. (2015). *Central America Regional Security Initiative: Background and Policy Issues for Congress* (Congressional Research Service Report). Washington, DC.
Open Society Justice Initiative. (2013). Judging a dictator: The trial of Guatemala's Rios Montt|Open Society Foundations (OSF). https://www.opensocietyfoundations.org/publications/judgi ng-dictator-trial-guatemala-s-rios-montt. Accessed 1 Sept 2016.
Paley, D. (2014). *Drug war capitalism*. Oakland: AK Press.
Quinones, S. (2014). Unaccompanied kids and unintended consequences. *Americas Quarterly*. http://www.americasquarterly.org/content/unaccompanied-kids-and-unintended-consequences.
Rabe, S. G. (2015). *The killing zone: The United States wages Cold War in Latin America*. New York: Oxford University Press.
Renwick, D. (2016). *Central America's violent northern triangle*. Washington, DC: Council on Foreign Relations. http://www.cfr.org/transnational-crime/central-americas-violent-northern-triangle/p37286.
Robinson, W. I. (2003). *Transnational conflicts: Central America, social change and globalization*. London: Verso.
Rodríguez, A. P. (2009). *Dividing the isthmus: Central American transnational histories, literatures and cultures*. Austin: University of Texas Press.
Rosnick, D., Main, A., & Jung, L. (2016). *An examination of LAPOP's impact assessment of US violence prevention programs in central America*. Washington, DC: Center for Economic and Policy Research.
Rothenberg, D. (2012). *Memory of silence: The Guatemalan truth commission report*. New York: Palgrave Macmillan.
Schneider, A. (2012). *State-building and tax regimes in central America*. New York: Cambridge University Press.
Smith, C. (1996). *Resisting Regan: The U.S. central America peace movement*. Chicago: University of Chicago Press.
Steinberg, M., Height, C., Mosher, R., & Bampton, M. (2006). Mapping massacres: GIS and state terror in Guatemala. *Geoforum, 37*(1), 62–68. https://doi.org/10.1016/j.geoforum.2005.02.003.
The White House. (2016). *FACT SHEET: The United States and Central America: Honoring our commitments*. Washington, DC. https://www.whitehouse.gov/the-press-office/2016/01/15/fact-sheet-united-states-and-central-america-honoring-our-commitments.
United States Institute of Peace. (1992). Truth commission: El Salvador. http://www.usip.org/publications/truth-commission-el-salvador.
United States Institute of Peace. (1997). Truth commission: Guatemala. http://www.usip.org/publications/truth-commission-guatemala.
United States Institute of Peace. (2012). Commission of inquiry: Honduras 1993. http://www.usip.org/publications/commission-inquiry-honduras-93.
World Bank. (2016). Poverty headcount ratio at $3.10 a day (2011 PPP) (% of population). http://data.worldbank.org/indicator/SI.POV.2DAY.

# Chapter 4
# Naming State Crimes, Naming the Dead: Immigration Policy and "The New Disappeared" in the United States and Mexico

**Christine Kovic**

In two events on different sides of the US-Mexico border, family members and activists remembered migrants who perished in their attempts to reach the United States. At the first, in Mexico City on August 19, 2013, the third anniversary of the massacre of 72 migrants in San Fernando, Tamaulipas, families of the dead presented their testimonies at the Permanent Tribunal of the *Pueblos* on Migration. The Tribunal, titled "Militarization of Borders, Criminalization, and Forced Disappearance of Migrants in Transit," opened with a reading of the names of the deceased. To mark the life of each of the 72 migrants, a person in the audience stood up after each name was read and responded in Spanish "*presente*" ("here"). Eventually, everyone in the room was standing, powerfully making visible the magnitude of loss.

The San Fernando massacre was a watershed event for making visible the violence against migrants who cross Mexico. Migrant deaths and kidnappings at the hands of narco-traffickers and common criminals, with the direct or indirect support of state agents, had taken place in many regions of Mexico for well over a decade before San Fernando. Yet government authorities in Mexico, Central America, and the United States had largely ignored or dismissed this violence. The discovery of 72 bodies at San Fernando, 58 men and 14 women from Honduras, El Salvador, Guatemala, Brazil, and Ecuador, however, could not be ignored, especially when immigrant rights activists denounced the events and media reports drew significant public attention to this violence. At the time of the Tribunal, 3 years after the killings, 12 of the dead remained unidentified, despite the fact that their bodies had been recovered immediately from within a warehouse, with their hands and feet bound, some stacked on top

C. Kovic (✉)
University of Houston-Clear Lake, Houston, TX, USA
e-mail: kovic@uhcl.edu



K.E. Latham, A.J. O'Daniel (eds.), *Sociopolitics of Migrant Death and Repatriation*, Bioarchaeology and Social Theory,
DOI 10.1007/978-3-319-61866-1_4

of one another. During their testimonies at the Tribunal, several Central American women reported having received remains that did not belong to them.

Two months after the Mexico City Tribunal, a second ceremony at the ecumenical Rothko Chapel in Houston, Texas, "welcomed the dead" on November 2, 2013, Day of the Dead. The Houston ceremony honored and remembered those who had died in Brooks County, Texas, from January 2012 through October 2013. Activists and representatives of religious groups and nongovernmental organizations, among others, stepped forward one-by-one to read aloud the names of the dead. The names filled a black binder. With five names to a page, they filled 40 pages, a total of 201 dead in 20 months.[1] Of the identified 10 are from Guatemala, 13 from Honduras, 28 from El Salvador, 40 from Mexico, one from Ecuador, one from Costa Rica, one from Dominican Republic, and two country unknown. The unidentified numbered 105, meaning that more than 50% remained unidentified at that time. These migrants are border crossers who likely died from dehydration and hyperthermia as they walked across the harsh Texas brush in attempts to circumvent the Border Patrol checkpoint near Falfurrias.

At these two events, family members, friends, and activists attempted to remember the dead, to demand that all the dead be identified, and to name these deaths as state crimes. Both events are acts of memory that illuminate the lives and the suffering of people whose deaths have otherwise been regarded as accidental and therefore apolitical. In other words, these events are acts of memory making, acts to politicize the loss of life among those who "don't count." Such memory making challenges state immigration and security policies that target the working poor and cause death.

By searching for the missing, placing photos of their loved ones in public places, and sharing stories of disappearances, family members work to keep the memory of their loved ones alive. In the process they work to raise awareness of conditions of their deaths and to "make count" those who literally go uncounted or, as undocumented migrants, are deemed socially unworthy of attention (Edkins 2011). Families and activists also labor to make visible the causes of border deaths. Like other acts of memory making in Latin America, remembering missing and dead migrants challenges the silences of absence and the denial of human rights.[2]

Acts of memory assert that migrant deaths are far from accidental; rather they are known outcomes of policies that criminalize the working poor and militarize borders. These policies are an integral but hidden part of the attrition through enforcement approach that has led US immigration policy for almost 20 years. The two sites of violence, Brooks County, Texas and San Fernando, Tamaulipas, Mexico, are separated by an international border and are 175 miles apart. Yet they are connected by underlying causes of death: immigration enforcement, a growing security complex,

[1] The list comes from Brooks County from October 2013; numbers of identified and countries are constantly revised as some are identified months or years later.

[2] In her writing about the *arpilleras* (woven cloths representing the circumstances of the disappeared in Chile), Marjorie Agosín notes that the disappeared under Pinochet were made to appear absent. She observes that "The *arpillera* presents a clear narrative and accuses those who have lived lives in opposition to human dignity" (2008: 35).

and neoliberal economic policies. These practices together create and reproduce structural violence, an indirect and often invisible form of violence that involves "chronic, historically entrenched political-economic oppression and social inequality" (Bourgois 2004: 426). In this case, inhumane border enforcement that targets migrants from the global south, "free" trade policies that displace small-scale farmers and urban workers, and immigration policies that criminalize migrants are root causes of border deaths.

Following pathways forged by families in search of missing loved ones and activists denouncing border deaths, this chapter spotlights that which is commonly missed in analyses of migrant deaths and disappearances: state policies that converge to create violence. It examines the extreme violence migrants experience at the US-Mexico border, in South Texas, and, for Central Americans, in crossing the nation of Mexico. It explores the reasons state-driven violence may be "missed," ignored, or simply dismissed as the fault of migrants themselves. Finally, it examines the ways migrants, their families and loved ones, and other members of civil society seek to identify the dead, protest the violence against migrants, and, in the process, demand the defense of immigrant rights. Data for this chapter are drawn from long-term ethnographic research in southern Mexico and South Texas and most recently as a collaborator of the Migrant Rights Collective and the Forensic Border Coalition.[3]

## The New Disappeared: Public Policy, Vertical Borders, and Migrant Death

Throughout their journeys, unauthorized migrants face great risk in their attempts to reach their US destinations. Central Americans in particular travel over 1,000 miles between Mexico's border with Guatemala to its northern border with the United States. While in Mexico, these migrants are defined as "irregular," meaning that they entered the country without a required visa. As such, they are subject to detention and deportation. "Irregular" migrants thus often hide from government authorities rather than seek protection from them. Intensified migration enforcement, the related need to circumvent checkpoints, and virtual impunity for those who commit crimes against migrants create dangerous conditions. Activists have labeled the Central American journey through Mexico a "vertical border" to illuminate the violence, surveillance, and dangers that migrants encounter while

[3] The Migrant Rights Collective was established in Houston in the Fall 2012 to address the growing numbers of migrant deaths in South Texas and support locating the missing and identifying the dead. The Collective works together with families in the Houston region who are searching for missing loved ones to achieve the following: (a) pressure authorities for policy changes at the state and federal level, (b) seek necessary services, and (c) give visibility to the issue of migrant deaths and unidentified human remains on the border. The mission of the Forensic Border Coalition (FBC) is to support families of missing migrants searching for their loved ones and to address problems related to the identification of human remains found near the US-Mexico border.

traveling through Mexico. Perhaps counterintuitively, crossing the Suchiate River (at Mexico's southern geographic border), between the state of Chiapas and the country of Guatemala, is in some ways the easiest part of the journey.

Undocumented Central American and Mexican migrants must additionally cross the highly militarized US-Mexico border, a site of increased enforcement in recent decades. As migrants attempt to circumvent checkpoints as far as 70 miles north of the border, hundreds perish each year, principally from heat exhaustion in the desert brush. Given that migrants perish in isolated regions of Texas and Arizona, many remains are never found. The official Border Patrol count of 6,570 border deaths from 1998 to 2015 certainly represents only a fraction of the total.[4] Indeed, the Border Patrol numbers do not include those who died or whose bodies were recovered in Mexico. Maria Jimenez (2009) names these "deaths by policy" to point to the role of US enforcement strategies in causing migrant deaths. In short, the state security apparatus in both countries targets rather than protects migrants.

In addition, neoliberal economic policies in Mexico that have displaced *campesinos* and urban workers have played an important role in migrant death. Neoliberal reforms implemented in Mexico in the 1980s and 1990s resulted in dramatic cuts in support for rural producers. With the North American Free Trade Agreement, "cheap" and highly subsidized corn produced in the United States flooded Mexico's markets. As the price of corn and other products dropped, it became ever more difficult for rural producers to survive and emigration from the countryside increased (Baker 2013). As David Bacon observes, "Without changing U.S. trade policy and ending structural adjustment programs and neoliberal reforms, millions of displaced people will continue to migrate, no matter how many walls are built on the border" (2014: 68).

## *Navigating Mexico*

Central Americans attempting to cross Mexico to reach the United States pay coyotes (those who guide migrants on their clandestine journey north) thousands of dollars to assist them in crossing; others jump freight trains to avoid the many checkpoints along migrant routes. On the freight train, migrants are vulnerable to rain, extreme heat, cold, and electrical wires. Human rights organizations in Mexico have documented myriad abuses against migrants including rape, assault, kidnapping, and extortion, among others. Migrants identify government agents such as police as being responsible for these abuses in a significant number of cases. While the Mexican government does not keep official data on the number of migrants who have disappeared or died in their journey (Paz Carrasco et al. 2016), a 2008 report by three organizations estimated that up to 400 Central Americans had died each year from 2005 to 2008 (Due Process of Law, Centro de Derechos Humanos Fray

[4] US Border Patrol, Deaths by Fiscal Year, https://www.cbp.gov/sites/default/files/assets/documents/2016-Oct/BP%20Southwest%20Border%20Sector%20Deaths%20FY1998%20-%20FY2016.pdf.

Matías de Córdova, and El Hogar de la Misericordia 2008: 14). These organizations note that the lack of information on the human costs of migration shows the lack of interest and concern for migrants themselves on the part of Mexican authorities. According to Official statistics, more than 20,000 people in Mexico were "disappeared" from 2006 to 2014, and migrants are a particularly vulnerable population, traveling in some of the most dangerous zones of Mexico and through isolated areas as they attempt to avoid detention (Paz Carrasco et al. 2016). Mexican activist Rubén Figueroa of the *Movimiento Migrante Mesoamericano* (Mesoamerican Migrant Movement) explains that there is an enormous undercount of migrants who have been killed or injured. "Not a week passes without our receiving information of an attack or homicide [of migrants]" (Petrich 2014). Migrants die in Mexico by drowning, falling from the freight train, car wrecks, and other so-called accidents. These deaths, rather than being accidents, are known outcomes of security policies that push migrants to travel in clandestine and dangerous conditions (Kovic 2010).

In 2014, Mexico initiated its Southern Border Program, which includes intensified militarization, migration enforcement, detention, and deportations, along with other strategies to close its border to Central American migrants. One strategy has been to attempt to stop migrants from riding the freight train by introducing raids where trains are stopped and people are forced off. Another is to improve the train tracks so that trains can travel at higher speeds, preventing migrants from jumping on. Human rights observers in Mexico note that the increased enforcement has caused migrants to travel in more dangerous conditions. The program is closely tied to US policy interests of preventing undocumented Central American migrants from reaching the US-Mexico border and entering the country. Indeed, the program is funded partially by the United States through the Mérida Initiative (Seelke and Finklen 2016). Under the new Border Program, Mexican authorities have detained record numbers of Central American migrants. For example, in 2015, Mexico deported more Central Americans than the United States (Villegas and Rietig 2015); it appears as though the United States is outsourcing border enforcement work to its southern neighbor.

## *Navigating South Texas*

More than 200 migrant border crossers died in Brooks County in 2012 and 2013 as they walked for miles in the heat attempting to skirt the checkpoint to avoid detection, detention, and deportation. In 2012 Texas had the highest number of migrant deaths ever recorded for the state since the US Border Patrol began tracking such deaths in 1998. The Border Patrol recorded 271 deaths in Texas in 2012 and 235 for 2013 (US Border Patrol 2016) . At the Sacred Heart Cemetery in Falfurrias, Texas, dozens of graves were marked with small tin plaques with black block letters. Labels reading "Unknown Female," "Unknown Remains," "Unknown Person," and "John Doe," among others, mark graves of the unidentified people found on the private ranchlands that surround the Falfurrias Border Patrol Checkpoint.

In 2012 and through part of 2013, Brooks county officials sent the remains of unidentified migrants to a funeral home where no DNA samples were taken before they were buried in these "pauper's graves" at Sacred Heart Cemetery. This took place even though Texas State law requires that authorities take DNA samples on all unidentified remains and "submit those samples to the center for forensic DNA analysis and inclusion of the results in the DNA database" (Texas Code Criminal Procedure 63.056). Families living in the United States, Mexico, Central America, and elsewhere were not able to locate the missing or even know if loved ones had died. As such, these migrants are some of *"los nuevos desaparecidos,"* ("the new disappeared"), a reference to the term "disappeared" from the 1970s and 1980s, naming those who were disappeared in the Civil Wars and repressive military regimes in Central and South America (Stephen 2008).[5] As was the case for the disappeared of previous decades, families with limited resources search persistently for news of their loved ones, seeking closure and knowledge of their whereabouts.

In May of 2013, forensic anthropologists from the University of Indianapolis and Baylor University began exhumations of the unidentified remains. The exhumation began late on a Sunday morning, and Rafael Hernández of Angeles del Desierto said a prayer for the dead and their families who were certainly searching for them. Within hours the exhumation team had reached the first remains. The remains rest in plywood boxes, sometimes with two or more bodies in a box. The team worked for weeks to eventually exhume 65 bodies for later identification.

The view of the open graves in the cemetery and knowing that many of the dead were Central Americans was reminiscent of the exhumations following the violence of the Civil War in Guatemala. In May 2013, the same month that the exhumations began in Falfurrias, General Rios Montt, who ruled Guatemala in 1982–1983, was convicted, at least temporarily, of genocide and crimes against humanity. News articles reporting on the trial often included images of exhumations of mass graves. At the trial, forensic experts of the Guatemalan Forensic Anthropology Foundation (FAFG) had presented evidence from exhumations of Ixil graves, contributing to his conviction of ordering the deaths of 1,771 Ixil Mayas during his rule. The exhumations in Guatemala set out to identify the dead and allow for families to bury loved ones. In addition they served as evidence that the killings were state crimes, intentionally organized by and carried out by the military regime.

In South Texas, the evidence of responsibility for migrant deaths is located beyond the graveyards. Exhuming the dead continues to be of great importance for identifying those who died and for creating a record of how many lives have been lost. However, the immediate cause of death is different than that in Guatemala; forensic evidence will not show that migrants were shot in the back or had their hands and feet bound before they were killed. Yet the causal link between the deaths of migrant men, women, and children and US border security policies is recognized and, in large part, intentional. The Immigration and Naturalization Services (INS) border enforcement policies of "Prevention-through-deterrence" date back to the 1990s with Operation

[5] Lynn Stephen writes of the "new disappeared, assassinated, and dead" to describe those who have met violence on the US-Mexico border in the contemporary period.

Hold the Line (El Paso, Texas 1993), Operation Gatekeeper (San Diego, California 1994), and Operation Safeguard (Arizona 1994, 1999), all established to concentrate border enforcement in densely populated urban areas (Dunn 2009). These policies were designed to create obstacles and difficulties to discourage undocumented immigration. As a result, migrants were "funneled" toward more dangerous crossing points such as the Arizona desert and South Texas brush, with deaths increasing 20-fold from 1990 to 2005 (Rubio Goldsmith et al. 2006). At the same time, no large-scale immigration reform has been passed to allow significant numbers of unauthorized immigrants to regularize their status since the 1980s, and more recent laws, including several passed in 1996, have increasingly restricted the rights of immigrants, both authorized and unauthorized alike.

## Pardoning the State, Blaming the Dead

Violence against undocumented migrants, including death, takes place in a highly politicized context. The US President-elect Donald Trump began his campaign by accusing Mexicans of being criminals; he proposed building a border wall and increasing border militarization and immigration enforcement. These proposals are not new. They only intensify decade-long bipartisan policies that have increasingly criminalized migrants, especially Mexicans and Central Americans, and have amplified border security with the goal of stopping undocumented migration (De León 2015; Gomberg-Muñoz 2012). In the current anti-immigrant context, the deaths of migrants at the US-Mexico border, which continue year after year, have become normalized. The deaths are commonly framed as the outcome of a crime –"illegal entry" – that migrants themselves are committing. As such, migrants themselves are blamed for putting themselves in danger. This emphasis on individual responsibility fits the neoliberal paradigm, an economic and political theory predominant in the contemporary world, in which the state's role is to guarantee "free" markets and conditions for investment, while "each individual is held responsible and accountable for his or her own actions and well-being" (Harvey 2005: 65).

Human rights abuses, by definition, are acts committed by states. In denouncing abuses, activists and non-governmental organizations seek to quantify abuses in counting and naming those who have been assassinated, tortured, and detained. They also seek to name those responsible for such abuses and demand justice. The missing Mexican and Central American migrants, like the disappeared of previous decades, make this quantification difficult if not impossible. In the 1960s–1980s, Latin American government officials not only challenged the numbers of those who had disappeared but also denied blame for them. In Argentina in the 1970s, General Videla famously stated that the disappeared were living clandestinely, supporting guerillas, and dedicating themselves to "subversion." In Guatemala, military officials argued that the disappeared had joined guerillas or moved to communist countries and were considered enemies of the state. In a different context, in the war on drugs in contemporary Mexico, government officials assume that those killed were involved in the drug trade in some manner, suggesting that they are somehow responsible for their own deaths. Mexican cartels "disappear" bodies in attempts to cover up the evidence of crimes. The official failure to count points to the politics behind measurement – both in terms of what is measured and what is ignored and how it is counted.[6]

News reports, government officials, and researchers commonly blame a series of non-state entities for violence suffered by migrants. The focus on the responsibility of coyotes, narco-traffickers, and even on the supposed recklessness and ignorance of migrants themselves covers up the fact that these deaths are state crimes. In one common narrative, migrants are blamed for reckless decision-making in traveling under dangerous conditions and for breaking the law and entering the United States without permission. For example, an article in the *American Journal of Public Health* by Sapkota et al. analyzes the risk factors for unauthorized migrants who died while entering the United States from Mexico, yet ignores the broader context in which deaths take place. The article notes that border deaths are "largely preventable." The authors recommend that "prevention strategies should target young Mexican men and focus on preventing them from conceiving plans to cross the border, discouraging them from using dangerous routes as crossing points, and providing search-and-rescue teams" (2006: 1282). This recommendation suggests that migrants have an alternative way to enter the United States and disregards the fact that people cross the border to reunite with family members, to return to their homes and jobs in the United States, or to flee violence in Mexico or Central America. The recommendation of preventing men from "conceiving plans" supports the individual responsibility model of neoliberalism, assuming that people can simply decide not to migrate. As such the recommendation ignores the violence in which people live – both physical and structural violence – and ignores the practically inexistent possibilities for large groups of Mexicans and Central Americans to migrate legally. Finally, the recommendation ignores the state's distinction between those deserving of the rights of citizenship and those who may provide profit through low-paid work precisely because they are "deportable" and disposable (De Genova and Peutz 2010).

In focusing only on the risks migrants take, researchers, policymakers, and others fail to acknowledge the limited possibilities for working poor migrants to enter the United States and the increasing dangers to migrants that are outcomes of security strategies. Politicians and the public alike argue that undocumented migrants must wait at the "back of the line" and enter the country legally, ignoring that it is all but impossible for working poor migrants to do so. Current US immigration laws provide almost no possibility for low-income migrants to obtain a visa to enter the United States. Family reunification is no longer a government priority and for many has been blocked as a legal option. The actual end of the line is for many migrants

[6] Anthropologists Sally Engle Merry and Susan Bibler Coutin examine knowledge systems as "part of conflicts rather than extrinsic to them"; they note that technologies "produce and reinforce hierarchies between what is 'knowable' and what is not" (2014: 1). Their work follows that of scholars such as Jean and John Comaroff who analyze the uses of numbers in "the construction of moral publics, so integral to debate about democracy, freedom, security, human rights" (2006: 211).

an unmarked grave in Mexico or the United States. In stark contrast, those with significant wealth can obtain visas to enter legally and even to obtain green cards in the United States. The EB-5 federal visa program allows foreigners who invest at least $500,000 and promise to create ten jobs to apply for a green card as noted in a recent New York Times article, "Want a Green Card? Invest in Real Estate."

Likewise, coyotes commonly are blamed for putting migrants at risk and in harm's way. Border Patrol agents refer to coyotes as the enemy that causes violence to or defrauds migrants, without attention to the structural forces that make coyotes necessary for reaching the United States and crossing the southwest. Most important, coyotes would not be needed at all if migrants could obtain a visa to enter the country legally. Yet when state agents in both Mexico and the United States locate migrants who are in danger, they are seen as "rescuing" them rather than as the very cause of the danger. To give but one example from the United States, on March 19, 2014, news media in Houston, Texas, reported that police officers found more than 100 people "crammed" into a small "stash house". Reportedly, coyotes held these Mexican and Central American migrants, demanding payment from family members, beyond the initial fee charged. The migrants were "rescued" by police, but turned over to Homeland Security, most likely to be deported. Brian Moskowitz of Houston's Homeland Security Operations noted that the case likely does not meet legal requirements as a trafficking case, which would allow those detained to file for a special visa.[7] This means they would be deported and have to begin their journey from Central America through Mexico and across the border again. The term "stash house" comes directly from language on drugs and narco-trafficking, linking the illicit drugs to illicit migrants.

All of these explanations of violence against migrants – blaming migrants for making poor decisions, for failing to follow laws, and for taking risks – miss the role of the state in creating the conditions of poverty and violence that migrants seek to escape, the lack of legal channels for migrants to use to enter the United States, and the enforcement policies in both Mexico and the United States that create dangers and cause death.

## Making Life and Death Visible

In response to migrant deaths and the large number of the missing, family members and activists work to make visible the violence against migrants. They challenge calls from policymakers for an increase in border security – a security defined only in terms of keeping migrants out of the nation, not in terms of protecting the life and well-being of migrants living in or attempting to reach the United States. With images of loved ones, family members and activists in the United States, Mexico, and Central America march to make the missing visible and protest policies that cause deaths.

---

[7] http://www.care2.com/causes/horrific-stash-house-highlights-desperation-of-illegal-immigration.html#ixzz30aS0ujMC.

Activists and families challenge the technologies of measurement and assessment commonly used by Border Patrol and other state agents to selectively count and quantify in ways that cause violence. Counting is central to the work of the US Customs and Border Patrol of the Department of Homeland Security. Yet what "counts" and who gets "counted" is counter to the concerns of families and activists. Border Patrol relies on statistics of "success" for continued funding. Its webpage provides tables, charts, and statistics in multiple forms including staffing by fiscal year, broken down by geographic sector: coastal border, northern border, and southwest border. It reports data on "immigration removals" that classify those convicted of a crime, country of origin, and the regions with the highest number of detentions. While Border Patrol "counts" migrants as "illegal aliens" who are apprehended at checkpoints, there is little effort to identify the dead. As noted, in Texas many unidentified persons have been buried without taking any DNA as required by state law. Even when DNA samples are collected, family members must enter their DNA in a database in order to make a match to identify the dead. Not only are many family members (residing in the United States, Mexico, or Central America) hesitant to submit samples, many law enforcement agencies in the United States refuse to take DNA samples from foreign nationals and fail to enter DNA profiles into databases that could facilitate identification.

While billions of dollars are spent each year to militarize and securitize the US-Mexico border, counties along the border, some of the poorest counties in Texas, lack funds to process and identify the dead.[8] The absence of standardized practices coupled with a lack of funds and political will to identify or even locate the dead means that many families may never know what happened to their loved ones. The low rate of identification is a powerful example of structural violence; because of inequalities of race, nationality, and class, migrants cross Mexico, the border, and south Texas in extremely dangerous conditions. For those who perish, their remains may never be recovered and if they are recovered, they may never be identified. As such, these migrants fit Judith Butler's (2010: 1) concept of "ungrievable," by the state, that is, their lives "cannot be apprehended as injured or lost if they are not first apprehended as living."

However, migrant deaths are grieved by family members and activists. In the summer of 2013, Houston activists, concerned about the deaths in Brooks County, worked to make border deaths visible as a concrete outcome of border militarization. Like activists and family members in Latin America in the past decades, remembering the dead and the disappeared connects to the human rights work of denouncing state violence and supporting immigrant rights. Long-time prison rights activist Pat Hartwell created a detailed Texas map with push pins marking each one of the 271 deaths recorded by the Border Patrol for the year 2012. She titled the map "Body Count" and included family photos of the missing and the dead. The Working Group to Prevent Migrant Deaths, later renamed the Migrant Rights Collective, created a

[8] The budget for US Border Patrol alone was 3.7 billion dollars for the Fiscal Year 2015. https://www.cbp.gov/sites/default/files/assets/documents/2016-Oct/BP%20Budget%20History%201990-2016.pdf,

series of posters with family photos of missing migrants, including their names and the date they disappeared to present at a series of public events from a hearing in Congress in Washington, DC, to a town hall meeting in Houston, and forums on immigrant rights. At a May Day vigil for immigrant and worker rights in 2013, activists placed dozens of white crosses to represent the dead in Houston's Guadalupe Park Plaza to mark and remember their lives. At this event, a woman from El Salvador shared a story of her nephew who was injured in Brooks County and could not continue the journey. She explained that when she went to the funeral home in Falfurrias to try to identify him, she was told she would have to pay thousands of dollars to exhume his remains. A Mexican migrant told of his cousin who had disappeared in northern Mexico due to violence in the region and whose whereabouts are unknown. Participants at the vigil placed a flower at the foot of each of the white crosses to remember those who had died. Members of the Working Group pointed out that while politicians in D.C. kept counting votes toward fictional immigration reform, people in Texas were counting bodies and disappeared.

Several slogans used at immigrant rights marches attempt to challenge the failure to count migrants as political actors. One example is "no somos uno, ni somos cien, somos milliones, cuentános bien" ("We are not one, we are not a hundred, we are millions, count us well"). In another example of turning around the power of numbers, the National Day Labor Organizing Network created the slogans "Not1More" to protest deportations and "2MillionTooMany" to denounce the record deportations that have taken place under the Obama Administration.

Just as Latin American women organized themselves in search of their missing family members in groups such as the Mothers of the Plaza de Mayo in Argentina and the Co-Madres (Mothers and Relatives of Political Prisoners, Disappeared, and Assassinated of El Salvador "Monseñor Romero"), migrant family members have formed organizations in Central America and Mexico to locate their loved ones and promote immigrant rights. For example, the Committee of Relatives of Deceased and Disappeared Migrants (Comité de Familiares de Migrantes Fallecidos y Desaparecidos, COFAMIDE), was initiated in 2006 in El Salvador to search for mothers, fathers, sons, and daughters who began their journey toward the United States who were never heard from again. COFAMIDE works in El Salvador, the United States, and Mexico to try to locate the missing migrants. The Honduran Committee for Disappeared Migrant Relatives (Comité de Familiares de Migrantes Desaparecidos) helps family members search for loved ones and also works to raise awareness about the difficulties migrants face, provide psychological assistance to migrants and their families, and support migrants that return with severe injuries, including limbs amputated by the freight trains, among other tasks. Members of these groups organize caravans throughout Mexico in search of their loved ones. In doing so, these women work to make the crimes against migrants visible and demand broad respect for immigrant rights.

The events described at the opening of this chapter are two of many ways that families and activists remember the lives of those who have died, demand that the dead be identified, and work to put an end to border deaths all together. In reflecting on the significance of forensic work in identifying the dead, Adam Rosenblatt notes that "mass grave investigations are described as an avenue toward some ethical or political goal ultimately meant to benefit *living* people" (2015: 157). For border deaths, exhumations and identifications serve to support the living families of the missing. Yet the human rights' work to prevent migrant deaths in the first place is required in addition to the work of identifications. While the deaths of thousands of migrants in Mexico's vertical border, along the US-Mexico border, and in South Texas are not visibly linked to repressive governments, they are nonetheless caused by policies of exclusion and rooted in discourses that dehumanize and criminalize. Security policies, ostensibly designed to protect members of the "homeland," push migrants to travel in dangerous conditions. Neoliberal economic policies limit the possibility of surviving with dignity in their sending communities. In this context, it might be relevant to question the meaning of "democracy," when governments not only allow but design policies that have led to the death of thousands.

## References

Agosín, M. (2008). *Tapestries of hope, threads of love: The Arpillera movement in Chile*. Lanham: Rowman & Littlefield.

Bacon, D. (2014). Immigrant labor, immigrant rights. *NACLA Report on the Americas, 47*(1), 64–69.

Baker, L. E. (2013). *Corn meets maize: Food movements and markets in Mexico*. Lanham: Rowman & Littlefield.

Bourgois, P. (2004). The continuum of violence in war and peace: Post-cold war lessons from El Salvador. In N. Scheper-Hughes & P. Bourgois (Eds.), *Violence in war and peace*. Malden: Blackwell.

Butler, J. (2010). *Frames of war: When is life grievable?* London: Verso.

De Genova, N., & Peutz, N. (2010). *The deportation regime: Sovereignty, space, and the freedom of movement*. Durham: Duke University Press.

De León, J. (2015). *The land of open graves: Living and dying on the migrant trail*. Berkeley: University of California Press.

Due Process of Law, Centro de Derechos Humanos Fray Matías de Córdova, & El Hogar de la Misericordia (2008). La crisis de derechos humanos en la frontera sur de México. Centro de Derechos Humanos Fray Matías de Córdova, Washington, DC/Tapachula.

Dunn, T. (2009). *Blockading the border and human rights: The El Paso operation that remade immigration enforcement*. Austin: University of Texas Press.

Edkins, J. (2011). *Missing persons and politics*. Ithaca: Cornell University Press.

Gomberg-Muñoz, R. (2012). Inequality in a "Postracial" era: Race, immigration, and criminalization of low-wage labor. *The DuBois Review, 9*(2), 339–353.

Harvey, D. (2005). *A brief history of neoliberalism*. New York: Oxford University Press.

Jimenez, M. (2009). *Humanitarian crisis: Migrant deaths at the U.S.-Mexico border*. San Diego: ACLU of San Diego & Imperial Counties and Mexico's National Commission of Human Rights.

Kovic, C. (2010). The violence of security: Central American migrants crossing Mexico's southern border. *Anthropology Now*, *2*(1).

Merry, S. E., & Susan, B. C. (2014). Technologies of truth in the anthropology of conflict. *American Anthropologist, 41*(1), 1–16.

Paz Carrasco, M. A., Cerda García, A., & Ledón Pereyra, A. (2016). *Mirar Las Fronteras Desde El Sur: Salud y migración en la frontera México-Centroamérica*. Guatemala-Mexico: Mesa de Coordinación Transfronteriza, Migraciones y Género, Universidad Autónoma Metropolitana-Unidad Xochimilco, voces Mesoamericanas, Acción con Pueblos Migrantes, A.C.

Petrich, B. (2014). Arriba al D.F. caravana de migrantes centroamericanos. *La Jornada*. April 23, 2014.

Rosenblatt, A. (2015). *Digging for the disappeared: Forensic science after atrocity*. Stanford: Stanford University Press.

Rubio-Goldsmith, R., McCormick, M. M., Martinez, D., & Duarte, I. M. (2006). *The 'Funnel Effect' and recovered bodies of unauthorized migrants processed by the Pima County Office of the Medical Examiner, 2990–2005. Report Submitted to the Pima County Board of Supervisors*. Tucson: Binational Migration Institute.

Sapkota, S., Kohl, H. W., Gilchrist, J., McAuliffe, J., Parks, B., England, B., et al. (2006). Unauthorized border crossings and migrant deaths: Arizona, New Mexico, and El Paso, Texas, 2002–2003. *American Journal of Public Health, 96*(7), 1282–1287.

Seelke, C.R., & Finklen, K. (2016). U.S.-Mexico security cooperation: The Mérida Initiative and Beyond. Congressional Research Service, 75700. https://www.fas.org/sgp/crs/row/R41349.pdf.

Stephen, L. (2008). Los Nuevos Desaparecidos y Muertos: Immigration, militarization, death and disappearance on Mexico's Borders. In B. Sutton, S. Morgan, & J. Novkov (Eds.), *Security disarmed: Critical perspectives on gender, race, and militarization* (pp. 79–100). New Brunswick: Rutgers University Press.

Texas Code of Criminal Procedure (n.d.). Chapter 63: Missing children and missing persons. http://www.statutes.legis.state.tx.us/Docs/CR/htm/CR.63.htm.

U.S. Border Patrol (2016). Southwest border deaths by Fiscal Year. U.S. Customs and Border Protection. https://www.cbp.gov/sites/default/files/assets/documents/2016-Oct/BP%20Southwest%20Border%20Sector%20Deaths%20FY1998%20-%20FY2016.pdf.

Villegas, R. D., & Rietig, V. (2015). *Migrants deported from the United States to the northern Triangle: A statistical and socioeconomic profile*. Washington, DC: Migration Policy Institute.

# Chapter 5
# Loss, Uncertainty, and Action: Ethnographic Encounters with Families of the Missing in the Central America-Mexico-United States Corridor

**Wendy A. Vogt**

Don Antonio walked through the front door to the office, and my stomach immediately dropped. I easily recognized him—his short stature, wrinkled and weathered skin, calloused feet in leather huaraches, woven bag over his shoulder, and tattered hat. He moved slowly but with purpose. He had become a regular visitor to the migrant shelter and organization where I worked. We knew what he was looking for, and each time he came to visit, we had the same answer. There were no new updates for him on the case of his son, Alex, who went missing while crossing the US-Mexico border earlier that year. Alex was last seen alive underneath a mesquite tree with his jacket tied around his waist. The two men who were with Alex, and who had traveled from the same Zapotec village in the Tlacolula District in the valley of Oaxaca, had since returned to Oaxaca after being deported by the US Border Patrol. The men were crossing what is known as the "Devil's Highway" in the Sonoran Desert of Arizona with a smuggler. Before leaving Alex underneath the tree, the smuggler took all the cash from Alex's wallet but left his ID card and placed it inside his jacket.

Don Antonio asked us how long it usually takes to find people in the desert. There are, of course, no simple answers to this question. He then speculated that maybe Alex was still alive and that is why his body has not been found. He told us that one of his family members reported they thought they might have seen Alex in Los Angeles but the details were unclear. We assured Don Antonio that if we found out any new information we would call him immediately. We would also be traveling to the village to conduct interviews with the other two men who were with Alex during the crossing to find out more information. Don Antonio nodded, he understood what we were saying, and he told us to be sure to stop by his home when we

W.A. Vogt (✉)
Department of Anthropology, Indiana University-Purdue University Indianapolis, Indianapolis, IN, USA
e-mail: wvogt@iupui.edu



K.E. Latham, A.J. O'Daniel (eds.), *Sociopolitics of Migrant Death and Repatriation*, Bioarchaeology and Social Theory,
DOI 10.1007/978-3-319-61866-1_5

visited. He left the office with no new answers, but I realized that during this time of extreme uncertainty, traveling to the city from his small rural village became his pilgrimage, his ritual, the one way he could be proactive as he grappled with the absence of his son.

Don Antonio is just one of thousands of family members across the Americas who live with the uncertainty of the fate of loved ones who have been detained, have disappeared, or have perished during their journeys to the north. This chapter shifts the focus from the politics of migrant death and repatriation from the US-Mexico border region to a wider geography of risk and violence that encompasses migrant transit routes and home communities within the Central America-Mexico-US corridor.

Long-term ethnographic research with both migrants in transit and migrant families illuminates the ways individuals, families, communities, human rights workers, scientists, and state actors become intimately linked as they grapple with the ever-changing contexts, logics, and production of migrant death. In doing so, I pay particular attention to how families cope with the uncertainty of missing loved ones. I argue that while disappearance has profound effects on the families of the missing, these responses are not monolithic. Families cope with the loss of loved ones in varied, sometimes surprising ways, demonstrating the breadth of both human resiliency and agency. Migrant families are not simply victims but engage state and non-state actors, institutions, and mediums as they confront the emotional, legal, and financial implications of loss. As the families of migrants negotiate these aftereffects, in some cases they create new openings for solidarity and engagement. I use these examples to develop an argument around the families of the missing as transnational actors, creating new meanings in anthropological understandings of transnational families.

## Searching Across Borders

When I set off to do fieldwork on the intersections between violence and migration in southern Mexico, I did not intend to encounter, much less do research on, the experiences of the families of missing migrants. My area of focus was—and still is—centered on the experiences of Central American migrants in transit through Mexico. My primary field site was a shelter located in the state of Oaxaca where I worked as a volunteer and conducted ethnographic research with migrants in transit and humanitarian aid workers. I also traveled to about a dozen other humanitarian aid shelters in southern Mexico and the Mexico-Guatemala border. In Mexico there is a network of over 50 shelters that offer room and board, medical attention, and in some cases legal help to Central Americans fleeing conditions of endemic poverty and everyday violence in Guatemala, Honduras, and El Salvador. The network of shelters has emerged in response to the multiple forms of violence Central Americans experience during their transit journeys. While en route, Central Americans regularly encounter extortion, assault, robbery, kidnapping, and death. While shelters are crucial in addressing the humanitarian crisis unfolding across Mexico, they are also contested spaces, where local residents fear migrants as outsiders.

Casa Guadalupe, the shelter where I worked in the city of Oaxaca, was also seen as a resource for local families. Casa Guadalupe began to attract the attention of local Oaxacans, many of them from indigenous Mixtec or Zapotec communities, seeking assistance on a variety of issues related to the migration and disappearance of their loved ones. It is important here to briefly outline the social context of migration in Oaxaca state. In addition to being one of the most ethnically diverse states, Oaxaca has the second highest poverty rate in Mexico and has one of the highest rates of out-migration. While migration has historically been a key livelihood strategy for indigenous Oaxacan families (Stephen 2007; Velasco Ortiz 2005; Kearney 2004; Lopez and Runsten 2004), shifts in US immigration policy over the past two decades have significantly impacted the ways both migrants and their families experience migration. Increased militarization of the US-Mexico border region (Nevins 2002; Andreas 2000; Dunn 1996; Heyman 1994) and the criminalization of unauthorized migration in the US (De Genova 2004) have not only made migrant journeys more dangerous and costly but also contribute to long-term family separation. Where Oaxacan migrants once worked as seasonal workers moving between Mexico and the US, many no longer risk making multiple crossing attempts (Holmes 2013). Moreover, legal restraints and the significant increase in raids and deportations of unauthorized migrants in recent years have also contributed to family separation (Abrego 2014; Boehm 2012).

Long-term family separation engendered by restrictive migration laws and border enforcement means that when family members go missing, financial and legal constraints often create barriers for local families searching for their loved ones. While in some cases the Mexican state facilitates cross-border actions, like the repatriation of identified remains of a deceased loved ones, there are no official state pathways or consistent forms of support to investigate missing loved ones who disappear during their crossings or while living in the US. Indeed, the Mexican state is heavily criticized for its incompetency in investigating its own citizens who have gone missing within Mexico. As such, the work of searching for missing loved ones in the US falls to the families themselves. While some families, especially those with resources and language skills, may take on the role of amateur detectives, most families, particularly in poor and rural areas, find themselves isolated in the context of a family disappearance.

While not widespread, in some cases civil society organizations like Casa Guadalupe emerged to support families grappling with the rippling effects of migration. As a volunteer and researcher at Casa Guadalupe and US citizen with English language skills, I was able to assist in several cases. For example, I tracked down inmate numbers and addresses of people detained in US federal detention facilities and assisted in transferring money out of immigrants' banking accounts post-deportation. I also traveled to family homes to conduct in-depth interviews, file missing person reports with organizations on the US-Mexico border, and collect DNA samples from relatives that may prove useful in the identification of human remains uncovered in the border region.

Through everyday life at the shelter working with both migrants in transit and the families of missing migrants, I began to see these trajectories and social issues not as separate but intimately related. On that summer day when Don Antonio arrived to the office, he greeted and shook hands with a young couple staying at the shelter. They smiled at him as they made phone calls to Guatemala, quietly speaking to their own parents and loved ones back home. I could sense Don Antonio's concern for the couple and when they left he said to me, "If I knew what was going to happen I would never have let my son go." Through this brief encounter between migrants headed to the US-Mexico border and the father of a young man who had likely died while crossing that very border, I began to reconceptualize what I initially thought about as two distinct flows and trajectories. These individuals, differentiated by citizenship, ethnicity, and age, were nevertheless connected within a larger geography of violence, uncertainty, and family separation engendered by the risks of contemporary mobilities.

## Geographies of Risk, Disappearance, and Death

Within this geography, the US-Mexico border region is the most visible site of migrant death and dying in the Americas. In recent years, scholars have begun to systematically examine the devastating human costs of US immigration policies along the border (Slack et al. 2016; De León 2015; Martinez et al. 2013). For example, in his recent book, Jason De Leon (2015) argues that the border has become a "state of exception" where US immigration policies, namely, Prevention Through Deterrence, strategically funnel unauthorized border crossers through harsh desert terrains where the desert acts as a weapon against migrants and their bodies. While the USA-Mexico border is a crucial space to witness the effects of state militarization, the human consequences of such policies and violence extend well *beyond* the border region.

Scholars of US immigration policies have sought to decenter the US-Mexico border as a privileged site of immigration enforcement. Since September 11, 2001, the political climate and approach to immigration enforcement in the US underwent a significant shift. Under a new homeland security framework, political borders have been reproduced in more localized and everyday forms of control. Rosas (2006) has conceptualized the sociopolitical "thickening" of the border, arguing for an understanding of the "plasticity of the exceptionality of the borderlands" through racialized practices of policing immigrant groups. In recent decades, we have seen this "thickening" of the US-Mexico border through militarization, policing, and surveillance into both communities in the US and throughout Mexico.

Elsewhere I have argued for analysis of what I call the "arterial border," the proliferation and intensification of US-supported state policing and militarization within Mexico's interior (Vogt 2017). US involvement in Mexico's immigration and border enforcement began in the 1980s during the Central American civil wars and has continued to the present day in response to periods of increased migration.[1] The proliferation of bordering practices along the highways and train routes that cut across Mexico like arteries has funneled migrants into more dangerous clandestine routes where abuse, extortion, sexual violence, kidnapping, and death at the hands of multiple actors are common. For Central American migrants in transit, the multiple borders they cross are sections of a larger whole that comprise their journeys. Migrants live in these liminal spaces of transit (Vogt 2013) for undetermined periods where they are susceptible to violence, disappearance, and death. As such, I argue for a more broadly conceptualized geography of risk and violence that extends beyond the US-Mexico border region and into spaces of home, transit, and destination. By expanding the geography of migrant death, we may move toward a more transnational and holistic understanding of effects of migration into households and communities across the Americas.

## Mexico: Home, Transit, and Destination

Padre Alejandro Solalinde, one of the most outspoken critics and defender of migrant rights in Mexico, publicly stated that "Todo Mexico es una fosa" (All of Mexico is a grave). Yet, as was pointed out to me by another priest who works along the Mexico-Guatemala border, for Central Americans, Mexico is a "cemetery without crosses" (Vogt 2013). Both these priests point to the fact that the Mexican state has very little accountability and virtually no track record in investigating the disappearances and deaths of both citizens and noncitizens. This became devastatingly apparent in the 2014 disappearance of 43 students in the town of Ayotzinapa and subsequent revelations that the disappearance was likely engineered by members of the state government in coordination with organized criminals. I traveled to Oaxaca just weeks after the students went missing. There were signs of protest and solidarity everywhere—street vendors with signs that read "Ayotzinapa, Your fight is my fight. Your pain is my pain. They were taken alive, we want them back alive!" On the front of the historic and spectacular Santo Domingo church in Oaxaca City, red graffiti marked "Fue el estado" (It was the state or the government did it), which has become a popular phrase in reference to Ayotzinapa but also signals the wider and more systemic forms of corruption and impunity in Mexico.

Since 2006 and the intensification of Mexico's war on drugs, death and disappearance have become more deeply integrated into public and everyday life in Mexico. An estimated 60,000–120,000 people have been killed, and the Mexican government reports at least 28,000 people missing, though human rights groups estimate that number is much higher because many families do not report for fear of reprisal. The Movimiento Migrante Mesoamericano (Mesoamerican Migrant

[1] For example, this type of militarization became most recently visible with the 2014 implementation of Mexico's Programa Frontera Sur, a result of US pressure on Mexico in the wake of the 2014 unaccompanied minor "crisis."

Movement) documents an estimated 24,000 bodies buried in unmarked graves in municipal cemeteries and 40,000 bodies of unidentified people in public morgues (Soler 2016). In March 2015, Mexico's attorney general (PGR) released a report documenting over 600 bodies discovered in 174 clandestine graves in 16 states in Mexico. Eighty percent of these bodies had not been identified. While many of the remains are thought to be victims of Mexico's drug war, at least some of the identified bodies, those uncovered in the northern Mexican state of Tamaulipas, were found to be of Central American migrants (Cancino 2015). While these numbers are only estimates, they speak to the gravity of the situation throughout Mexico. Mexico's drug war has wreaked havoc on the lives of everyday people, but we cannot underestimate the ways it has also transformed migrant routes and the experiences of Central American migrants in transit, people who have even less recourse to legal protections in Mexico.

There are no official systematic efforts to document and record the numbers of Central Americans who have died in transit, but reports by human rights organizations give us a clue into the extent of such violence. Based on early reports by Mexico's Human Rights Commission on the numbers of Central Americans who disappeared in mass kidnappings (Comisión Nacional de los Derechos Humanos 2011), migrant rights advocacy groups estimate that between 70,000 and 120,000 migrants have disappeared between 2006 and 2016 (Soler 2016). This figure may include migrants who have been kidnapped, have been forced into illicit economies, have been detained, have perished, or have lost communication for other reasons. But the systematic targeting of Central Americans was made crystal clear in August 2010 with the discovery of 72 mostly Central American migrants found executed on a ranch in the northern state of Tamaulipas, Mexico. I remember reading the news of what was to become known as "the Tamaulipas massacre," wondering if any of the migrants I had met and interviewed just weeks before were among the dead. Indeed, it would have likely taken them that amount of time to reach the northern border. As I contemplated this reality, my mind turned to the families of those 72 individuals and to the families of missing migrants across the Americas who were likely wondering the same thing.

## Rippling Effects of Loss and Uncertainty

In the absence of formal monitoring systems to document and combat the widespread violence and impunity suffered by migrants in transit, how do families grapple with the uncertainty surrounding the loss of their loved ones? In migration studies, there is an important body of literature on transnationalism and transnational families. Scholars have examined the arrangements, practices, experiences, and affective ties between parents and children located in different physical spaces. In such a framework, "physical absence is compatible with social presence and participation" (Carling et al. 2012). Migrants engage multiple "répertoires" (Coe 2014) to make sense of and negotiate the realities engendered by family separation.

Yet one area that is lacking from this research is the ways families make sense of and experience the absence of family members who are physically and legally separated not only by national borders and state policies but also by the uncertainty and silence that accompany migrant disappearance and death. The literature on transnational families focuses on the physical absence of family members from shared households and spaces, but these family members still exist in the world. What happens when family members go missing? How do the social relations and practices of care, affect, and transnational parenthood continue despite these absences? I argue that the theoretical framework of transnational families is useful in understanding not only the social ties and arrangements between family members connected across borders but also the rippling effects of migrant disappearance and loss on the families of migrants.

In 2008, I conducted a series of interviews with a woman named Doña Tere, the mother of a man who went missing while living in Texas. He had been living in the US for 5 years and maintained regular contact with her through weekly phone calls. But the phone calls stopped coming and she started to worry. She then received an anonymous phone call telling her that her son had been killed in a prison located in Ciudad Juarez, the border town across from El Paso. Doña Tere provided details of her attempts to locate her son in both Texas and Juarez, the cast of characters with which she has been in contact, and the tidbits of information she has been able to cobble together. She gave us all the phone numbers she had, and we spent weeks calling his neighbors and friends and local prisons trying to find him. Eventually Doña Tere decided she needed to look for him herself. She borrowed money from family members and spent months waiting for a tourist visa so she could travel to Dallas. As she waited, she often came to the office to run ideas by us. One of her ideas was to rent a car and purchase a loudspeaker so that she could use it to call his name in the neighborhood where he lived. Toward the end of my fieldwork, Doña Tere did eventually make the trip to Texas. She rented the car and the loudspeaker, though she returned with no answers. Over the course of our interviews, Doña Tere expressed a deep sense of pain and suffering associated with the uncertainty of her missing son. Despite the deafening silence of his absence, every time she heard a key in the front door of her home, she thought it might be her son, finally returning home.

A commonality between both Mexican and Central American families was the sense of uncertainty surrounding the loss of their loved ones. The theory of ambiguous loss, "A situation of unclear loss resulting from not knowing whether a loved one is dead or alive, absent or present" (Boss 2004:554), has become the hallmark framework in understanding these contexts. Ambiguous loss theory was coined by Pauline Boss in the 1970s and is correlated to symptoms of depression, anxiety, and family conflict. Where conventional practice is driven by demands for truth and closure, for many families coping with ambiguous loss, truth may never be found. Thus, psychologists have developed a set of therapeutic guidelines including normalizing ambivalence, tempering the need to control, and discovering hope (Boss 2006). While the theory of ambiguous loss has been applied primarily in US contexts, for example, in the aftermath of 9/11, scholars have also started to use it to understand the effects of loss on families in global contexts as well. Indeed, the International Committee of the Red Cross has adopted the theory of ambiguous loss to understand the effects of disappearance on families. While the theory of ambiguous loss is useful in gauging some of the immediate psychological effects of loss for families, migrant loss can have rippling effects into communities as well. I share the details from another case in order to demonstrate the wider social effects of migrant loss. At times, the uncertainty that accompanies a missing migrant can create ruptures within families and in local communities. I began this chapter with the story of Don Antonio Marquez, the father looking for his son, Alex, who went missing in the early summer of 2009 while crossing the Sonoran Desert in Arizona. Two months after Alex went missing, I traveled to his hometown to interview members of the Marquez family and the other two migrants, David and Jose, who were the last people to see him alive. The Marquez family who live in a predominately Zapotec village of less than 5,000 people in the valley of Oaxaca did not want their son Alex to migrate to the USA. However, David and Jose had made contact with a coyote who was going to help them cross and convinced Alex to go along with them. This coyote recruited migrants through the central speaker system common in small rural Oaxacan villages. Several weeks after their departure, David and Jose returned to the community without Alex. They had been detained and deported by US Immigration officials after flagging down a Border Patrol vehicle just north of Ajo, Arizona. David was the very last person to see Alex and was the one who had to tell his parents what happened to them during their four days crossing the desert.

Along with one of my coworkers at Casa Guadalupe, I visited David in his family home. We entered his house and were greeted by an older man with a terrible eye infection and two young children dressed in dirty clothes. They led us into the main room, where chickens roamed on the dirt floors. David was willing to talk to us about his experience, but the conversation was difficult. Not only was the crossing a traumatic event for him, but the after effects for his family and community have caused significant distress. As he spoke, he plucked dried kernels from an ear of corn and shook them in the palm of his hand, periodically throwing them on the ground for the chickens to eat. The group of three contracted the smuggler in their hometown, and after several long bus rides to Sonora, Mexico, they crossed the border near Sonoita, located between Tucson and Yuma. They didn't know it, but this stretch of land is known as the "Devil's Highway"; trails once used by prospectors on their way to look for gold in California are now used by smugglers and unauthorized migrants making their way north (Urrea 2005). As he described the strikingly beautiful and terrible landscape, David mentioned passing the debris of old bombs, most likely the southernmost edge of US Military Barry M. Goldwater bombing and gunnery range. He also described a large rock they had to climb over, marked with white crosses on it. Later, when David would draw a picture of their journey to send to humanitarian aid groups working on the border, this rock and crosses would feature prominently.

The smuggler gave the three young men white pills to take, which he promised would give them more energy for the crossing. But after four days of walking with very little water and food, several people in their group were severely dehydrated and blistered. Alex was the worst. The smuggler told Alex that he could not go on, and when they reached Ajo, he would leave him there. But Alex insisted that he wanted to continue with the group. The smuggler agreed, but soon he became so weak and dehydrated, and he could not continue. At that point Alex begged them to leave him. David described Alex lying underneath a tree in the desert with his jacket wrapped around his waist. He said he was still breathing when he left, leaving some hope that he may have survived. David also said that before they left Alex, the coyote took his wallet and all his money, leaving only his identification card.

Since his return, David has had a difficult time emotionally and socially. He carried the stigma and the guilt of returning home. The Marquez family blames him for leaving Alex in the desert and does not understand why he could not carry him with the rest of the group. As David spoke, he said that they do not understand how tired and weak he was after walking for four days with almost no water. He barely survived the journey himself. I also interviewed David's father who said that the Marquez family was making threats against them. David's father said that Alex and his parents were in a dispute before he left, and perhaps he was still alive but has not called because he was still angry with them. David's family attempted to locate the coyote from their village for answers but found his house abandoned. He had moved on and no one knew where. When I interviewed Alex's parents at their home, they were distraught and asked many questions, and his mother cried profusely. They asked how long it would take to find him and what is the normal amount of time. There were no easy answers to their questions. As far as I know, Alex's remains have not been recovered. 2009 was one of the deadliest summers for migrants crossing the Tucson sector of the US-Mexico border. The Pima County Medical Examiner's office examined the remains of 190 unidentified border crossers that year (Martinez et al. 2013). As scholars and activists have argued, the remains that are actually uncovered are thought to be only a portion of the total number of people who died while crossing the border.

This story exemplifies some of the uncertainty and heartbreak experienced by families of missing migrants and illustrates how migration can create fractures within local communities. Alex's family still held out some hope that they would find him and that he might even return. At the very least, they hoped to find some closure and to bring his body back home where he belonged. And yet, the goals of bringing remains home are not shared uniformly among all families of the missing. In 2013, I returned to Mexico where I accompanied one of my colleagues and a local priest to a rural village in the mountainous region of Oaxaca's Sierra Sur. Our mission that day was to deliver the news to a family that the remains of their loved one, Artemio, had been recovered in the desert of Arizona. His remains were at the medical examiner's office in Tucson, and the Mexican consulate needed the family to sign the appropriate forms to have his body repatriated. We spent the day traveling the windy road up to the village and finally located his house, a small wooden house with dirt floors with a small fire slowly burning outside. We reached the house where we encountered Artemio's mother, wife, and two children. The priest reiterated to the family that they were almost 100 % certain that this was a match for Artemio and that the science was conclusive. But the mother resisted and shrugged her shoulders. "Ni modo" (oh well, it doesn't matter); she said over and over again. She then stated, "How can you take some saliva from my mouth and use that to tell me that my son is dead?" She said she simply did not believe them and that as a mother she knew in her heart that her son was still alive. The science behind DNA testing simply did not translate to this family, and we left that day without getting the form signed. Artemio's body would remain in the US, most likely buried in a communal grave. In this example, we see the limits of forensic science as it is applied in real world contexts. This work is not just about science; it is about a matrix of people connected between and across borders and boundaries. For it to be successful, there need to be more resources and attention not just to the remains of the missing but also to the wider familial and social networks of the missing. As migrant crossings become more clandestine and dangerous, it is crucial for social scientists to recognize the ways transnational families are being reshaped not only by family separation and deportation but also by disappearance and death.

Since the bulk of my fieldwork was completed in 2013, I have started working with a new organization founded in 2014 called CAMINOS (Centro de Acompañamiento a Migrantes, Oaxaca), which was founded by a former colleague at Casa Guadalupe. CAMINOS was created with the explicit goal of assisting the families of migrants in Oaxaca. This includes assisting the families of migrant farmworkers, of deported migrants, and of the missing. At the time of this writing, CAMINOS had over 80 open cases of missing family members. More research is needed with organizations like CAMINOS to understand the effects of state policies and contemporary conditions in the everyday lives of individuals, families, and communities. What we can see so far is that while conditions are often devastating, people are resilient and find new ways to come together, organize, and seek answers and justice.

## Solidarity and Activism Among Families of the Missing

While the framework of ambiguous loss is useful in capturing the experiences of many families of the missing, it is also important to recognize the steps that families are taking in searching for their loved ones. For some, like Don Antonio, this meant taking a second-class bus from his rural village to the city to check on the status of his son's case. Yet, for others, we have witnessed remarkable forms of solidarity and activism among the families of the missing.

Across Mexico, regional civil society organizations have been created by the families of the missing as new forms of social networking and activism. A number of social media sites such as Facebook have also become important to organizing efforts for the families of the missing. There are Facebook profiles dedicated to individual people who have gone missing, including children. There are other Facebook groups with thousands of members where the families of the missing post photographs and information on their missing loved ones, people who went missing while crossing the border, or people suspected of being deported.[2] People also use

[2] For example, one group "Desaparecidos Que Murieron Tras Perseguir El Sueño Americano" has over 25,000 members (https://www.facebook.com/groups/775009732596941/).

Facebook as a space to share photographs of bodies that have been recovered in helping to locate and inform family members. People include information such as age; last place seen alive; identifying markers such as birthmarks, tattoos, and dental work; and phone numbers of family members. Members often respond in the comments with words of encouragement, blessings, or simply "compartido" (shared) in their locations. Through these social media sites, we see how the rippling effects of migrant disappearance extend beyond physical spaces and communities and through cyberspace.

In addition to these new forms of social networking and solidarity, transnational organizations, Mexican citizens, and local civil society organizations are developing new pathways to bring together forensic science and humanitarian efforts around the missing. Since 2009, in coordination with a multinational group of partners, the Argentine Forensic Anthropology Team (EAAF) has also started working along the southern and northern borders in Mexico in an effort called Proyecto Frontera to recover the remains of Mexican and Central American migrants who have perished during their transit journeys (Délano Alonso et al. 2016; Schwartz-Marin and Cruz-Santiago 2016). In the US, the Colibrí Center for Human Rights works directly with families and forensic scientists to search for the missing and identify the dead (http://www.colibricenter.org/).

In Mexico a new humanitarian organization called Citizen-led Forensics (Ciencia Forense Ciudadana) was established in 2014 to create a mechanism where "citizens can systematize and co-govern forensic technologies" including the operation of an online forensic database to register the cases of missing persons and a DNA biobank that contains the samples of families of the disappeared (http://cienciaforenseciudadana.org.) There are efforts underway in Mexico on the part of organizations of the families of missing migrants and other human rights groups to push for a national DNA database for the missing in Mexico. Ernesto Schwartz-Marin and Arely Cruz-Santiago, researchers of Citizen-led Forensics, argue that this is an example of the ways everyday citizens are transgressing expert and political boundaries by "resignifying forensic practices which are generally the monopoly of the state" (Schwartz-Marin and Cruz-Santiago 2016).

At the local level, people are utilizing forensic science in their efforts to find answers. In 2016, a group of mothers and family members in the state of Veracruz, frustrated with the lack of action and accountability on behalf of the state, took measures into their own hands when they uncovered over 100 unmarked graves in a field adjacent to a residential neighborhood. The LA Times called these families, which originally formed from a WhatsApp chat group and has more than 50 members, "amateur forensic anthropologists" (McDonnell 2016).

In addition to these actions in Mexico, we also see the emergence of groups and organizations working on a transnational level to search for missing migrants. One of the most compelling displays of solidarity and action around the disappearances and deaths of migrants in Latin America comes of out the work of several organizations in Central America comprised of the families of missing migrants. These organizations coordinate an annual caravan that traces the steps of their missing loved ones through transit routes across Mexico. In 2009, I accompanied the caravan of the Central American mothers of missing migrants in southern Mexico. The caravan was largely organized by the Salvadoran organization Asociación Comité de Familiares de Migrantes Fallecidos y Desaparecidos de El Salvador (Committee of Relatives of Dead and Disappeared Migrants, COFAMIDE).

A group of about a dozen families carried large cardboard posters with the photographs of their missing loved ones. Some had children go missing only years before, others for decades. I interviewed several of the families and listened to them as they passed around a microphone sharing their personal testimonies. During a march in the Oaxacan transit town of Ixtepec, one mother handed out printed flyers with the photo of her missing son as she still held out hope that she would find him. Indeed, the caravan has been successful in locating several family members living in Mexico. During a caravan in November 2011, one mother was able to locate her son who had been imprisoned in Chiapas for the past 7 years. As these mothers retraced the movements of their missing children, they spatially expressed the rippling effects of clandestine migration. The migration of individuals impacts family, community, and nation. They wanted to witness this journey and to know the landscapes where their children, and thousands of others like them, have disappeared.

Latin American women have a strong historical tradition of drawing on their roles as mothers and caregivers to make strategic alliances in various political movements. Examples of such women's activism include most famously the Asociación Madres de Plaza de Mayo who protested against their disappeared children in Argentina's Dirty War (1976–1983) and the Committee of Mothers and Relatives of the Political Prisoners, Disappeared, and Assassinated of El Salvador "Monseñor Romero" (CO-MADRES) who protested their missing family members in El Salvador's civil war (Stephen 1995). Through making their own histories known, these women refuse to let their children be forgotten. Furthermore, while the women who are at the front lines of these movements for migrant rights are suffering, they are neither suffering alone nor solely in private. Rather, they are making their suffering visible, through the media, in public marches, events, and their annual caravan, to compel people to see not only what they have gone through, as women and family members who have lost a loved one, but to raise awareness on the structural and state conditions that contribute to violence against migrants. Their actions illuminate the ways transnational families are being transformed and how the uncertainty associated with migrant loss and death spans both the private and public realms of intimate and civic life.

## Conclusion

As this chapter has demonstrated, migrant journeys continue on after death. They continue on in the labs and databases of multiple organizations and human rights groups located along national borders, in transit towns, in home communities, and at family dinner tables. Where Mexican and Central Americans have historically encountered violence during their transit journeys, as states implement harsher securitization programs, they now face more systematic forms of disappearance and death. In this paper I suggest that the everyday violence and death experienced by Mexicans and Central Americans must be understood as part of the same trajectory of violence and death along the Central America-Mexico-US corridor. This geography of risk and violence reflects state and structural policies that privilege sovereignty and power over human life and dignity. Yet in light of these changing and difficult contexts, migrant families engage a number of state and non-state actors and practices as they grapple with the effects of the loss of a loved one. The transnational ties that connect families across borders become interwoven into the everyday fabric of family and community life across the Americas. Yet, as we have seen over the last several years around the borders of Europe, the humanitarian crisis around dangerous transit journeys and migrant death is not unique to the Americas (Mediterranean Missing Project 2016). As states, scientists, and citizens around the world grapple with the immediate and lingering effects of migrant death, it is crucial that at the very least, the families of the missing are involved.

## References


Abrego, L. J. (2014). *Sacrificing families: Navigating laws, labor, and love across borders*. Palo Alto: Stanford University Press.

Andreas, P. (2000). *Border games: Policing the U.S.-Mexico divide*. Ithaca: Cornell University Press.

Boehm, D. (2012). *Intimate migrations: Gender, family, and illegality among transnational Mexicans*. New York: NYU Press.

Boss P. (2004). Ambiguous loss research, theory, and practice: Reflections after 9/11. *Journal of Marriage Family, 66*(554), 551–556.

Boss, P. (2006). *Loss, trauma and resilience: Therapeutic work with ambiguous loss*. New York: Norton.

Cancino, F. (2015). Fosas clandestinas, en 16 estados del país. El Universal.

Carling, J., Menjívar, C., & Schmalzbauer, L.. (2012). Central themes in the study of transnational parenthood. *Journal of Ethnic and Migration Studies, 38*(2), 191–217.

Coe, C. (2014). *The scattered family: Parenting, African migrants, and global inequality*. Chicago: The University of Chicago Press.

Comisión Nacional de los Derechos Humanos. (2011). Informe Especial Sobre Secuestro de Migrantes en México. *Comisión Nacional de los Derechos Humanos*.

De Genova, N. (2004). The legal production of Mexican/migrant 'Illegality'. *Latino Studies, 2*(2), 160–185.

De León, J. (2015). *The land of open graves: Living and dying on the migrant trail*. Berkeley: UC Press.

Délano Alonso, A., Galbraith, P. D., & Nienass, B. (2016). Bringing the dead back into society: An interview with Mercedes Doretti. *Social Research: An International Quarterly, 83*(2), 511–534.

Dunn, T. (1996). *The militarization of the U.S.-Mexico border 1978–1992: Low-intensity doctrine conflict comes home*. Austin: Center for Mexican American Studies, University of Texas at Austin.

Heyman, J. M. (1994). The Mexico-United States border in anthropology: A critique and reformulation. *Journal of Political Ecology, 1*, 43–65.

Holmes, S. (2013). *Fresh fruit, broken bodies*. Berkeley: University of California Press.

Kearney, M. (2004). *Changing fields of anthropology: From local to global*. Lanham: Rowman & Littlefield Publishers, Inc.

Lopez, F. H., & Runsten, D. (2004). Mixtecs and Zapotecs working in California: Rural and urban experiences. In G. Rivera-Salgado & J. Fox (Eds.), *Indigenous Mexican migrants in the United States*. La Jolla: Center for U.S.-Mexican Studies, UCSD.

Martinez, D., Reineke, R., Rubio-Goldsmith, R., Anderson, B., Hess, G., & Parks, B. (2013). A continued humanitarian crisis at the border: Undocumented border crosser deaths recorded by the Pima County Office of the Medical Examiner, 1990–2012. *The Binational Migration Institute, The University of Arizona*.

McDonnell, P. (2016). 'Mexico is one big cemetery': The search for the secret graves of 'the disappeared'. *Los Angeles Times*.

Mediterranean Missing Project. (2016). 'Like a part of a puzzle which is missing': The impact on families of a relative missing in migration across the Mediterranean. Mediterranean Missing: Understanding the Needs of Families and the Obligations of States. *The Mediterranean Missing Project*.

Nevins, J. (2002). *Operation gatekeeper: The rise of the "Illegal Alien" and the making of the U.S.-Mexico boundary*. New York: Routledge.

Rosas, G. (2006). The thickening borderlands: Diffused exceptionality and 'Immigrant' social struggles during the 'War on Terror'. *Cultural Dynamics, 18*(3), 335–349.

Schwartz-Marin, E., & Cruz-Santiago, A. (2016). Pure corpses, dangerous citizens: Transgressing the boundaries between experts and mourners in the search for the disappeared in Mexico. *Social Research: An International Quarterly, 83*(2), 483–510.

Slack, J., Martínez, D., Lee, A. E., & Whiteford, S. (2016). The geography of border militarization: Violence, death and health in Mexico and the United States. *Journal of Latin American Geography, 15*(1), 7–32.

Soler, M. S. (2016). Central American Migration. https://movimientomigrantemesoamericano.org.

Stephen, L. (1995). Women's rights are human rights: The merging of feminine and feminist interests among El Salvador's mothers of the disappeared (CO-MADRES). *American Ethnologist, 22*(4), 807–827.

Stephen, L. (2007). *Transborder lives: Indigenous Oaxacans in Mexico, California, and Oregon*. Durham: Duke University Press.

Urrea, L. A. (2005). *The Devil's highway: A true story*. New York: Back Bay Books.

Velasco Ortiz, L. (2005). *Mixtec transnational identity*. Tucson: University of Arizona Press.

Vogt, W. (2013). Crossing Mexico: Structural violence and the commodification of undocumented central American migrants. *American Ethnologist, 40*(4), 764–780.

Vogt, W. (2017). The arterial border: Negotiating economies of risk and violence in Mexico's security regime. *International Journal of Migration and Border Studies, 3*(2–3), 192–207.

# Chapter 6
# The Geography of Migrant Death: Implications for Policy and Forensic Science

**Gabriella Soto and Daniel E. Martínez**

## Introduction

A preponderance of evidence indicates a high correlation between the current paradigm of US border enforcement and a rise in undocumented migrant deaths in the USA-Mexico borderlands. While many of our colleagues in this volume focus on their involvement in identifying migrant remains, this chapter explores the multifaceted implications of the geography of death. Where do migrants die? Over more than two decades of border enforcement following the existing strategic regime, has the geography of death shifted? If so, what are the implications of this shift? What can geographic analyses of the changing locations of migrant death tell us about the efficacy of current border strategy?

Following other contributions to this volume, we work from the premise that death does not occur in a vacuum. The sociopolitical and geographic circumstances of migrant deaths necessitate particular attention and care. Each discovered migrant body prompts a series of medicolegal and social responses. But under the current circumstances, migrant deaths recurrently appear in clusters, often meriting mass casualty responses continuing over months and years. What is the impact of migrant deaths on the particular places where those deaths occur?

We begin first with a brief discussion of the key moments in the evolution of border security leading to the present. In particular, we situate our analysis from the US Border Patrol's (USBP) implementation of Operation Blockade (Hold-the-Line) in El Paso, Texas, in 1993; it is at this time that US border enforcement strategy

G. Soto (✉)
School of Anthropology, University of Arizona, Tucson, AZ, USA
e-mail: sotog@email.arizona.edu

D.E. Martínez
School of Sociology, University of Arizona, Tucson, AZ, USA
e-mail: danielmartinez@gwu.edu



K.E. Latham, A.J. O'Daniel (eds.), *Sociopolitics of Migrant Death and Repatriation*, Bioarchaeology and Social Theory,
DOI 10.1007/978-3-319-61866-1_6

came to rely on dangerous geography as a force multiplier for border control. Next, we move from a broad interstate analysis of trends in migrant deaths to a more localized analysis of deaths in Pima County, Arizona, and Brooks County, Texas. These two counties have become loci of what is known as the "funnel effect," described as USBP's continued push of migration into more difficult and dangerous territory. In this effort, we undertake map-based analysis using geographic information system (GIS) software, ArcGIS 10.3.

## The Prevention Through Deterrence Strategy

> "Gatekeeper and Hold the Line…are great examples of how we did all this [work to implement new strategic plans] and [migration] shifted. So, at one moment we can say we have operational control in the area, and the next minute it will change." (Testimony of U.S. Border Patrol Chief Mark Morgan 2016)

In a September 2016 congressional hearing on border security, newly appointed USBP Chief Mark Morgan explained how, despite years of evolution in border strategy, the basic issues stay the same. Undocumented migration continues, and, to this end, migrants adapt to the border security barriers they encounter. Here, there is an acknowledgment and stated expectation that migration patterns will continue to experience active geographic transition to avoid and overcome enforcement efforts. In this section, we unpack this statement, tracing the specific policy evolution in border security cited by Morgan. We also problematize the statement, recognizing that shifting patterns of migration are the direct and intended results of a strategy specifically aimed at funneling undocumented migration into treacherous territory meant to serve as a natural barrier.

The evolution of the contemporary era of border militarization can track its beginning to the 1986 Immigration Reform and Control Act (IRCA). Considered to be the last comprehensive immigration reform bill passed by the US Congress, it effectively legalized the status of nearly three million undocumented immigrants by 1992 (Massey et al. 2002). With massive legalization and its simultaneous increase of sanctions against employers who knowingly hire undocumented workers, the passage of IRCA led to mounting political pressures that (a) something be done to stem subsequent undocumented immigration and (b) immigration enforcement be moved from the US interior to the southwestern border. At the same time, however, IRCA also contributed to increased border enforcement efforts by expanding USBP's budget and staffing numbers (Durand and Massey 2004; Andreas 1998), a trend that would continue well into the 2010s.

Couched in the broader context of the "war on drugs" in addition to immigration enforcement, the Office of National and Drug Control Policy commissioned a 1993 study by Sandia National Laboratories—a private physical security system company—to assess ways in which the USA could increase security along its southwestern border (Cornelius 2001; Andreas 2000; US General Accounting Office [GAO] 1994) . The security company suggested that the USA shift its focus from interdiction (i.e., apprehending border crossers and seizing contraband) to deterrence via physical infrastructure and interior checkpoints throughout the southwest (Cornelius 2001; GAO 1994).

That same year, the El Paso Sector of the USBP implemented Operation Blockade, which consisted of heavily enforcing and patrolling the urban downtown border of El Paso, Texas, and Juárez, Chihuahua (Dunn 2009; Cornelius 2001; Andreas 2000). Although later renamed Operation Hold-the-Line due to political pressure[1] (Dunn 2009; Cornelius 2001; Andreas 1998), the aim of this new strategy was to deter would-be undocumented immigrants by increasing and concentrating the presence of USBP vehicles in a well-traversed corridor frequented by undocumented border crossers (UBCs). Operation Hold-the-Line was deemed an overnight success, as apprehensions in the El Paso Sector decreased by 76% between fiscal year (FY) 1993 and 1994 (Cornelius 2001).

However, research conducted by the Population Research Center (1994) found that Operation Hold-the-Line primarily deterred local "unauthorized 'commuter migrants'" who crossed the border on a daily basis from Ciudad Juárez to work in El Paso's service sector but did little to deter undocumented migrants from the interior of Mexico who continued to rely on *coyotes* and shifted their routes outside of the city (Cornelius 2001). Moreover, USBP apprehensions immediately increased in the adjacent Tucson Sector as they decreased in the El Paso Sector (GAO 1994), further suggesting that undocumented migrants simply changed their routes to less scrutinized border areas. Nevertheless, given immediate "success" in the El Paso Sector, Immigration and Naturalization Services (INS) implemented "prevention through deterrence" strategy in July 1994. Predicated on a notion of general deterrence, and using language put forth by Sandia National Laboratories, the aim of prevention through deterrence was to dissuade aspiring migrants by phasing in efforts to block entry from traditional and known migration routes; Operation Hold-the-Line was implemented in the El Paso Sector in 1993, followed by Operation Gatekeeper in the San Diego Sector in 1994, Operation Safeguard in the Tucson Sector in 1995, followed finally by Operation Rio Grande in 1997 in South Texas (Dunn 2009; Andreas 2000, 1998). USBP anticipated new enforcement efforts would deter many would-be migrants from crossing. The harsh physical terrain in remote areas of the border would also give US authorities a tactical advantage to pursue and apprehend any otherwise undeterred UBCs (Andreas 1998, 2000; US Border Patrol [USBP] 1994).

Post-9/11, USBP operations shifted from the Department of Justice to the Department of Homeland Security; the change brought a rebranded version of prevention through deterrence known as "defense-in-depth" that capitalized on inland

[1] The Mexican government protested the connotations of the word "blockade," implying a total sealing of the border. Operation Blockade went underway of the Mexican and US governments coincidentally negotiated the terms of the North American Free Trade Act (NAFTA) that was to open the border to free trade. The coexisting policies of blockading of people while opening of the border to the distribution of goods lay bare some uncomfortable realities, and the moniker "blockade" brought these seeming contradictions to the surface (Andreas 1998; Cornelius 2001; Dunn 2009).

enforcement efforts (Nevins 2010; USBP 2004; Dunn 1996). Importantly, the political environment post-9/11 renewed fervor for USBP expansion and infrastructure building, in large part prompted by the recommendations issued from the 9/11 Commission Report (Congressional Research Service 2008; The Library of Congress 2005; Kean and Hamilton 2004), and linked the strategic mission of USBP to the prevention of international terrorism. It also popularized the notion that all undocumented border crossers were potential terrorists and thus high-priority threats to national security (The Library of Congress 2005). In effect, a doctrine of low-intensity conflict came to dominate the border zone, a phenomenon known as border militarization (Dunn 1996). A key feature of this doctrine broadly, and border militarization specifically, is that "military forces take on police functions, while police forces take on military characteristics" (Dunn 1996).

Defense-in-depth continued to rely on border wilderness as a natural barrier. It was clear that (a) it was not possible to rely on the deployment of forces directly on the line of a nearly 2,000 mile border and that (b) migrants were bypassing security on the border anyways, and this reality could be used to the agency's strategic advantage (US Customs and Border Protection [USCBP] and US Border Patrol [USBP] 2012; USBP 2004). Defense-in-depth thus moved border control forces further inland to increase the time and territory over which USBP could detect and interdict UBCs. Reliance on wilderness and the move inland engendered increases in USBP's annual budget and staffing, the expansion of border fencing, and the deployment of infrared cameras, flood lighting, and other high-tech equipment along border and at checkpoints throughout the southwestern United States, as well as the deployment of greater numbers of interior checkpoints.

## Migrant Deaths Along the USA-Mexico Border

Several scholars suggest that increased border militarization did little initially to deter undocumented migration but was effective in redistributing migration into less enforced areas along the border (Onrrieus 2004; Dávila, Pagán, and Soydemir 2002; Cornelius 2001), a phenomenon known as "the funnel effect" (Binational Migration Institute [BMI] 2006) . The funnel effect refers to the increase in migrant deaths in regions that had previously experienced relatively low rates of migration and deaths in prior years (BMI 2006; Eschbach et al. 1999, 2003; Cornelius 2001). The true number of migrant deaths along the USA-Mexico border is unknown, and there is no comprehensive, exhaustive count of migrant deaths across the USA-Mexico border over time. Rather, estimates of migrant deaths consist of those that have come to the attention of US authorities, medical examiners, medical investigators, or other county officials. For these reasons, we draw on estimates compiled by two main sources in this chapter: USBP estimates for the FY 1998–2015 period and medical investigator reports from the Pima County Office of the Medical Examiner's (PCOME) between FY 1990 and 2015. Additionally, we rely on the death statistics collected by Border Patrol in Brooks County, Texas, compiled in map form by the

*Corpus Christi Caller* newspaper between 2011 and 2014, though this record is incomplete as we will explain further below.

According to USBP estimates, 6,571 migrants died while attempting to cross the USA-Mexico border between FY 1998 and 2015. Migrant deaths have remained relatively high despite a decrease in apprehensions over time (Figs. 6.1, 6.2, and 6.3). This apprehension data is often used by scholars as a proxy for undocumented migration flow (Martínez et al. 2014; Espenshade 1995).

Generally speaking, the migrant death rate across the border has remained high over time, except in the case of FY 2014 and 2015.[2] However, the death rates for these years are likely skewed for two reasons. First, FY 2014 was the initial year on record that the number of non-Mexicans apprehended by the USBP exceeded those of Mexicans (USCBP 2016b). Data suggest that much of this increase was driven by the apprehension of family units and unaccompanied children from Central America. High level of violence in the Northern Triangle (i.e., Guatemala, El Salvador, and Honduras) led to a notable increase in the number of Central American family units and unaccompanied children crossing the USA-Mexico and presenting themselves to US authorities as an effort to seek asylum in the summer

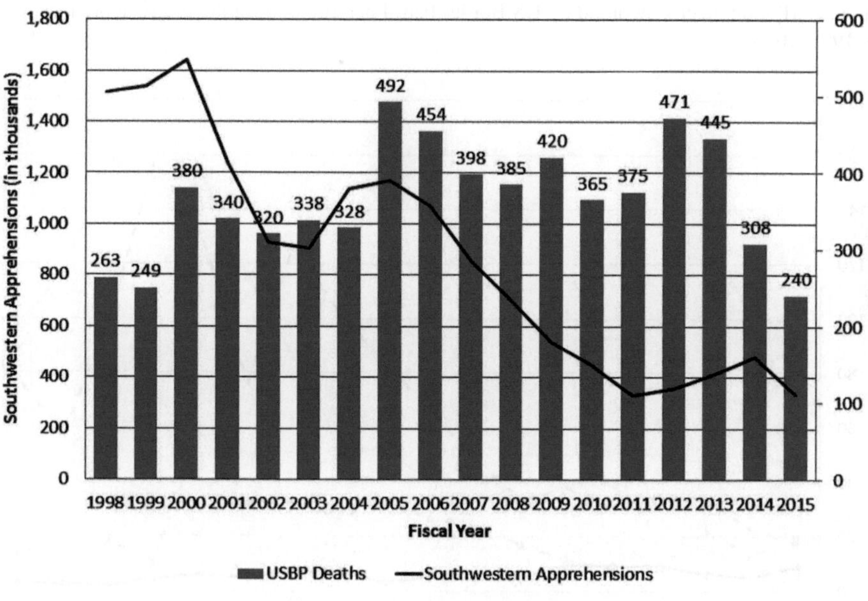


**Fig. 6.1** Migrant deaths recorded by US Border Patrol relative to southwestern apprehensions, FY 1998–2015

[2]We calculated the migrant death rate by dividing annual USBP migrant deaths estimates by the number of annual southwestern apprehensions and multiplying the quotient by 100,000 to standardize the rate.

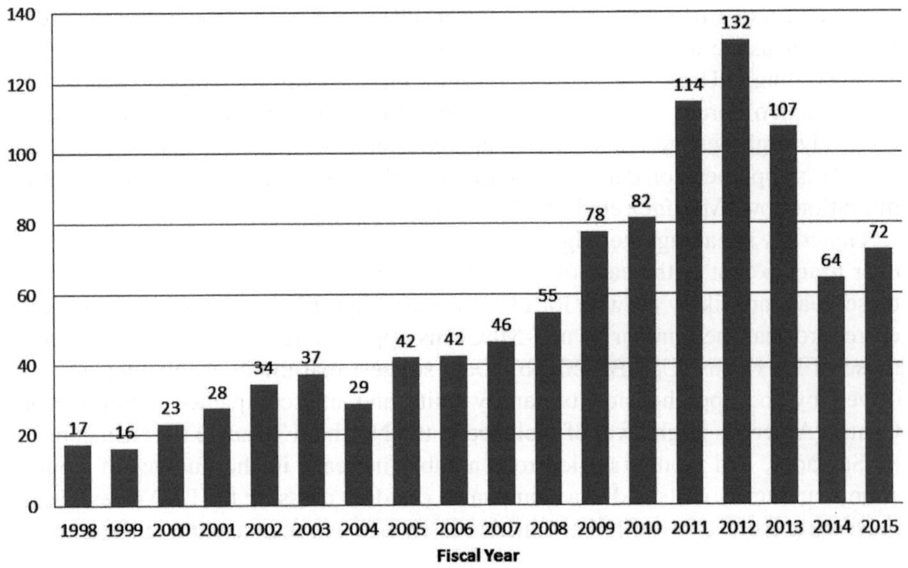


**Fig. 6.2** Migrant deaths recorded by US Border Patrol per 100,000 southwestern apprehensions, FY 1998–2015

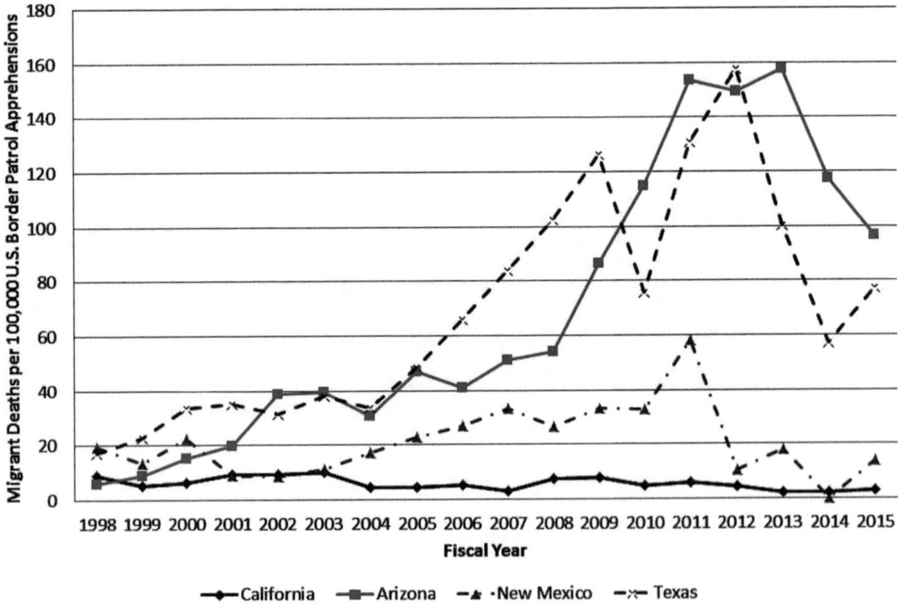


**Fig. 6.3** Approximate migrant death rate by state, FY 1998–2015

of 2014 (American Immigration Council 2016). According to US Customs and Border Protection (USCBP) (2016b), 68,445 members of family units were apprehended along the southwestern border in FY 2014, compared to just 14,855 in FY 2013, which represents a 361% increase year-over-year. Nearly 74% of the family unit members apprehended in FY 2014 were from Guatemala, El Salvador, or Honduras (USCBP 2016b).

Second and in a similar vein, 68,451 unaccompanied children were apprehended in the same year, up from 38,759 the previous year (USCBP 2016b). Again, just over 75% of the unaccompanied children apprehended in FY 2014 were from the Northern Triangle. Although they register as apprehensions, Central Americans who turn themselves over to US authorities immediately after entering the United States are at lower risk for death when compared to migrants attempting to avoid detection, thus likely downward biasing the approximate death rate for FY 2014. We also have reason to believe that the true migrant death rate in FY 2015 is higher than as suggested in Fig. 6.2 due to concerns regarding the validity of USBP's migrant death estimates for that particular year.[3]

In sum, the true number of migrant deaths along the USA-Mexico border is unknown. However, according to USBP estimates, at least 6,571 migrants have died while attempting to cross into the United States since FY 1998. And although apprehensions have decreased substantially over the past decade, the rate of migrant deaths appears to have remained relatively high.

## The Changing Geography of Death

Undocumented migrants continue to die at high rates along the USA-Mexico border despite a relatively steady decrease in undocumented migration since FY 2005. The geography of migrant death has changed considerably over the past two decades. Prior research illustrated that increasing border enforcement in different sectors effectively redistributed migration into less enforced areas along the border, subsequently leading to an increase in migrant deaths in regions that experienced relatively lower rates of death in prior years (Martínez et al. 2013, 2014; BMI 2006; Eschbach et al. 1999, 2003; Cornelius 2001). Reineke and Martínez (2014) illustrate that although migrant deaths have remained high, and possibly increased

[3] Specifically, we find a significant disparity between the number of migrant deaths reported by the US Border Patrol in the Tucson Sector in FY 2015 and those recorded by PCOME in Tucson, Arizona. A prior report found that migrant deaths recorded by USBP and the PCOME between 1998 and 2012 were highly positively correlated ($r = 0.98$; $p < 0.000$), with USBP's estimates slightly exceeding those recorded by PCOME because the former covers a larger jurisdiction than the latter (Martínez et al. 2013). However, the USBP only reported 63 migrant deaths in the Tucson Sector in FY 2015, compared to 136 deaths recorded by the PCOME. which is an entity that has consistently investigated border-crosser deaths since at least 2001 using a rigorous methodology (Anderson 2008; Anderson and Parks 2008). This disparity suggests that the migrant death rate for FY 2015 depicted in Fig. 6.2 could potentially be as high as 94 per 100,000 apprehensions.

slightly over time, they have also in fact fluctuated geographically across the border. For example, in the mid-to-late-1990s, migrant deaths were concentrated in California and Texas (including El Paso)—averaging roughly 100 deaths per year in each state—likely due the high volume of border crossings in the San Diego and El Paso sectors. However, beginning in the early 2000s, migrant deaths decreased in California and Texas and increased substantially in Arizona. This shift coincided with an increase in apprehensions in the region as a direct result of the USBP's use of prevention through deterrence strategy (Martínez et al. 2013, 2014; BMI 2006). By the early 2010s, migrant deaths remained high in Arizona but once again rose in Texas as border crossings increased in the Rio Grande Valley Sector.

Figure 6.3 (below) further illustrates the changing geography of migrant death by plotting approximate death rates across time in California, Arizona, New Mexico (i.e., El Paso Sector data) and Texas using USBP migrant death estimates and apprehension statistics. As noted, migrant death rates were lower in the late 1990s across the border but increased significantly in Arizona and Texas between FY 2004 and 2012.

## *Changing Demographics of Border Crossers and Efforts to Identify the Dead*

The geography of death also pertains to the home origins of border crossers. For instance, between FY 2000 and 2009, only 11% of UBCs positively identified by PCOME were of Central American origin. However, this share increased to nearly 17% in FY 2010–2015 ($p < 0.01$). This shift in decedents' region of origin is consistent with Border Patrol apprehensions in the Tucson Sector during the same time periods. Between FY 2000 and 2009, approximately 7% of migrants apprehended in the Tucson Sector were what the USBP calls "other than Mexicans" (USCPB 2015), the majority of whom were likely from Central America. However, between FY 2010 and 2015, around 32% of apprehensions in the same area were non-Mexicans (USCBP 2015). Interestingly, this suggests that Central Americans appeared to be *overrepresented* among UBCs relative to their share of apprehensions in the FY 2000–2009 time period but *underrepresented* between FY 2010 and 2015, the latter which may partially be explained by increasing rates of Central American family units and unaccompanied children turning themselves over to US authorities in an effort to seek asylum.

Finally, the changing geography of death also refers to deceased migrants' country of residence. Increased border enforcement has disrupted seasonal migration patterns and increased permanent settlement among undocumented migrants (Massey et al. 2015). The US undocumented population has remained steady at approximately 11 million people over the past 5 years (Passell and Cohn 2016). Formal removals (i.e., "deportations") have increased since 2002 and have actually outpaced voluntary returns since FY 2011 (Office of Immigration Statistics 2016).

In other words, interior immigration enforcement efforts, driven largely by the "war on terror" and programs such as Secure Communities and 287(g), have resulted in the mass deportation of migrants with social ties to this country, many of whom possess a strong resolve to return to their loved ones in the United States. A recent study of repatriated Mexican migrants, for example, found that 66% of respondents who considered their "home" to be located in the United States believed they would cross the border again. This was compared to 48% of those who said their home was located in Mexico (Slack et al. 2015).

## Evidence from the Arizona-Sonora Region: A Case Study

The volume and rate of migrant death has increased substantially in southern Arizona over the past two decades (Fig. 6.4) (Martínez et al. 2013, 2014; BMI 2006). The increase in migrant deaths in southern Arizona was certainly due, in part, to increased undocumented migration in the region. Nevertheless, this was not simply just a function of crossing activity in the region. The approximate migrant death rate in the Tucson Sector—denoted by the solid trend line—increased exponentially after FY 2000 as well, reaching an all-time high in FY 2015 (Fig. 6.4). This strongly suggests that the duration and difficulty of the journey have intensified over the years as migrants have had to traverse even more rugged and remote areas in order to avoid detection by US authorities.

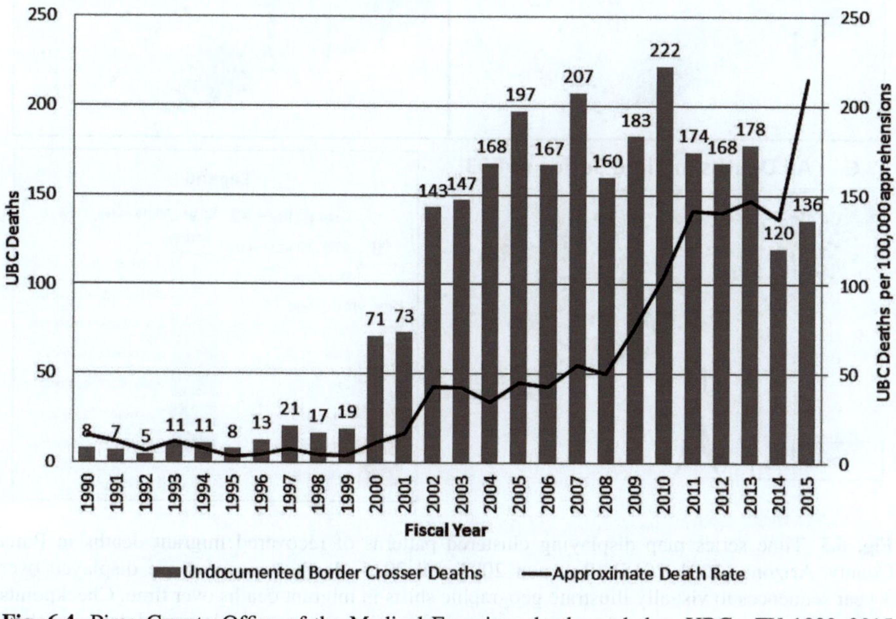


**Fig. 6.4** Pima County Office of the Medical Examiner deaths coded as UBCs, FY 1990–2015 ($N = 2{,}634$)

Kernel density analysis can be used to visually understand the geographic shifts in migrant death clusters (Fig. 6.5). Kernel density refers to a statistical formula for analyzing geographic data, which uses a quadratic formula to place a highest density of points or features at its center and then expands outward to show the relative

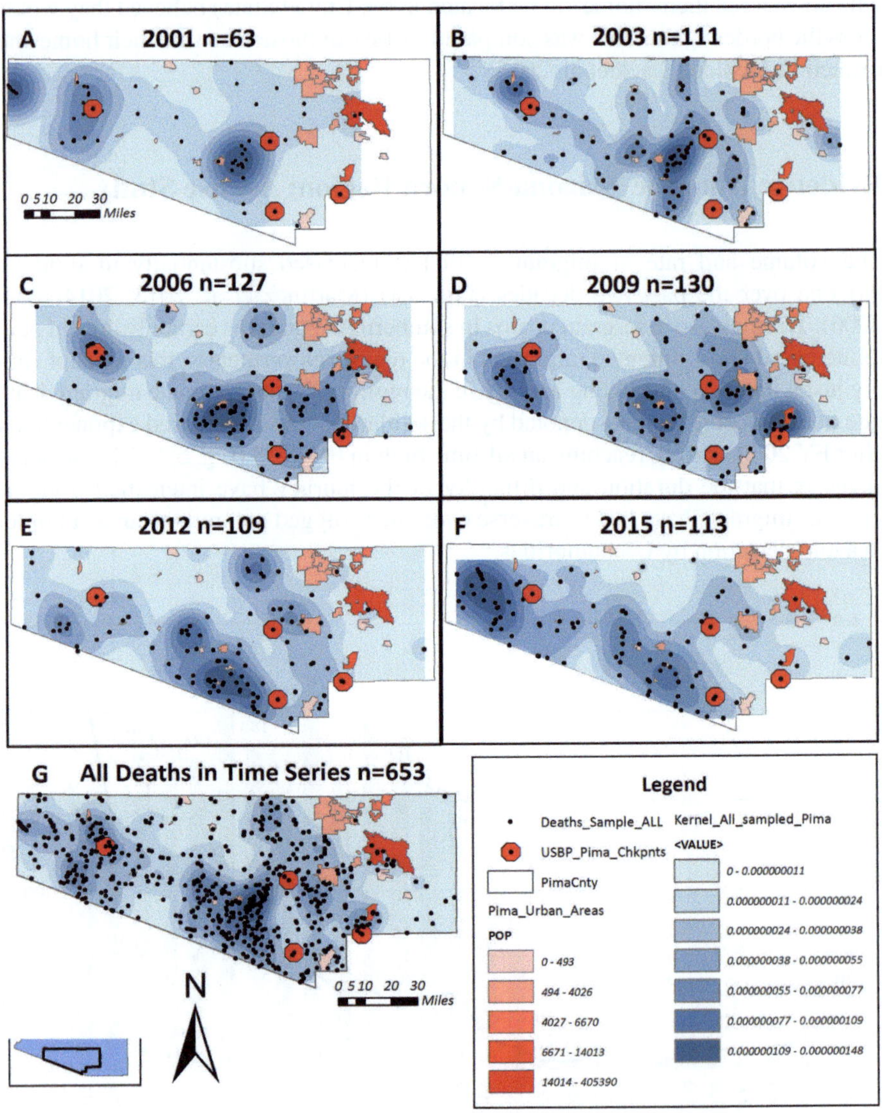


**Fig. 6.5** Time series map displaying clustered patterns of recovered migrant deaths in Pima County, Arizona (2001–2015). Between 2003 and 2015, deaths recovered are displayed over 3-year sequences to visually illustrate geographic shifts in migrant deaths over time. Checkpoints displayed are those known to the authors, though there is not an accessible record dating each of these checkpoints. Some may not have existed for all the years shown

density of points or features in its neighborhood (O'Sullivan and Unwin 2010). Importantly, when we discuss trends in clusters of migrant deaths over time, to some extent we also see death locations as a proxy for evaluating migration patterns within Pima County. We see the locations of Border Patrol highway checkpoints as proxies to represent the funneling effect of border enforcement, where migration patterns are driven around such locations. This is visible in Fig. 6.5. Where clustered deaths occur is where migration too is most likely occurring. This assumption is complicated for several reasons, one of which is that migration does occur in remote areas and when a body is found it is often by happenstance. Therefore, it is not a given that the year a body is recovered corresponds with the year a person died or by extension years in which the given area served as an active migration corridor (Binational Migration Institute [BMI] 2015; Martínez et al. 2013). Migration corridors in increasingly difficult areas were not used at all until recently; they are almost wholly products of the funneling effect of border security.

Absent other assumptions, Fig. 6.5 illustrates that in some years remains are recovered in certain areas and not others. Over time, clusters of deaths reoccur in areas where death rates were apparently lower or absent in intervening years. We extrapolate these trends to understanding the prolonged exercise of the prevention through deterrence or defense-in-depth strategies. In Pima County, where deaths and migration have occurred at their highest rates in recent years, the effects of border strategy have seemingly managed to follow migration trends, focusing efforts where border crossings are highest, ultimately pushing undocumented crossings into other areas. And this recurs in circular fashion. Recall USBP Chief Mark Morgan's description of the situation in 2016, "…at one moment we can say we have operational control in the area, and the next minute it will change" (Testimony of U.S. Border Patrol Chief Mark Morgan 2016). We see changing clusters of deaths as the effects of this security reality in a county-level microcosm, where the risk appears correlated with a continued funneling of migration to more difficult territory.

## Evidence from South Texas/Northeastern Mexico

While a range of data has been collected over years in Arizona to illuminate causes and trends for migrant deaths occurring in the state, Texas is a different story. There are many reasons for this, including the fact that Texas counties cover relatively small areas relative to Pima County and the fact that there are so many of them. Forty counties in Texas are located within 100 miles of the USA-Mexico border, compared to six counties in Arizona located within 100 miles of the border, five counties in California, and five counties in New Mexico. Texas also shares the largest land border with Mexico of any border state, with over 1,200 miles of border compared to Arizona's nearly 700 miles of border.

Since 2011, Brooks County in Southwest Texas—one of the smaller counties at 944 square miles—has come under particular scrutiny. There is only one significant population center in Brooks County, the town of Falfurrias, with a population of just under 5,000. The majority of the acreage of Brooks County is privately owned ranchland. The expanse of private land complicates efforts to organize humanitarian efforts to distribute aid to migrants in transit, (Eddie Canales of Houston Unido, personal communication). The county is located 70 miles north of the USA-Mexico border (US Census Bureau 2010). 2012 was the first year since the early 1990s that Texas saw the majority of recovered migrant remains for all of the border states at 271 individuals (59% of total migrant deaths along the border), 129 (48%) of which were recovered from Brooks County, reflecting a 73% increase from the preceding year (Houston United/Houston Unido 2013). Thirty-six percent of the migrant remains recovered in Brooks County are currently unidentified (Houston United/ Houston Unido 2013) . Importantly death statistics from Texas are generated by USBP, where we have already discussed the border agency's partial measure of deaths (BMI 2006).

Geographically, a plotting of migrant deaths in Brooks County (Fig. 6.6) shows their orientation in circular fashion around the county's one checkpoint. USBP itself describes the area around the region's main checkpoint as surrounded by "rough terrain" and "crude vegetation" (USCBP 2016a; Houston United/Houston Unido 2013) where it is relatively easy for migrants to both hide and lose their way. Comparisons to geographic trends coming from Pima County correspond with the early expansion of a funnel effect, on a smaller regional scale. Figure 6.6 displays a partial time series of deaths in Brooks County based on data published in *Corpus Christi Caller.* Metrics from the *Caller* were used because the newspaper provided consistent notes regarding the accuracy of each of the recorded death locations, rating the coordinates associated with each discovered migrant body on a scale from low to high, and also noted when a body was discovered but coordinates were not recorded.

The *Caller* only recorded deaths over a limited time period, from 2011 to early 2014, numbering 290 individuals. Of these, 19% of bodies had no associated map coordinates. These included deaths from 2011 to 2014. In fact, all confidence designations occur over all of the years in this sample; the recording of death locations did not become more consistent over time. Four-and-a-half percent of recovered remains had "low confidence" locations, and 22% had "medium confidence" locations. "Low" and "medium confidence" locations commonly mean that coordinates were taken for a recovered body but likely only after remains were moved to a road for its transportation to a mortuary (BMI 2015). Fifty-four-and-a-half percent of coordinates for recovered remains in Brooks County were rated "high confidence." This means that during recovery of a migrant's remains, geographic coordinates were taken exactly where the remains were found. Figure 6.6 includes only individuals for which the coordinates of recovery were rated high confidence. This is to ensure that the geographic representations of death densities align as closely as possible with the actual geography of death. Otherwise, the map mirrors those created for Pima County (Fig. 6.5), using a kernel density analysis to view trends in locations where migrant remains were recovered.

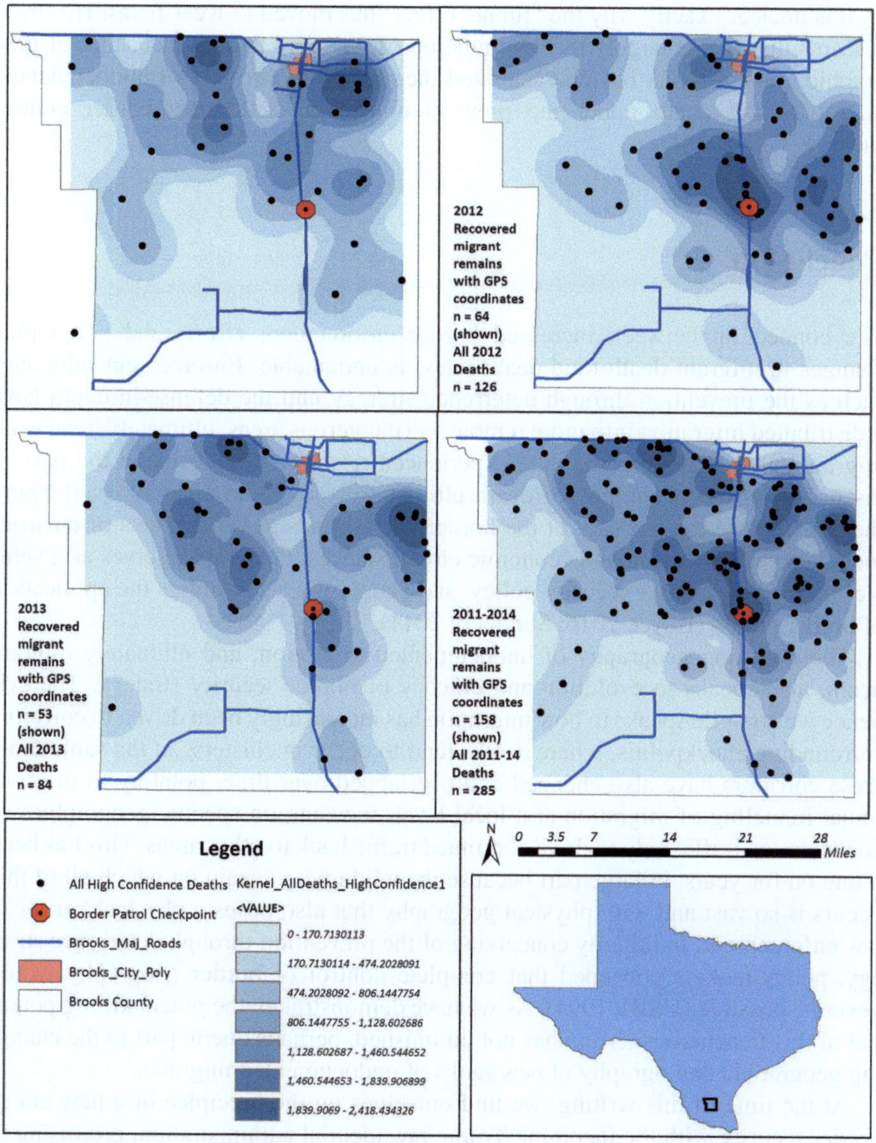


**Fig. 6.6** This time series map examines clustered patterns of recovered migrant deaths in Brooks County, Texas, between 2011 and 2014

It is unclear exactly why the "funnel effect" has moved to west Texas. However, it seems that this is largely the continuation of the more than two decades of geographic transition that has characterized the changing corridors of undocumented migration and death under the prevention through deterrence border control strategy.

## Conclusion

The connection between increased border enforcement efforts and geographic changes in migrant death (and death rates) is undeniable. Enforcement initiatives such as the prevention through deterrence strategy and the defense-in-depth have redistributed migration into more remote and dangerous areas, ultimately increasing migrant death in regions that had experienced relatively low levels in the past. A discussion of the geography of death ultimately leads to an array of overlapping themes because the territory of the border corresponds to varying sets of environmental, social, political, and economic circumstances. Geography serves as a vehicle for enacting border security policy, and geography also inhibits the application of border policy (Boyce 2016; Sundberg 2011).

The changing geography of undocumented migration, and ultimately migrant death, also speaks to evolution and efficacy of border security strategy. The evidence we compile speaks to how migration has increasingly been driven to corridors surrounding checkpoints, where deaths tend to occur in clusters. At the same time, these corridors have also changed and overlapped over time, pointing to the continual funneling of migration at a local level, focusing on specific geographies of concentrated traffic only to drive continued traffic back to other areas. This has been going on for years, in large part because the wilderness terrain on which all of this occurs is so vast and with physical geography that also poses a physical barrier to law enforcement. In initially conceiving of the prevention through deterrence strategy, policy-makers conceded that complete control of border geography would never be possible (USBP 1994). As we have demonstrated, the potent killing potential of this treacherous terrain has not diminished, perhaps due in part to the changing geographic demography of new ranks of undocumented migrants.

At the time of this writing, we find ourselves on the precipice of a new era of border security with the incoming Trump presidential administration, promising to increase the ranks of border agents and build a wall (not acknowledging nearly 700 miles of wall already exist) at Mexico's expense. We are concerned for a repetition of the strategic mistakes that have proven so deadly in the past. Instead of reconceptualizing a violent border strategy, this administration indicates that it will merely enhance the existing practices. If history is any indication, this will lead to even greater loss of life.

## References


American Immigration Council. (2016). *Understanding the Central American refugee crisis: Why they are feeling and how US policies are failing to deter them (special report)*. Washington, DC: American Immigration Council.

Andreas, P. (1998). The US immigration control offensive: Constructing an image of order on the southwest border. In M. M. Suarez-Orozco (Ed.), *Crossings: Mexican immigration in interdisciplinary perspectives* (pp. 341–356). Cambridge, MA: DRCLAS/Harvard University Press.

Andreas, P. (2000). *Border games: Policing the US-Mexico divide*. Ithaca: Cornell University Press.

Anderson, B. E., & Parks, B. (2008). Symposium on Border Crossing Deaths: Introduction. *Journal of Forensic Sciences, 53*(1), 6–7.

Anderson, B. E. (2008). Identifying the Dead: Methods Utilized by the Pima County (Arizona) Office of the Medical Examiner for Undocumented Border Crossers: 2001-2006. *Journal of Forensic Sciences, 53*(1), 8–15.

Binational Migration Institute. (2006). *The "funnel effect" and recovered bodies of unauthorized migrants processed by the Pima County Office of the Medical Examiner, 1990–2005*. Tucson: University of Arizona.

Binational Migration Institute. (2015). *Protocol development for the standardization of identification and examination of UBC bodies along the US-Mexico border: A best practices manual*. Tucson: University of Arizona.

Boyce, G. (2016). The rugged border: Surveillance, policing and the dynamic materiality of the US/Mexico frontier. *Environment and Planning D: Society and Space, 34*(2), 245–262.

Congressional Research Service. (2008). *The REAL ID act of 2005: Legal, regulatory and implementation issues (CRS report for Congress)*. Washington, DC: Congressional Research Service.

Cornelius, W. A. (2001). Death at the border: Efficacy and unintended consequences of US immigration control policy. *Population and Development Review, 27*(4), 661–685.

Dávila, A., Pagán, J. A., & Soydemir, G. (2002). The short-term and long-term deterrence effects of INS border and interior enforcement on undocumented immigration. *Journal of Economic Behavior & Organization, 49*(4), 459–472.

Dunn, T. J. (1996). *Militarization of the United States-Mexico border, 1978–1992*. Austin: CMAS Books.

Dunn, T. J. (2009). *Blockading the border and human rights: The El Paso operation that remade immigration enforcement*. Austin: University of Texas Press.

Durand, J., & Massey, D. S. (Eds.). (2004). *Crossing the border: Research from the Mexican migration project*. New York: Russell Sage Foundation.

Eschbach, K., Hagan, J., Rodriguez, N., Hernandez-Leon, R., & Bailey, S. (1999). Death at the border. *International Migration Review, 33*, 430–454.

Eschbach, K., Hagan, J., & Rodriguez, N. (2003). Deaths during undocumented migration: Trends and policy implications in the new era of homeland security. *In Defense of the Alien, 26*, 37–52.

Espenshade, T. J. (1995). Using INS border apprehension data to measure the flow of undocumented migrants crossing the US-Mexico frontier. *International Migration Review, 29*, 545–565.

Kean, T. H., & Hamilton, L. (2004). *The 9/11 commission report: Final report of the national commission on terrorist attacks upon the United States*. Washington, DC: National Commission on Terrorist Attacks upon the United States.

Houston United/Houston Unido. (2013). *Searching for the living, the dead, and the new disappeared on the migrant trail in Texas*. Houston: Houston United/Houston Unido.

Martínez, D., Reineke, R., Rubio-Goldsmith, R., Anderson, B. E., Hess, G., & Parks, B. (2013). *A continued humanitarian crisis at the border: Undocumented border crosser deaths recorded by the Pima County Office of the Medical Examiner, 1990–2012*. Tucson: Binational Migration Institute, University of Arizona Department of Mexican American Studies.

Martínez, D. E., Reineke, R., Rubio-Goldsmith, R., & Parks, B. O. (2014). Structural violence and migrant deaths in southern Arizona: Data from the Pima County Office of the Medical Examiner, 1990–2013. *Journal on Migration and Human Security, 2*(4), 257–286.

Massey, D. S., Durand, J., & Malone, N. J. (2002). *Beyond smoke and mirrors: Mexican immigration in an era of economic integration*. New York: Russell Sage Foundation.

Massey, D. S., Durand, J., & Pren, K. A. (2015). Border enforcement and return migration by documented and undocumented Mexicans. *Journal of Ethnic and Migration Studies, 41*(7), 1015–1040.

Nevins, J. (2010). *Operation gatekeeper and beyond: The war on "illegals" and the remaking of the US-Mexico boundary*. New York: Routledge.

Office of Immigration Statistics. (2016). *2014 yearbook of immigration statistics*. Washington, DC: US Department of Homeland Security.

Orrenius, P. M. (2004). The effect of US border enforcement on the crossing behavior of Mexican migrants. In J. Durand & D. S. Massey (Eds.), *Crossing the border: Research from the Mexican migration project* (pp. 281–289). New York: Russell Sage Foundation.

O'Sullivan, D., & Unwin, D. (2010). *Geographic information analysis* (2nd ed.). Hoboken: John Wiley & Sons, Inc..

Passel, J.S., & Cohn, D. (2016). Unauthorized immigrant population stable for half decade. Pew Research Center. Retrieved from http://www.pewresearch.org/fact-tank/2016/09/21/unauthorized-immigrant-population-stable-for-half-a-decade/.

Population Research Center. (1994). *Illegal Mexican migration and the United States/Mexico border: The effects of operation hold the line on El Paso/Juarez*. Washington, DC: U.S. Commission on Immigration Reform.

Reineke, R., & Martínez, D. E. (2014). Migrant deaths in the Americas (United States and Mexico). In*Fatal journeys* (pp. 45–83). Geneva: International Organization for Migration.

Slack, J., Martínez, D. E., Whiteford, S., & Peiffer, E. (2015). In harm's way: Family separation, immigration enforcement programs and security on the US-Mexico border. *Journal on Migration and Human Security, 3*(2), 109–128.

Sundberg, J. (2011). Diabolic caminos in the desert & cat fights on the Río: A post-humanist political ecology of boundary enforcement in the United States-Mexico borderlands. *Annals of the Association of American Geographers, 101*(2), 318–336.

Testimony of U.S. Border Patrol Chief Mark Morgan. (2016). Moving the line of scrimmage: Re-examining the defense-in-depth strategy: Hearings before committee on homeland security, subcommittee on border and maritime security, house of representatives, 114th Congress.

The Library of Congress. (2005). *Immigration: Analysis of the major provisions of the REAL ID act of 2005 (CRS report for Congress)*. Washington, DC: Congressional Research Service.

US Border Patrol. (1994). *Border Patrol Strategic Plan: 1994 and Beyond*. Washington, D.C.: US Border Patrol. Retrieved from http://cw.routledge.com/textbooks/9780415996945/gov-docs/1994.pdf.

US Border Patrol. (2004). *National border patrol strategy*. Washington, DC: US Customs and Border Protection.

US Census Bureau. (2010). Brooks County, Texas. In *QuickFacts*. Washington, DC.

US Customs and Border Protection, & US Border Patrol. (2012). *2012–2016 border patrol strategic plan. The mission: Protect America*. Washington, DC: US Customs and Border Patrol.

US General Accounting Office. (1994). *Border control: Revised strategy is showing some positive results. (GAO/GGD-95-30)*. Washington, DC: GAO.

US Customs and Border Protection. (2015). *Fiscal Year 2015 CBP Border Security Report*. Washington, DC: US Customs and Border Protection. Retrieved from https://www.dhs.gov/sites/default/files/publications/CBP%20FY15%20Border%20Security%20Report_12-21_0.pdf.

US Customs and Border Protection. (2016a). Falfurrias Station. In *Border Security*. Washington, D.C.: US Customs and Border Protection. Retrieved from https://www.cbp.gov/border-security/along-us-borders/border-patrol-sectors/rio-grande-valley-sector-texas/falfurrias-station.

US Customs and Border Protection. (2016b). *United States Border Patrol Southwest Family Unit Subject and Unaccompanied Alien Children Apprehensions Fiscal Year 2016*. Washington, DC: US Customs and Border Patrol. Retrieved from https://www.cbp.gov/newsroom/stats/southwestborder-unaccompanied-children/fy-2016.

# Chapter 7
# Follow the Power Lines Until You Hit a Road: Contextualizing Humanitarian Forensic Science in South Texas

**Alyson J. O'Daniel**

In May 2016, I sat and talked with Ryan, a forensic scientist-in-training and intern with the South Texas Human Rights Center (STHRC). Although Ryan had been an intern with the STHRC for fewer than 9 months, he was already practiced at navigating complexities associated with the work of migrant identification and repatriation in southern US borderlands. As we sat in the Texas State University "dry lab," volunteers from the University of Indianapolis (UIndy) pieced together the skeletal remains of a perished migrant. Ryan, moving back and forth between email messages concerning a potential search and rescue operation in Falfurrias and the task of analyzing what remained of the dead in San Marcos, stopped to share with me stories and experiences of his work as a uniquely positioned actor in this effort.

Ryan's position was unique, in part, because his time was more or less equally divided working with living relatives of missing migrants as well as the remains of the dead. To him, it was particularly clear that the forensic science of migrant death was but "one tiny part of this whole huge process," though an important part nonetheless. Ryan joined the Texas-based migrant identification initiative as a graduate student volunteer assisting in exhumation and skeletal analysis of unidentified remains from the Sacred Heart Cemetery in Falfurrias. He had later been brought aboard the STHRC to use his knowledge of forensic identification to assist families who were themselves navigating the bureaucracy of repatriation on behalf of missing loved ones. Yet, on his very first day on the job, Ryan found himself confronted with a powerful case that represented what he would later understand as the unchartered terrain characterizing his role and the process of migrant identification in Texas more generally. As he explained,

A.J. O'Daniel (✉)
Anthropology Department, University of Indianapolis, Indianapolis, IN, USA
e-mail: odaniela@uindy.edu


K.E. Latham, A.J. O'Daniel (eds.), *Sociopolitics of Migrant Death and Repatriation*, Bioarchaeology and Social Theory,
DOI 10.1007/978-3-319-61866-1_7

> I took a call that was from this guy's dad. The kid was my age and his dad was reporting him missing so that we could search for him. The last phone call he [the father] got was to say that he [his son] was too sick to go on. He said, 'I know I'm like 10 miles from Falfurrias.' And that was all we had to go on. …A lot of times, they're [migrants] told, 'just follow the power lines until you hit a road' and so that's all we might know; that they are following the power lines…

As Ryan and I reflected on the uncertain navigation strategy of "just following the power lines," he further explained that those involved with humanitarian assistance efforts were essentially following the power lines too. He elaborated that "we are doing our best to address what's happening at the border, but the information and resources we have are minimal." While the power lines illuminated at least a pathway forward, the broader landscape of migration, rescue, death, and identification continued to seem dizzyingly vast.

This chapter explores in broad strokes the complex navigations of forensic scientists in the dizzying landscape of migrant death and repatriation in South Texas. I use Ryan's discussion of power lines as a metaphor to focus attention on state policies, practices, and ideology structuring crisis response. That is to say that I am intent on illuminating the broad, systems level social conditions under which forensic scientists in this setting endeavored to do the work of migrant identification. At the same time, however, I also invite readers to consider how the work of forensic scientists was power laden. By this I mean to spotlight how values of humanitarianism and virtues of professional authority imbued forensic scientists with the power to collectivize migrant death and repatriation as locally significant advocacy issues. Highlighting that forensic scientists endeavored to shift crucial resources and public attention to and from particular aspects of migrant death and repatriation, I assert that ethnographic attention to processes of forensic scientific practice in this crisis setting may also be an important means of following the power lines, so to speak.

Attention to power in this context is significant because forensic science is often understood as functioning apart from broader sociopolitical frameworks and traditions; its value in the American medicolegal system, for example, is partially derived from the idea that science and its practitioners are objective, neutral observers of "natural fact." However, when applied in settings of humanitarian crisis, the social nature of forensic scientific practice becomes clearer. For example, in his ethnography of international forensic science investigation, Rosenblatt (2015:xvii) highlights ways in which forensic investigation in settings of humanitarian crisis "is political all the way down." Spotlighting the complexities of working with transitional governments, the international legal system, host universities, families and other mourners, and local media outlets in the aftermath of human rights atrocity, Rosenblatt posits that forensic investigations are calculated balancing acts that unfold in a complex landscape of stakeholders (2015:80). Forensic scientists therefore are mediators of knowledge production, at times crafting narratives more strategic, calculated, and contextually minded than "uncovered" as scientific discovery of natural fact. Through what contextual conditions might the power dynamics of humanitarian forensic identification at the border be understood? And, through what strategies and processes might forensic scientists enact, reproduce, or disrupt power? The following provides basis for posing these questions, illuminating future research directions concerning the forensic science of migrant identification along the way.

## Research Methods and Setting

This opportunity to explore sociopolitical complexities of migrant identification arose in the context of collaboration between me and Dr. Krista Latham, a forensic scientist from the University of Indianapolis involved in the South Texas migrant death crisis response. Generally, our collaborative work was aimed at pinpointing challenges and best practices for forensic work applied in settings of humanitarian crisis among student-centered forensic investigation teams. For the past 3 years, Dr. Latham has traveled to South Texas with carefully selected teams of undergraduate and graduate student volunteers to assist in migrant identification. They have worked collaboratively with teams from Baylor University and, most recently, Texas State University's Operation Identification initiative (OPId). Their trips may be characterized as "short bursts" (lasting 10–14 days at a time) of intensive labor and immersive learning. I was invited as a participant and observer on my first "short burst" assignment in May 2016. My goal on this trip was to document, to the extent possible, the complicated networks of individuals, agencies, and ideas into which students were thrust during their work in Texas.

During this initial 10-day trip, I used research strategy informed by "rapid assessment ethnography." Such an approach facilitated identification of key insights concerning contexts, conditions, and experiences of work among the UIndy team of migrant identification volunteers. Essentially, "rapid assessment ethnography" triangulates a variety of qualitative (and often quantitative) research strategies to collect targeted information under severe time constraints (Handwerker 2001; Scrimshaw et al. 1991). While participant observation and informal conversations provided the backbone of my data collection strategy, I complemented the method with interviews among three key informants and analysis of gray and scholarly literature pertaining to the crisis in South Texas. In addition, I drew heavily from the nuanced insights of Dr. Latham to interpret and contextualize my observations concerning power dynamics and informants' narrative explanations of their experiences with this crisis response. Thus, the analysis presented here should be understood as a set of general findings pointing a way forward for future anthropological investigation and deliberation. The intention here is to thus sharpen focus on under-discussed dimensions of migrant death in South Texas.

## Global Contexts: Capitalism, the State, and Migrant Death

As previous chapters in this volume explain, conditions of contemporary capitalist expansion are important for understanding mass death at the USA-Mexico border. The term "neoliberalism" has been widely used by scholars to describe the series of sweeping economic policies and an accompanying ideological stance spread around the world throughout the 1980s and the 1990s (Richland 2009; Kotz 2002). In its most basic sense, the term refers to the adoption and spread of a market-centered style of governance wherein the state plays a role limited to the protection of private property and the facilitation of a "free market" economy. The general ideological position undergirding neoliberalism suggests that state interference in economic markets hinders development and growth (Harvey 2005) and that the state should therefore provide for the well-being of its citizens through the creation and maintenance of a free market economy (Di Leonardo 2008). Privatization, market deregulation, and the planned shrinkage of government safety net programs have been key strategies characterizing neoliberal economic reform (Kim et al. 2000).

As highlighted in Chaps. 3, 4, and 5 of this volume, the imposition and adoption of neoliberal policies in countries across Latin America have had profound effects on labor markets, social resources, conditions of everyday life, and, central to this volume, decisions and experiences of migration. In this vein, scholars have painstakingly documented the local intensification of poverty and the exacerbation of vulnerability (Damian and Boltvinik 2006; Reygadas 2006), as well as extraordinary conditions of violence as some of the legacies of neoliberalism in Latin America (Esparza et al. 2013; Ungar 2006). Their work highlights current migration and refugee crises as outgrowths of these conditions and, therefore, as outgrowths of neoliberal economic strategy as it articulated with historical conditions of exploitation, political instability, and material inequality (see Chap. 3, this volume).

The migration literature further makes clear that, ironically, while neoliberalism creates conditions amenable to the free movement of capital, money, goods, and services across national borders, the movement of people across national boundaries has been increasingly restricted (Kotz 2002). Thus migrants may experience violence and inequality in their home communities as well as in the liminal spaces of their journeys (Vogt 2013) and in the borderlands of their countries of destination (De León 2015). The role of global capitalism in the migration crisis, it seems, has been understood largely in relation to the role that the political economy has played in producing persistent deprivation and volatility compelling migrant and refugee border crossing. While this dimension of state policy and capitalist practice has rightly spotlighted attention on myriad forms of violence engendered by recent forms of capitalist development, little focus has been afforded to contexts and processes of humanitarian forensic identification as part of the contemporary human migration story.

## Forensic Science in a Neoliberal Context

### *Ideology and Humanitarian Science: Joining the Ranks of the Citizen Volunteer*

As many anthropologists working in US communities have noted, virtues of volunteerism and community service have become central alternatives to state action in the neoliberal era (Hyatt 2001:203). This is because economic strategies of privatization, market deregulation, and government disinvestment required a fundamental reconfiguration of the relationship between citizens and the state (Ferguson 2006; Goode 2002; Goode and Maskovsky 2001). This reconfiguration gained popular support through ideological emphasis on individualism, deservedness, and a call to civil society's "return" as the key to solving persistent social problems (Hyatt 2001). Disinvestment in antipoverty programs and the restructuring of full-time, union-backed labor markets into part-time, insecure work have increased pressure on local communities and charitable organizations to fill the gaps between diminishing safety net resources and the growing need to access public support. At the same time, entrenched conditions of poverty and social inequality have been depoliticized as instances of individual failure and moral ineptitude (Goode and Maskovsky 2001). In this way, neoliberal ideals of personal responsibility and rugged individualism accompanying economic reform measures serve to place burdens of care and social change onto individual actors (O'Daniel 2016; Biehn 2014; Hyatt 2001). Put another way, citizen volunteers are now expected to engage a range of functions and roles previously filled by the state (Bloom and Kilgore 2003).

In this climate, the role of "citizen volunteer" has been naturalized as the logical or even preferred response to social crises of our times. From Islamic charitable giving in Egypt (Atia 2013) to the homeless shelter industry in the United States (Lyon-Callo 2004), a major thrust of neoliberal governance seeks to privatize responsibility for the well-being of individuals and populations. As Foucault (1991) theorized, governance, in part, refers to how the state shapes and guides the conduct of people; it is also how people are then compelled to govern themselves. Science has long played a constructive role in the art of justifying, organizing, and compelling self-governance and self-regulation. That is to say that scholarly and medical disciplines have served as vehicles for managing populations and defining civic morality and moral personhood (Hess and Frickel 2014; Pasquino 1991; Hacking 1986). Forensic science, as a branch of the US criminal justice system, is rather obviously no exception to the imbrication of science and governance. Yet forensic scientists who choose to join the voluntary sector of migrant identification do so as *presumably* self-governing individuals operating in some ways outside of medicolegal structures and authority traditionally associated with their work. Humanitarian forensic science therefore may be shaped and guided by ethical standards, social values, and material conditions in some ways distinctive to their roles as citizen volunteers. They are, in other words, social agents acting within and on a global political economy that shapes the migrant death crisis as well as its response.

## *Local Material Realities and the Moral Call for Humanitarian Science*

It is through interconnected processes of international migration, dwindling social resources, escalating militarization of the border, and depoliticization of inequality that Brooks County, Texas, and its County Seat, Falfurrias, came to require the help and support of forensic volunteers. Historically, Brooks County has been home to large-scale cattle ranching operations. A focus on dairy-producing livestock and cattle feed farming helped to insulate the county from widespread economic disaster associated with the Great Depression (as cited in Texas State Historical Association 2016). In the mid-1930s, the discovery of extensive gas and oil reserves also helped many local cash-poor farmers to survive the Depression's aftermath. The 1950s and 1960s ushered in a period of economic diversification; commercial cotton farming and "truck farming" (including vegetables and melons) became increasingly important to the local economy, though cattle ranching remained the key agricultural focus. Brooks County and its county seat, Falfurrias, continued to grow throughout the 1970s and 1980s. The Texas Historical Society (2016) even boasts that by the mid-1980s, the county had "two doctors, two dentists, a hospital with facilities for thirty-one, …[and more]."

By 2016, local legal economy in Falfurrias continued to focus on employment via cattle ranching and oil production. The US Border Patrol had also emerged as a significant source of jobs. Although the Falfurrias, Texas, checkpoint had been in operation since 1940, by 2002 the checkpoint had grown to a three-acre compound with an administrative building and detention and processing centers (US Customs and Border Protection 2016) . In a context of relative growth, a new national-brand hotel, a handful of fast-food chain restaurants, a regional chain grocery store, and a few gas stations outfitted with restaurants, convenience stores, and gift shops accommodated the needs of local residents as well as visiting laborers associated with the oil industry. Yet the modern design and apparent newness of the hotel's exterior provided stark contrast to low-income residential housing well worn by sun and decades of occupancy.

Falfurrias was home to just under 5,300 people in the 2000 census and had a median annual household income of $15,000. Roughly 46 % of the population lived below the federal poverty line (Texas Association of Counties 2016) . Since then, there has been some population decline (4,981 individuals counted in the 2010 census) and growth in annual household income ($17,200 according to 2015 US Census Bureau estimates). Yet, as the Brooks County Deputy Sheriff explained, the county and the city both remained "cash strapped" and grossly under-equipped to deal with "mass death at their doorstep." Indeed, in 2014, Brooks County was so cash strapped that it suspended healthcare coverage for all of its employees (as cited in Police Executive Research Forum 2016, p. 11). For years, what are believed to be small numbers of unidentified perished migrants had been buried using whatever private and public resources local officials and volunteers could piece together. The lack of formal and systematic medicolegal procedures for attending to unidentified migrant death ultimately left the remains and their handling at the discretion of private landowners and public servants unequipped to usher them through an identification and repatriation process. However, in 2012, when migrant deaths reached unusually high proportions, the county and private citizens could no longer shoulder the escalating resource burden; the financial, administrative, and material costs of migrant death were simply not accommodated in federal, state, county, and city budgets.

The lack of government-sponsored resources to handle the growing numbers of unidentified dead initially resulted in burials that may seem to some as haphazard, even callous. For example, UIndy-led exhumations have uncovered multiple bodies in the same grave, remains buried in trash bags, unmarked burials, and bodies for whom there turned out to be neither death investigation nor records of burial. At first thought, these conditions seem startlingly disrespectful; it would be easy to dismiss such practices as evidence of xenophobic disregard for human life. To this point, scholars have highlighted how notions of deservingness and personal responsibility contribute to the widespread belief that poor and undocumented migrants are indeed "alien others" whom we must fear will take "our" jobs, use "our social resources, and morally bankrupt "our" culture and society (O'Leary et al. 2014; Chavez 2013). The demonization of migrants in popular and political discourse may well contribute to burial practices that Dr. Tim Gocha described as "second class treatment for non-citizens." Yet, in light of diminishing access to state resources, persistent local poverty, and the relatively recent escalation of migrant death awareness, dismissing unidentified migrant burial practices as evidence of personal animosity for migrants is perhaps to overestimate the agency of local actors and to underestimate the systemic nature of the problem. Instead, as Dr. Spradley preferred to characterize the situation, "I truly believe that people [in border counties] are dealing with this situation the best way they can, but when you have a problem this big with very few resources, how you deal with it is very constrained and may not be what's optimal." To put it another way, local response to migrant death had been improvised in the absence of state resources and in the face of powerful political economic processes that have long depoliticized conditions of global capitalism creating the crisis.

Given a lack of state and local resources, the burden of attending to migrant death had been essentially privatized as the purview of citizen volunteers. The call to action for forensic investigators, as scientists themselves explained, was initially humanitarian and, for many, was driven by a morally inflected sense of professional obligation. As Dr. Latham explained in a 2014 blogpost entitled "sacrifice[1]":

> I will get to hug and kiss my son again, but there are hundreds of mothers whose children are buried unidentified in the Sacred Heart Burial Park who cannot say the same thing. I cannot imagine the agony of not knowing where my child is or not knowing if he is safe or even still alive. The thought that I may never see his sweet smile or hear his voice say "I love you" would be unbearable for me. While these mothers may not be able to hear their children's voices or hug them one more time, at least we can help find their sons and daughters and return them home to be reunited with their families. Their families deserve to mourn and grieve over the loved ones they have lost. This is the type of closure that we as forensic scientists can bring to these mothers.

For many volunteers like Latham, the work of migrant identification and repatriation represents one way that forensic scientists can use their professional expertise to ease suffering and promote the welfare of others. It may be seen as a calling to serve less fortunate families based on empathy. Or, it may also be seen as a calling to act based one's sense of moral obligation or civic duty. While one volunteer spoke of the crisis as "an injustice that needs to be righted," another described her volunteer efforts in more neutral terms, saying "I always thought about the work we're doing as service to our local, state, national, and international community." In any case, volunteers felt a general sense of professional responsibility to define and address a

[1] The blog post can be found at this link: https://beyondborders.uindy.edu/?s=sacrifice.

problem that otherwise seemed to blur boundaries of social ownership. Who is accountable to the problem of unidentified perished migrants? What resources should be used for attending to this problem? What does/should solutions to unidentified migrant death look like? In the face of these questions, forensic scientists devoted their personal time, energy, resources, and attention to the unidentified dead.

## Advocating for Social Change: Publicizing the Private Response

Texas State University scientists quickly learned that attending to the problem of unidentified dead far exceeded the basic forensic goal of identification and the humanitarian goal of repatriation. Local response and remedy for attending to escalating migrant death proved dispersed and complicated. When asked how she came to understand the systemic challenges of migrant identification in South Texas, Dr. Spradley remembered:

> I think it was on a Saturday, and [a colleague from Colibri] told me about this particular case. There were two men who were traveling together. One of them got sick and his travel companion had to leave him behind. …So his travel companion found his family in Houston and said 'okay, we left [him] here [at a particular spot]. So the family drove down to Brooks County and looked at the pictures and the clothing description was exactly what the travel companion had described. So the funeral home that handled the transportation and burial said, 'well you're going to have to do DNA analysis and that's going to cost you $2000. And, if you want the body exhumed, that's going to cost you money too because we don't have a DNA sample.' Of course, by law they were supposed to do all of those things, but they didn't. We reached out to the Argentine Forensic Anthropology Team and it turns out they had a family reference sample for [this man's] family. They were going to pay for DNA testing and for exhumation. Well, then nobody remembered where [he] was buried. And that was the first time I got a sense that this was really, really complicated.

As Spradley described, challenges of migrant identification went far beyond the "usual" complications of skeletal analysis and DNA testing. Complicating factors included local lack of knowledge concerning policy-mandated procedures for documenting and handling unidentified remains, county-by-county differences in resources and burial and identification protocol, challenges of working with international consulates, and barriers to sharing information between FBI, the national missing persons registry, and international missing persons databanks. The sense that South Texas migrant identification issues were "really, really complicated" was conveyed to me through various stories consistently throughout my time with identification experts and volunteers in Texas. Dr. Gocha explained the complexity this way:

> There's so many different entities that are intertwined in different ways. The project is bigger than skeletal analyses. The project really is: how can we find where these migrant deaths are located, working with the forensic border coalition, how many migrant deaths are happening every year and where are they buried? And then, what are the practices for how they're buried and *then* getting permission to exhume them? Only then do you get to

processing and the analyses and sending samples off for DNA testing. Then you're waiting for all that while working with the DNA laboratories in the US versus outside the US and then working with the different legal jurisdictions in Texas and internationally. It's all in this bigger and bigger context.

As both forensic scientists quoted above pointed out, the project of migrant identification had been as much about mapping and navigating the many bureaucratic channels pertaining to the unidentified dead as it was about applying scientific methods for identification purposes.

Even once methods of identification had been applied and a positive identification had been made, there were additional rules concerning release of information and remains set forth in state and national medicolegal systems. For example, Texas followed what locals described as "the JP system." The "JP system" refers to a system of medicolegal governance wherein deaths are reportable to a Justice of the Peace who, in turn, may determine whether death investigation by a medical examiner or coroner is warranted. This is in contrast to the "Coroner System" or "Medical Examiner System" wherein deaths are reported directly to a coroner or a medical examiner. At the time of this research, there were only four Justices of the Peace that served all of Brooks County. In addition, Brooks County did not have its own Office of the Medical Examiner. Without an Office of the Medical Examiner, the Justices of the Peace were charged with the task of handling the county's deaths, as well as other matters including hearing class C misdemeanor cases, civil cases, and landlord/tenant disputes (Texas Association of Counties 2016). Other public resources and personnel for attending to the unidentified dead were virtually nonexistent. In a county typically prepared to handle the remains of its estimated average three deaths per year, the influx of perished migrants represented a serious strain on a local medicolegal system otherwise untested in a mass death scenario. The novelty of the situation coupled with the personnel challenges it posed ultimately helped to explain why in May 2016 there were identifications made from remains found in Brooks County that were ineligible for release, despite positive laboratory identification; a Justice of the Peace was unavailable to change names on the death certificates and/or sign required forms.

Given the challenges forensic scientists faced in locating unidentified dead, gaining access to information, and otherwise steering remains through the repatriation process, volunteers in this effort necessarily engaged with the intensive social labor of advocacy. At the heart of this advocacy has been the creation of narrative and practice that humanizes migrants, problematizes status quo burial practices, and collectivizes responsibility for migrant identification among many actors across and including the state, as well as across national boundaries.

Humanization of perished migrants was an important step in defining unidentified perished migrants as a social problem worthy of attention and resources. For example, student volunteers in the Forensic Anthropology Center at Texas State University (FACTS) are given the opportunity to "process" personal artifacts belonging to perished migrants. I observed as University of Indianapolis graduate students carefully washed the clothing and accessories belonging to an unidentified migrant whose bodily remains were drying in the "wet lab." I looked on as documentarians filmed and the graduate students grew quiet. Dirt-caked bundles reeking of decomposition fluid gradually became first jeans and boots and then undergarments and a shirt. I noted the clumsy hands of one graduate student, the awkwardness of somehow carefully scrubbing. The work was delicate and the students were somber. As one student hung a pair of socks on an outdoor clothes line a few yards away, I asked the other, "What are you thinking as you process the clothes?" "That these are the last time someone will wash this woman's clothes. That this is something someone's mother would usually do for them," she replied. While in the lab conducting skeletal analyses, migrants were typically "cases" or "remains," especially until analysis had been completed. However, processing the clothes was differently humanizing, a moment where students could allow themselves the chance to wonder who the migrants had been in life and, in turn, who might be missing them now. As Dr. Gocha explained,

> Processing the personal items is a whole other layer of humanizing. I think it's good for students, especially, to understand why this is important and why some of the circumstances around this have to change. They get to understand up close that these were people who had lives and families and will probably be missed.

Several news stories, documentaries, and public events such as "Missing in Harris County Day" emphasized the families and former lives of unidentified perished migrants and a corresponding social obligation to improve the identification and repatriation process on their behalf. Perished migrants weren't simply the dead; they were family members deeply missed and intensely mourned.

The work of collectivizing responsibility for migrant identification was subtle at times. The 2016 Missing in Harris County Day, for example, included a guest speaker panel that brought together forensic scientists, medical examiners, and families of missing loved ones to highlight the work of migrant identification as a humanitarian plight in context of a "mass disaster." The language of mass disaster was consistently used by Texas State University scientists, even when volunteers from UIndy sometimes used the language of human rights or social justice. The use of "mass disaster," explained Dr. Spradley, was a deliberate choice made locally that conveyed the sense that migrant death represents "a scenario in which a local jurisdiction is overwhelmed by the amount of deaths in a particular time period and they don't have enough money or personnel to process it." Linguistically framing migrant death in this way focused attention away from politically divisive debates concerning border crossing and rights and toward more unifying themes coalesced around resource access and local infrastructure. Such an approach could potentially build buy-in for stakeholders who were positioned around issues of migrant death in diverse and sometimes incompatible ways.

Through their careful outreach and education work, forensic scientists have been instrumental in building relationships between previously disparate entities and actors in Texas. For example, key players in the South Texas migrant identification network have, with the help of key players in the Arizona-based migrant identification network, established a nongovernmental organization through which to lobby for state-level systems change and national response in the form of disaster relief funding. The Forensic Border Coalition (see also Chap. 11, this volume) was created as a way to present "a unified front" in matters of legislation and policy that might aid in streamlining the identification process and supporting the work from exhumation to analysis and repatriation. The FBC's work at the time of this research included advocating for policy change related to administration of death certificates, creation of a technical report outlining the systemic nature of migrant identification challenges, and lobbying senators in Washington, DC, in hopes of procuring funds to alleviate the financial burdens posed by identification and repatriation. In this capacity, at least some forensic scientist volunteers have leveraged their knowledge, expertise, and social capital into formal advocacy roles and positions of power that may ultimately serve as vantage points from which to restructure local medicolegal systems, national policy regarding migrant death and repatriation, and international entities relating to the migrant death crisis. These citizen volunteers, in other words, seek to enlist the state among the ranks of their cause.

## Closing

The forensic science of migrant identification and the work of repatriation offer a crucial vantage point from which to understand important conditions and processes in the story of contemporary human migration. Attention to the work of forensic scientists in this crisis setting illuminates ways in which the social life of migrants endures beyond death in the borderlands in part as humanitarian cause and subject of advocacy. Forensic scientists have emerged as critical mediators in the social lives of perished migrants, directing attention to migrant death, telling difficult stories of state-wide resource scarcity and neglect, and advocating for systems-level change. While many of the volunteers encountered during this work highlight that scientific methods of identification are and must be neutral, the acts of identification and repatriation are most certainly acts born of power. An anthropology of migration and migrant death must therefore direct attention to power lines in US-based landscapes of migrant death and identification, including those leading us through difficult terrains of critical self-reflection.

## References

Atia, M. (2013). *Building a house in heaven: Pious neoliberalism and Islamic charity in Egypt*. Minneapolis: University of Minnesota Press.

Biehn, T. (2014). Who needs me most? New imperialist ideologies in youth-centered volunteer abroad programs. In M. C. Forte (Ed.), *Good intentions: Norms and practices of imperial humanitarianism* (pp. 77–87). Montreal: Alert Press.

Bloom, L. R., & Kilgore, D. (2003). The volunteer citizen after welfare reform in the United States: An ethnographic study of volunteerism in action. *VOLUNTAS: International Journal of Voluntary and Non-profit Organizations, 14*(4), 431–454.

Chavez, L. (2013). *The Latino threat: Constructing immigrants, citizens, and the nation*. Stanford: Stanford University Press.

Damian, A., & Boltvinik, J. (2006). A table to eat on: The meaning and measurement of poverty in Latin America. In E. Hershberg & F. Rosen (Eds.), *Latin America after neoliberalism: Turning the tide in the 21st century?* (pp. 144–170). New York: The New Press.

De León, J. (2015). *The land of open graves: Living and dying on the migrant trail*. Berkeley: University of California Press.

Di Leonardo, M. (2008). Introduction: New global and American landscapes of inequality. In J. L. Collins, M. Di Leonardo, & B. Williams (Eds.), *New landscapes of inequality: Neoliberalism and the erosion of democracy in America* (pp. 3–20). Santa Fe: School for Advanced Research Press.

Esparza, M., Huttenbach, H. R., & Feierstein, D. (Eds.). (2013). *State violence and genocide in Latin America: The cold war years*. New York: Routledge Press.

Ferguson, J. (2006). *Global shadows: Africa in the neoliberal world order*. Durham: Duke University Press.

Foucault, M. (1991). Governmentality. In G. Burchell, C. Gordon, & P. Miller (Eds.), *The Foucault effect: Studies in governmentality* (pp. 87–104). Chicago: University of Chicago Press.

Goode, J. (2002). From new deal to bad deal: Racial and political implications of U.S. welfare reform. In C. Kingfisher (Ed.), *Western welfare in decline: Globalization and women's poverty* (pp. 65–89). Philadelphia: University of Pennsylvania Press.

Goode, J. G., & Maskovsky, J. (Eds.). (2001). *New poverty studies: The ethnography of power, politics, and impoverished people in the United States*. New York: New York University Press.

Hacking, I. (1986). Making up people. In T. C. Heller, M. Sosna, & D. E. Wellbery (Eds.), *Reconstructing individuality: Autonomy, individuality and the self in western thought* (pp. 222–236). Stanford: Stanford University Press.

Handwerker, W. P. (2001). *Quick ethnography: A guide to rapid multi-method research*. New York: Altamira Press.

Harvey, D. (2005). *A brief history of neoliberalism*. New York: Oxford University Press.

Hess, D.J., & Frickel, S. (2014). Introduction: Fields of knowledge and theory traditions in the sociology of science. In D. J. Hess, & S. Frickel (Eds.), *Fields of knowledge: Science, politics, and publics in the neoliberal age. Political Power and Social Theory, 27*, 1–30. Bingley: Emerald.

Hyatt, S. B. (2001). From citizen to volunteer: Neoliberal governance and the erasure of poverty. In J. Goode & J. Maskovsky (Eds.), *New poverty studies: The ethnography of power, politics, and impoverished people in the United States* (pp. 201–235). New York: New York University Press.

Kim, J. Y., Millen, J. V., Irwin, A., & Gershman, J. (2000). *Dying for growth: Global inequalities and the health of the poor*. Monroe: Common Courage Press.

Kotz, D. M. (2002). Globalization and neoliberalism. *Rethinking Marxism, 14*(2), 64–79.

Lyon-Callo, V. (2004). *Inequality, poverty, and neoliberal governance: Activist ethnography in the homeless sheltering industry*. Toronto: University of Toronto Press.

O'Daniel, A. (2016). *Holding on: African American women surviving HIV/AIDS*. Lincoln: University of Nebraska Press.

O'Leary, A. O., Deeds, C. M., & Whiteford, S. (2014). Introduction. In A. O. O'Leary, C. M. Deeds, & S. Whiteford (Eds.), *Uncharted terrains: New directions in border research methodology, ethics, and practice* (pp. 1–22). Tucson: University of Arizona Press.

Pasquino, P. (1991). Criminology: The birth of a special knowledge. In G. Burchell, C. Gordon, & P. Miller (Eds.), *The Foucault effect: Studies in governmentality* (pp. 235–250). Chicago: University of Chicago Press.

Police Executive Research Forum. (2016). *Responding to migrant deaths along the southwest border: Lessons from the field*. Washington, DC: Ford Foundation.

Reygadas, L. (2006). Latin America: Persistent inequality and recent transformations. In E. Hershberg & F. Rosen (Eds.), *Latin America after neoliberalism: Turning the tide in the 21st century?* (pp. 120–143). New York: The New Press.

Richland, J. B. (2009). On neoliberalism and other social diseases: The 2008 sociocultural anthropology year in review. *American Anthropologist, 111*(2), 170–176.

Rosenblatt, A. (2015). *Digging for the disappeared: Forensic science after atrocity*. Stanford: Stanford University Press.

Scrimshaw, S. C. M., Carballo, M., Ramos, L., & Blair, B. A. (1991). The AIDS rapid anthropological assessment procedures: A tool for health education planning and evaluation. *Health Education Quarterly, 18*(1), 111–123.

Texas Association of Counties. (2016). Brooks County profile. http://www.txcip.org/tac/census/profile.php?FIPS=48047. Accessed 7 July 2016.

Texas State Historical Association. (2016). Brooks County. https://tshaonline.org/handbook/online/articles/hcb16. Accessed 1 Aug 2016.

Ungar, M. (2006). Crime and citizen security in Latin America. In E. Hershberg & F. Rosen (Eds.), *Latin America after neoliberalism: Turning the tide in the 21st century?* (pp. 171–192). New York: The New Press.

US Customs and Border Protection (2016). Falfurrias Station. https://www.cbp.gov/border-security/along-us-borders/border-patrol-sectors/rio-grande-valley-sector-texas/falfurrias-station. Accessed 12 Sept 2016.

Vogt, W. A. (2013). Crossing Mexico: Structural violence and the commodification of undocumented Central American migrants. *American Ethnologist, 40*(4), 764–780.

# Part II
# Producing and Situating Forensic Science Knowledge

# Chapter 8
# Digging, Dollars, and Drama: The Economics of Forensic Archeology and Migrant Exhumation

**Krista E. Latham and Ryan Strand**

Migrant deaths in South Texas have reached mass disaster numbers. Ultimately, these increasing numbers have led to imbalances and shortcomings in funding, resources, and media attention directed at assisting with this humanitarian crisis. Where funding is lacking from government agencies, private donations from civilians and foundations indirectly supplement resources to assist local law enforcement responsible for identifying remains. Volunteer forensic scientists have been providing their time and skillsets so that funding limitations do not hinder best practice investigative protocols. However, media channels directed at educating the public on the scarcity of resources shape resource and financial imbalances when they focus on visually dramatic, "on-the-ground" efforts and ignore funding challenges of laboratory analyses. This chapter examines the implications of these imbalances from the perspective of the volunteer forensic anthropologist, who is present both "on the ground" and "behind the scenes," in order to provide an understanding of the amount of work and preparation involved in these identification efforts. It suggests that limited knowledge about this specialized forensic work can translate into funding disparities between the various identification efforts and that media has a crucial role to play in the politics of funding. Therefore, a detailed discussion of the identification process is included to raise awareness about a process that is not fully understood by those outside the field. This chapter explores the efforts of university volunteers before, during, and after large-scale exhumations of unidentified migrants that took place in 2013 and 2014 in Brooks County, TX, and places their work within a broader sociopolitical framework. It positions the

K.E. Latham (✉)
Biology and Anthropology Departments, University of Indianapolis, Indianapolis, IN, USA
e-mail: lathamke@uindy.edu

R. Strand
South Texas Human Rights Center, Falfurrias, TX, USA
e-mail: sthrc.ryan@gmail.com



K.E. Latham, A.J. O'Daniel (eds.), *Sociopolitics of Migrant Death and Repatriation*, Bioarchaeology and Social Theory,
DOI 10.1007/978-3-319-61866-1_8

forensic scientist at the intersections of politics, economics, and social practice shaped by sociopolitical conditions in the Texas borderlands.

## Forensic Archeology

Forensic anthropologists have a tailored yet widely applicable skillset incorporating expertise in the human skeleton, archeological techniques, and practice within a medicolegal setting. These skills make the anthropologist vital to the exhumation and investigation of migrant deaths in borderlands. Archeology is the controlled recovery of the physical evidence and remains of past peoples. It applies a purposeful and systematic approach to preserve the context of the information located at the archeological site. Forensic archeology is the application of archeological principals and techniques within a medicolegal and/or humanitarian context (Dupras et al. 2012; Blau and Ubelaker 2009). The utilization of forensic anthropologists with archeological training to recover human remains and associated evidence at deposition sites rather than law enforcement personnel is not an insult to the capabilities of various law enforcement agencies but rather is a reflection of practicality.

At a crime scene where a suspicious death is located, archeological technique is employed as a means to locate, recover, and carefully document each item's position in three dimensional space. This allows for later reconstruction of the death scene, which is essential in interpreting how the individual came to be in that location, how long they were there, how they may have died, and their identity. Forensic archeology can be utilized at crime scenes where the body is deposited on the ground surface, as well as crime scenes where the individual has been buried. The excavation of burials is especially complex and requires the use of small hand tools like masonry trowels, spoons, and brushes to slowly remove dirt and fill from the burial shaft and leave all human remains and artifacts in their original position. The use of large shovels or machinery should only occur under special supervised circumstances. Archeologists are also trained in stratigraphy, a branch of geology that studies soil composition. This allows the archeologist to recognize soil disturbances, which is essential in differentiating grave fill versus sterile soil and is utilized in locating burials. Forensic archeologists must also be trained in human osteology, the study of the human skeleton. Oftentimes the skeleton being investigated within the medicolegal system is not in pristine condition. Rather it is significantly altered from its living form, such as degraded, scattered, fragmented, and/or burned. Formal osteological training allows the forensic archeologist to recognize human bone in many conditions and contexts (Cheetham and Hanson 2009; Stoutamire 1983).

Minimally, the forensic archeologist needs formal training in recording provenience (creating maps and photography), archeological technique for the excavation and recovery of remains and evidence, geology, anatomy, and chemistry. It is not efficient in terms of time or money for every law enforcement agency to train one of their personnel to do forensic archeology as these types of cases are rare in most jurisdictions. It is much more practical to consult with a forensic archeologist when decomposed or skeletonized remains are encountered by law enforcement agencies. Most forensic anthropologists practicing in the USA consult on single homicide cases. They assist in the systematic recovery of a single individual body from the death scene. It is usually rare for forensic anthropologists to work scenes where multiple bodies are located or comingled.

## Forensic Archeology and Humanitarian Crises: A Brief History

While the majority of cases that forensic anthropologists assist with are single homicide cases, mass grave and mass disaster scenarios across the globe have more recently required the unique skillset of forensic anthropologists. The use of international forensic science experts in humanitarian efforts began in 1984 when the American Association for the Advancement of Science (AAAS) deployed experienced forensic anthropologists to Argentina to assist in identifying thousands of the "disappeared" during the junta regime that lasted from 1976 to 1983 (Fondebrider 2009). The importance of forensic science-based human rights investigations has grown over the past 30 years as forensic experts continue to volunteer their time to identify victims of human rights violations across the planet. The unique expertise of a forensic archeologist in identifying burials and systematically exhuming burials positions them as essential to such investigations.

Forensic archeologists have been utilized to locate and/or excavate large mass graves containing victims of ethnic, religious, and political conflict. Careful and systematic exhumation allows them to uncover information that can be instrumental in identification of the victims and interpreting trauma visible on the skeleton. This may in turn be essential evidence in the prosecution of those committing the atrocities. Additionally, since archeologists are anthropologists, they are often trained to approach their work in ways that are appropriate for the religious and cultural worldviews of the deceased. This is especially important during the politically and emotionally charged process of mass grave exhumation, where media, government officials, nongovernment organizations, and others are all watching and carefully monitoring the process (Rosenblatt 2015).

In Latin America, hundreds of thousands of people went missing between 1960 and 1991. These individuals were detained or kidnapped and killed, and their bodies subsequently disappeared. In many instances, the bodies were buried in cemeteries as "John Does" or unmarked, buried in mass graves in clandestine locations or in military compounds, thrown in wells, dropped from aircraft into the ocean, and burned or destroyed by chemicals (Fondebrider 2009). This resulted in thousands of families searching for information regarding their missing loved ones and the need for a scientific approach to locate and recover the bodies of the dead.

In 1984, the *Equipo Argentino Antropologia Forense*/Argentine Forensic Anthropology Team (EAAF) was formed in response to requests by the Grandmothers of Plaza de Mayo, a nongovernmental human rights organization searching for children that disappeared with their parents during the previous political regime. The EAAF began efforts to locate, recover, and identify the "disappeared," with one of their goals being the implementation of exhumation techniques that preserved context and prevented the destruction of evidence. This grew from the fact that hundreds of individuals had been exhumed before the creation of the EAAF and many were damaged and commingled in the process. The EAAF started as a group of enthusiastic anthropology students who were guided and trained by Dr. Clyde Snow, a prominent US forensic anthropologist, who combined traditional archeological and forensic anthropology techniques to conduct the exhumations (Fondebrider and Scheinsohn 2015; Fondebrider 2009; Doretti and Snow 2003). Thus, the creation of the EAAF signaled the first formal recognition of the importance of forensic archeological technique in a humanitarian crisis setting.

In 2006, a multidisciplinary forensic team at the Servicio Medico Legal (SML) in Chile began the task of identifying a large number of unidentified "disappeared" that were buried in Patio 29. Patio 29 comprises 320 plots and is located in the country's largest cemetery, Cementerio General. The military dictator of the previous political regime ordered bodies of the "disappeared" to be secretly buried in this location. In 1991, after appointment of President Aylwin, the military was charged with overseeing exhumation of the remains. During these efforts, only 108 of the original graves were located, and 126 individuals were recovered. After information surfaced that many of the individuals buried in Patio 29 had been misidentified, the human rights identification division of the SML was completely restructured to include forensic archeologists, osteologists, and dentists (DeVisser et al. 2014). Patio 29 played an essential role in identifying the need for trained archeologists to conduct the exhumations of the victims of the Pinochet regime.

Forensic archeologists have also assisted in other types of mass death events, including air craft, train or bus crashes, bombings, and natural disasters. Disaster response of this kind is complicated and requires coordination of multiple agencies to address the disaster site, the disaster morgue, and the family assistance center. Forensic archeologists play a prominent role in the recovery of mass disaster victims at the disaster site. For example, forensic archeology was utilized after the burning of the Branch Davidian compound (Waco, TX) in 1993; after multiple aircraft crashes, including USAir flight 427 (Pittsburgh, PA), United Airlines Flight 93 (Somerset, PA), and Korean Air Flight 801 (Guam), at the World Trade Center Towers after the events of September 11, 2001; and in New Orleans after Hurricane Katrina (Sledzik 2009; Fulginiti et al. 2006; Saul and Saul 2003; Ubelaker et al. 1995).

## Brooks County, Texas: A Case Study in Volunteer Mass Disaster Assistance

While a terrorist bombing or aircraft crash would be followed by governmental resources to assist in the identification of the dead, there are many silent mass disasters in the USA that are being addressed by large-scale volunteer efforts. The

**Table 8.1** Number of migrant remains recovered in Brooks County, TX, from 2009 to 2016: These numbers represent bodies that were discovered and likely underrepresent the actual number of migrant deaths in the county during this time period

| | Recovered bodies 2009–2016 | | | | | | | |
|---|---|---|---|---|---|---|---|---|
| | 2009 | 2010 | 2011 | 2012 | 2013 | 2014 | 2015 | 2016 |
| January | 4 | 1 | 0 | 1 | 7 | 7 | 11 | 3 |
| February | 6 | 0 | 2 | 3 | 5 | 5 | 7 | 3 |
| March | 4 | 1 | 5 | 1 | 4 | 3 | 5 | 5 |
| April | 1 | 1 | 3 | 4 | 4 | 5 | 0 | 5 |
| May | 5 | 3 | 6 | 5 | 8 | 5 | 3 | 6 |
| June | 5 | 3 | 6 | 18 | 7 | 12 | 3 | 5 |
| July | 11 | 2 | 9 | 25 | 16 | 7 | 2 | 12 |
| August | 12 | 7 | 10 | 20 | 19 | 8 | 2 | 5 |
| September | 8 | 2 | 10 | 23 | 6 | 3 | 2 | * |
| October | 3 | 0 | 3 | 15 | 5 | 0 | 6 | * |
| November | 1 | 0 | 5 | 9 | 2 | 4 | 1 | * |
| December | 1 | 0 | 6 | 5 | 4 | 2 | 7 | * |
| Totals: | 61 | 20 | 65 | 129 | 87 | 61 | 49 | 44* |
| Grand total | 472* | | | | | | | |

* = no data at this time

humanitarian crisis currently occurring in US counties near the Mexico border is described by those working there as a mass disaster situation (see Chap. 7, this volume). While different from what might typically be considered a mass disaster, an event that generates mass death within a very short period of time, the strain of the large number of deaths on local medicolegal systems is at mass disaster proportions. For example, the number of unidentified migrants recovered from Brooks County, TX, in 2012 is documented at 129 (Table 8.1). This number is similar to the number of deaths that would need to be investigated if a commercial aircraft were to crash in that county.

Many mass disasters generate state and federal funding to assist with the recovery and identification of the victims by forensic specialists and law enforcement. However, poor border counties are faced with large numbers of deaths and no assistance for the recovery and analysis of these unidentified individuals. Faced with no funding for costly forensic analyses, Brooks County officials made the decision to dedicate portions of the Sacred Heart Burial Park (Falfurrias, TX) to burial of the migrants until they could afford proper forensic analyses. In 2013 and 2014, teams from the University of Indianapolis and Baylor University traveled to Falfurrias to begin exhuming the migrant remains to start them on their journey toward identification (Fig. 8.1). Over 100 individuals were exhumed during the two field seasons.

The county utilized forensic archeologists for the exhumations for a variety of reasons. When the individuals were buried, a small metal marker was used to designate the burial location (Fig. 8.2). Over time the markers were destroyed or moved resulting in a situation where it was unknown exactly how many individuals were buried at Sacred Heart Burial Park and the exact location of each burial. Therefore,

**Fig. 8.1** During the summers of 2013 and 2014, teams from the University of Indianapolis and Baylor University conducted forensic archeological excavations in areas of the cemetery containing the remains of unidentified migrants (University of Indianapolis photo by Guy Housewright)

a systemic excavation of the entire plot dedicated to migrant burials was required. Additionally, proper archeological technique would ensure preservation of burial context. The burials represent secondary deposition locations, and context is essential in this case for preserving any and all information related to the burial event and the unidentified decedent. This can later assist in identification purposes as all antemortem and postmortem information is collected and compared following an identification hypothesis. For example, if the body bag is not labeled with a law enforcement case number, burial context and location could possibly be compared with burial records to assist in recovery of this lost information to link the individual to a law enforcement case file. Therefore, documenting the location of each burial within the cemetery and the association between burials and/or burials and artifacts can be instrumental in identification in this situation.

## The Journey Toward Positive Identification

The exhumation seasons in Brooks County, Texas, were short but intense, with archeologists spending about 10 days in the field each year. While the process of exhumation was physically and emotionally exhausting for those conducting the excavations, the process of exhuming the unidentified migrants represents the shortest segment of the identification journey. The long and arduous task of laboratory

**Fig. 8.2** Small metal markers were used to designate the migrant burial locations. The amount of information displayed on the markers was not consistent and could contain any combination of descriptive data including demographic information, date of recovery, location of recovery, or Electronic Death Record numbers (University of Indianapolis photo by Krista Latham)

analysis, the collection of family reference information, and the repatriation process represent a much longer portion of the journey home for these individuals (see Chap. 11, this volume). Media outlets and public attention tend to focus on visually dramatic settings of exhumation. Therefore, little of the difficult repatriation journey is covered by the media or understood by state and federal government agencies.

When human remains are discovered in Texas, the justice of the peace or medical examiner can request any series of analyses to be performed that can assist in cause/manner of death determination and identification. Traditionally, autopsies are often ordered for remains with soft tissue present while anthropological analyses are often ordered for skeletal remains. A forensic odontologist may also be consulted to analyze the teeth in order to make comparisons between the teeth of the unidentified individual and available antemortem dental records for identification purposes. Other forensic specialists may be consulted based on the circumstances of the particular case. Autopsies traditionally cost around $1,500, if not more, and this cost is paid by the county. Currently autopsy services are not volunteered for the migrant remains in the same way that anthropological services are volunteered. For counties where over 50 bodies are found every year, postmortem examination costs can dramatically affect the overall county budget as the county scrambles to cover costs. County employees, including those employed at agencies involved in these investigations, often have their salaries and benefits reduced in order to compensate for these costs (Saslow 2014).

Positive identification of individuals buried in Sacred Heart Burial Park is ultimately due to DNA matches. As per Texas state law, a small sample of bone or tooth is sent to a federally funded forensic DNA laboratory for the generation of a DNA profile. This profile can then be compared to reference samples from the missing person or their family members. With federal funding, these DNA analyses are performed at no direct cost to the county. However, if additional tests are requested by investigators, a private lab is often utilized. If the county cannot cover the expenses, the costs are often covered by grant money through a nongovernment organization. Additionally, new methods are constantly being developed to assist with the identification process. Teeth, bone, and hair samples can be used to perform stable isotope analysis (Chesson et al. 2017). This molecular technique can help narrow the geographic origin of the unidentified person. As well, bone can be sampled for histological analysis to assist with age estimation. Histology utilizes bone growth and remodeling patterns to estimate the age of the person at death (Crowder et al. 2017). To date, the individuals who have received these additional tests did not cost the county because the services were voluntarily conducted and covered by private funding (see Bartelink Chap. 10). However, it is important to note that specialized tests like isotope analysis can cost over $1,000 per individual, and the ability of the forensic anthropologist to conduct these tests is due to grant funding. Applying for and obtaining grant funding is costly in terms of the time investment the applicant devotes to the grant application process.

Because many identification hypotheses are formed as a result of DNA analyses, DNA reference samples are an extremely important component of the identification process. Most DNA reference samples are in the form of family reference samples, which are saliva or blood samples submitted by family members to be compared with DNA samples processed from unidentified human remains. If a positive DNA association occurs between a sample from an unidentified individual and reference samples from the family, best practices suggest that all possible antemortem and postmortem data are compared for consistency. Antemortem data are often derived from missing persons' reports filed by the family with law enforcement agencies and/or nongovernment organizations. Examples of data collected in these reports can include date of last contact, demographic data (age at the time of last contact, height, weight, etc.), and personal effect data. These data are then compared against postmortem data, such as date of recovery of remains, condition of the remains when found, biological profile data derived from forensic anthropological analyses, and personal effects found with remains. If no inconsistencies are found between antemortem and postmortem data, or once any inconsistencies are explained, then a full identification report can be written detailing all scientific analyses conducted for the case. This identification report is sent to the appropriate jurisdictional authority responsible for the inquest for formal acceptance of the identification, and an authorization for release of remains to the family is signed by the jurisdictional authority.

If the identified individual is a foreign national, then the family has the option to have the remains repatriated to the family residing in the foreign national's country of origin. The repatriation process is coordinated by the foreign national's consular office. Repatriations must occur through a funeral home, chosen by either the family or the consular office, depending on the consular policies. After obtaining authorization for release of the remains, the agency in custody of the remains coordinates with the chosen funeral home to facilitate the repatriation. Many cases have a death certificate filed under the name of "Unidentified" or "John/Jane Doe," in which an amendment to the death certificate is necessary before the remains can be repatriated. Once the death certificate is changed and the remains are transferred to the funeral home, the funeral home will repatriate the remains to the family with assistance from the consular office. The costs of repatriation are often covered by consular offices, meaning that the expense is covered to an extent by the country of origin. However, this funding fluctuates with each country's budget for consular services, resulting in costs to the family to have their loved one repatriated. Oftentimes the volunteer forensic anthropologists are contributing to multiple tasks within the identification journey in their quest to identify and subsequently repatriate identified remains (see Chap. 11, this volume).

An identification can be defined differently depending on the perspective taken. In other words, the answer to the question "What is/constitutes an identification?" can vary depending on whether the question is asked to a forensic scientist, a jurisdictional authority, or family and friends of a missing loved one. For a forensic scientist, an identification is based on the results of analytical tests. The specific number and type of forensic tests performed for any given case will vary depending on location and available resources. Within this context, a scientific identification is the conclusion of a series of analyses that verifies the identification hypothesis.

Jurisdictional authorities (justice of the peace, law enforcement agent, consulate, etc.) are concerned with the legal aspects of the identification. They rely on a "positive" result from the forensic analysis and entrust the forensic scientists' opinion, in order to move forward with the legal processes they are required to uphold. Within this context, an identification is the conclusion of an inquest that initiates the legal processes necessary for repatriation/final disposition.

Regardless of the outcomes of scientific analyses or jurisdictional declarations, an identification must be accepted by the family and friends of a missing loved one for the entire identification process to be completed. In other words, the family and friends of a missing loved one must be convinced, not told, that their loved one has been identified. Distrust in government and/or law enforcement systems can result in distrust in the results reported from these agencies. In these cases, families often rely on evidence they can visually recognize, like personal effects, to confirm an identification. Careful consideration must be taken to clearly explain how the identification was made because, for the family and friends of a missing loved one, an identification is closure.

## Planning the Exhumations

Planning the mass exhumation of individuals who perished during a humanitarian crisis requires much more than ordering shovels and other archeology supplies. Proper permissions must be obtained from the appropriate legal authorities. It must be determined that the well intentions of the forensic archeologists fit within the framework of what the family desires. In other words, it must be taken into consideration whether or not family members would want their loved ones exhumed and identified. While some may assume that all families would want their loved one identified and sent home, the reality is that some cultural groups prohibit or discourage postmortem handling of the body. Such culturally inappropriate handling may doom their loved one to unrest forever (Rosenblatt 2015). After these preliminary considerations are addressed, the field season can be planned with an estimation of how much work should occur and what supplies are needed. The teams working at Sacred Heart Burial Park traveled long distances. Travel arrangements and accommodation plans were made. Equipment management required planning months in advance due to the fact that some equipment could not be transported via plane and therefore had to be acquired in Texas. The work also involved coordinating and preparing a large number of students. While they were trained in proper archeological technique, their safety had to be considered while performing manual labor in high temperature and high humidity conditions, with additional safety hazards like scorpions, fire ants, and snakes considered. It is at this step that monetary costs are the most obvious in terms of travel and supplies; however, the hidden costs of time and personal safety are often not considered.

Furthermore, the exhumations required the coordination of multiple agencies and organizations. This coordination may prove more difficult than it appears since each organization has different configurations, missions, motivations, and access to resources. For example, exhumations at Sacred Heart Burial Park were performed by Baylor University and the University of Indianapolis. However, the Brooks County Sheriff's Office and the Brooks County Justices of the Peace were involved in authorizing the exhumations and the subsequent analyses for their inquests. Texas State University assisted in the processing and curation of many remains. Baylor University, University of Indianapolis, Texas State University, University of North Texas Center for Human Identification (UNTCHI), and the Defense POW/MIA Accounting Agency (DPAA) all assisted with anthropological analyses. UNTCHI and the EAAF provided DNA analyses. Finally, countless law enforcement agencies and nongovernment agencies assist with the investigations that are still open. Coordinating the efforts of these agencies requires an understanding of the relationships (or lack thereof) between these agencies. While not directly related to the planning of the exhumation process, an understanding of future necessary collaborations is extremely beneficial to the planning of exhumations.

The exhumations were conducted to increase chances of identification by performing analyses that were not performed prior to burial due to lack of resources or lack of knowledge of particular tests. Therefore, following exhumations, development of best practices/standard operating procedures (SOPs) and education for all involved parties of these best practices/SOPs are key to preventing the need for future exhumations. These best practices/SOPs must be both sustainable and adaptive to changing resources and jurisdictions while still promoting practices that offer the highest chances for identification. Changing existing practices requires political legwork. For example, following exhumations in Brooks County, the commissioner's court approved the motion to have all remains discovered in Brooks County sent to a medical examiner for autopsy instead of a mortuary. This approval was likely only successful as the result of political pressure on the ground in Falfurrias, TX.

After exhumations, data regarding location and analyses for each individual must be organized and managed. A database with query options should be developed to (1) document all possible information regarding each case exhumed, (2) track workflow for all analyses performed, including both location and time, and (3) allow for active comparisons against antemortem data such as missing persons reports. While many agencies have their own databases regarding cases that they work with, options should be available in the case that these individual databases/agencies do not actively communicate or cross-reference cases. A centralized database that tracks post-exhumation workflow (skeletal analysis, DNA analysis, etc.) is a general best practice in that it can both track workflow to promote efficiency and create a detailed timeline for every exhumed case. Furthermore, a centralized database can also include information discovered regarding pre-exhumation data if available (recovery reports, autopsies before burial, etc.)

Ensuring that all efforts are made for identification requires understanding the stakeholders involved and the relationships between them. Prior to exhumations, the county's historical and current protocols need to be understood in order to determine how many remains could be exhumed and what details of the remains might be available (location of recovery, previous tests performed, etc.). Next, jurisdictional authorities must be convinced that exhumations need to take place and that all data related to these exhumations will be documented and reported back to these authorities. This step often requires time and the development of trusting relationships. Following exhumations, additional political work is necessary to ensure that best practices are being followed for the analyses of all exhumed cases.

## Public Awareness and Funding: Critical Intersections

Given the multifaceted nature of migrant identification, one of the most crucial, but underappreciated, roles of forensic anthropologists is to secure resources for their work. There are monetary costs associated with equipment, travel, and scientific tests. By bringing awareness to the crisis and their work, it is possible to secure donations from individuals interested in supporting various facets of the initiative including the humanitarian, educational, and scientific aspects. Attention and awareness can come from the motivation of the forensic anthropologist in terms of lectures and presentations or can be the by-product of media attention.

**Fig. 8.3** Multiple media sources were present at the Sacred Heart Burial Park to document the exhumation process. Their cameras were often focused on some of the most emotional and delicate moments of the work, such as the removal of remains from the graves. This image captures the media's proximity as forensic scientists respectfully documented the remains (University of Indianapolis photo by Rachel Gravens)

The excavation seasons in Sacred Heart Burial Park attracted major media attention (Fig. 8.3). There were few days that we were not being filmed, photographed, or questioned. While some outlets appeared truly interested in bringing awareness to the humanitarian crisis on the border, others seemed obviously there to produce shock value. Some journalists made requests to pose, reenact, or change protocol for a "good shot," which we quickly denied. We dodged tripods and were shushed near microphones and asked to stop working so interviews could take place. On more than one occasion, we had to remind media outlets that they should be respectful of the dead and their families, and on some occasions, they were told they had to stop because they were negatively impacting our work at the cemetery.

While we lost count of the number of various new outlets on scene during the exhumations, media attention to the laboratory analyses has been scant. The exhumations were indeed an important starting point in the journey to identification for these migrants, but the laboratory analyses are a long and underappreciated process. Even though many people are unaware of the process of forensic archeology, even more are unaware of the many laboratory techniques and the countless hours that go into a forensic identification. Uneven media attention to the varied aspects of identification and repatriation contributes to this deficit in public knowledge and attention. It is likely the laboratory analyses would not garner the same response from their viewers as the exhumations and therefore the reason why the exhumations drew more attention than the laboratory work. The exhumations occur among the backdrop of a local cemetery littered with colorful flowers and are a flurry of activity as forensic archeologists uncover the dead. The act of removing a body from the ground is both somber and dramatic. Contrast this with the sterile backdrop of a forensic laboratory, where scientists are slowly and deliberately analyzing the bones and teeth of the skeleton. This process, while vital to identification, is not as intuitively exciting for lay audiences as the cemetery exhumations.

A similar pattern emerged regarding funding, with more attention and resources donated toward the exhumations than toward the laboratory work. While some of the individuals participating in the field season were students taking a field course and professors getting paid for instructing the course, others were volunteers. Travel, lodging, food, and field gear were all paid for out of pocket or funded through various grants and fund raising events for the volunteers. The forensic anthropology laboratory analyses are also volunteer events, with time and resources being donated by the professionals. However, there are some aspects of the forensic investigation that are expensive and require funding that sometimes poorly paid university professors cannot afford. For example, biohazard disposal and personal protective equipment associated with processing, DNA analyses, and isotope analyses can average thousands of dollars per unidentified individual. Yet, donations are much more likely to fund exhumations over laboratory work.

This brings into question the motivation of the funders. Many donations came from the friends and family of the field team, signifying their support for their loved one in doing this humanitarian work. Additional funding came from the University of Indianapolis Provost, who seemed equally concerned about assisting with the crisis and providing her students with a global citizenship experience. Other donations came from fundraising efforts (http://beyondborders.uindy.edu/support-our-trip/), but progress in identifying the dead requires large funding bodies, and there are few available funds for this type of work. Educational funding is available for data collection and academic pursuits; however, it is not appropriate to use this crisis as a test of the scientific method. There are additional funds available for forensic analyses, but many of these do not extend to non-US nationals. Finally, humanitarian aid is available for the living migrant refugees but not to identify the dead. This leaves forensic scientists working in the Texas borderlands vulnerable to funding bodies to continue their volunteer work, as money is needed for everything from field supplies and travel expenses to processing costs, personal protective equipment, lab supplies, educational outreach, surveying, meeting with families, visiting consulates, and other analytical tests.

## Summary

At this point, we must ask ourselves what is the answer to addressing the forensic side of this crisis? Unfortunately, there is no answer that addresses everything in every situation. Would it be better to replace the volunteers with governmental entities? On the one hand, those with governmental standing will have greater access to resources and permissions that are not granted to volunteers. However, they do not have the freedom to modify their policies and adapt to new and unforeseen circumstances. Currently, making progress requires both the governmental and volunteer groups to work together. The volunteers have found ways to bring attention to the work and garner some monetary resources by positioning themselves as both the forensic scientists qualified to do the work and the humanitarian volunteers obligated to do so. This complex set of interactions has allowed them to operate as knowledge producers on the one hand as they relate the stories of the dead and as consumers on the other hand as they utilize resources to conduct the scientific work. They both create and influence narratives of migrant death as they work to identify those that have perished and repatriate their remains home to family members.

With immigration being a hot political topic, the media will continue to cover the mass deaths and forensic work in the Texas borderlands as they see fit. Local law enforcement and forensic scientists must continue to wrestle with the fact that media outlets are in the business of getting viewers and not necessarily the business of reporting the news. News is meant to be informational yet viewers are grabbed by emotions like shock, fear, or outrage. On the one hand, attention and awareness can come from media attention and potentially bring much needed resources to a crisis situation. On the other hand, the biased lens of the media and their lack of fact checking have, in many cases, caused more harm than good by reporting embellished dramatic accounts, ultimately resulting to misleading inaccuracies. For example, many outlets comingled stories of the increased numbers of unaccompanied migrant minors with stories of the cemetery exhumations, thus leading many to believe there were a large number of children in the cemetery. But that is not the case. It is difficult for those on the ground to see how our actions get reported, or rather distorted, by the time they get to the general public. In June 2014, one of the authors reflects on this very subject in a blog post entitled "Broken" (http://beyond-borders.uindy.edu/2014/06/08/broken/) "Today I watched as the media that came to talk about the mistreatment of these individuals during life disrespect them during death. They interrupted our work, attempted to put tripods and equipment in the holes we were digging and in effect exploited and sensationalized them. I wondered how they could report on this story without really feeling it."

In the end, the story that needs to be told is the story of the lives lost and the families in mourning. In order to bring aid and resources to communities that are desperate for resources, we need to find ways to tell their stories in a way that does not exploit them. The need for forensic archeologists to continue exhumations in the Texas borderlands and forensic scientists to continue working on identifications is great, and their jobs will not be complete in the near and foreseeable future.

## References

Blau, S., & Ubelaker, D. H. (2009). Forensic anthropology and archaeology: Introduction to a broader view. In S. Blau & D. H. Ubelaker (Eds.), *Handbook of forensic anthropology and archaeology* (pp. 21–25). Walnut Creek: Left Coast Press.

Cheetham, P. N., & Hanson, I. (2009). Excavation and recovery in forensic archeological investigations. In S. Blau & D. H. Ubelaker (Eds.), *Handbook of forensic anthropology and archaeology* (pp. 141–149). Walnut Creek: Left Coast Press.

Chesson, L., Tipple, B., Youmans, L., O'Brien, M., & Harmon, M. (2017). Forensic identification of human skeletal remains using isotopes: A brief history of applications from archaeological dig sites to modern crime scenes. In K. Latham, E. Bartelink, & M. Finnegan (Eds.), *New perspectives in human skeletal identification*. New York: Elsevier.

Crowder, C. M., Adronowski, J. M., & Dominguez, V. M. (2017). Bone histology as an integrated tool in the process of skeletal identification. In K. Latham, E. Bartelink, & M. Finnegan (Eds.), *New perspectives in human skeletal identification*. New York: Elsevier.

DeVisser, E. M., Latham, K. E., & Intriago Leiva, M. (2014). The contribution of forensic anthropology to national identity in Chile: A case study from Patio 29. In D. L. Martin & C. P. Anderson (Eds.), *Bioarcheological and forensic perspectives on violence*. New York: Cambridge University Press.

Doretti, M., & Snow, C. C. (2003). Forensic anthropology and human rights: The Argentine experience. In D. W. Steadman (Ed.), *Hard evidence, case studies in forensic anthropology* (pp. 290–310). Upper Saddle River: Prentice Hall.

Dupras, T. L., Schultz, J. J., Wheeler, S. M., & Williams, L. J. (2012). *Forensic recovery of human remains: Archeological approaches* (2nd ed.). New York: CRC Press.

Fondebrider, L. (2009). The application of forensic anthropology to the investigation of political violence: Perspectives from South America. In S. Blau & D. H. Ubelaker (Eds.), *Handbook of forensic anthropology and archaeology* (pp. 65–74). Walnut Creek: Left Coast Press.

Fondebrider, L., & Scheinsohn, V. (2015). Forensic archaeology: The Argentinian way. In W. J. M. Groen, N. Marquez-Grant, & R. Janaway (Eds.), *Forensic archaeology: A global perspective*. Chichester: Wiley-Blackwell.

Fulginiti, L. C., Warren, M. W., Hefner, J. T., Bedore, L. R., Byrd, J. H., Stephan, V., & Dirkmaat, D. C. (2006). Anthropology responds to Hurricane Katrina. *Proceedings of the American Academy of Forensic Sciences, 12*, 305.

Rosenblatt, A. (2015). *Digging for the disappeared: Forensic science after atrocity*. Stanford: Stanford University Press.

Saslow, E. (2014). In poorest county in Texas, at center of US border crisis, Brooks County sheriff's deputies go it alone. The Monitor. http://www.themonitor.com/news/local/in-poorest-county-in-texas-at-center-of-us-border/article_f0b3bfc2-25a0-11e4-8644-0017a43b2370.html. Accessed 6 Oct 2016.

Saul, F. P., & Saul, J. M. (2003). Planes, trains and fireworks, the evolving role of the forensic anthropologist in mass fatality incidents. In D. W. Steadman (Ed.), *Hard evidence, case studies in forensic anthropology* (pp. 266–277). Upper Saddle River: Prentice Hall.

Sledzik, P. (2009). Forensic anthropology in disaster response. In S. Blau & D. H. Ubelaker (Eds.), *Handbook of forensic anthropology and archaeology* (pp. 374–387). Walnut Creek: Left Coast Press.

Stoutamire, J. (1983). Excavation and recovery. In D. Morse, J. Duncan, & J. Stoutamire (Eds.), *Handbook of forensic archeology and anthropology* (pp. 20–47). Tallahassee: Rose Printing Company.

Ubelaker, D. H., Owsley, D. W., Houck, M. M., Craig, E., Grant, W., Woltanski, T., Fram, R., Sandness, K., & Peerwani, N. (1995). The role of forensic anthropology in the recovery and analysis of Branch Davidian Compound victims: Recovery procedures and characteristics of the victims. *Journal of Forensic Sciences, 40*(3), 335–340.

# Chapter 9
# Expanding the Role of Forensic Anthropology in a Humanitarian Crisis: An Example from the USA-Mexico Border

**Angela Soler and Jared S. Beatrice**

A humanitarian emergency arises when such an event affects vulnerable populations who are unable to withstand the negative consequences by themselves. 'Vulnerability' refers to a reduced capacity of individuals or groups to resist and recover from life-threatening hazards, and is most often connected to poverty. That is, poor populations are more likely to be more vulnerable to man-made or natural disasters. –Humanitarian Coalition

## Forensic Anthropology, Humanitarian Aid, and Human Rights Investigations

Since the formation of the Argentine Forensic Anthropology Team (EAAF) in the mid-1980s, forensic anthropologists have been engaged in humanitarian aid and the forensic investigation of human rights violations around the world (Komar and Buikstra 2008; Fondebrider 2004). Forensic anthropology teams such as EAAF, the Guatemalan and Peruvian Forensic Anthropology Teams, as well as Physicians for Human Rights and the International Committee of the Red Cross have been called to respond to crises worldwide, demonstrating the significant contributions of forensic anthropology to humanitarian response and human rights investigations. Aside from expertise in recovering and examining highly decomposed, skeletonized, and fragmentary remains, forensic anthropologists are in the unique position of being

The views and opinions expressed in this chapter are the author's own and do not reflect the opinions of the New York City Office of Chief Medical Examiner or the City of New York.

A. Soler (✉)
Office of Chief Medical Examiner, New York, NY, USA
e-mail: drangelasoler@gmail.com

J.S. Beatrice
Department of Sociology and Anthropology, The College of New Jersey, Ewing, NJ, USA
e-mail: beatricj@tcnj.edu

 
K.E. Latham, A.J. O'Daniel (eds.), *Sociopolitics of Migrant Death and Repatriation*, Bioarchaeology and Social Theory,
DOI 10.1007/978-3-319-61866-1_9

both impartial forensic scientists and broadly trained anthropologists (Burns 1999). Human rights investigation experts argue that comprehensive anthropological knowledge is essential in the humanitarian context to maintain scientific integrity while at the same time working with sensitivity among different cultures and oppressed communities (Fondebrider 2004; Doretti and Snow 2003). Furthermore, combining a community- or population-wide approach typical to anthropological research with the individual-specific analysis typical of medicolegal death investigations can provide a more holistic account of events in human rights investigations. For example, forensic experts investigating mass graves document injuries on each individual but also analyze group-level patterns of trauma to provide a scientifically accurate reconstruction of violence enacted against a community.

Similar to the medicolegal investigative framework, the primary purpose of the forensic investigation in a humanitarian response is to "collect, preserve, and objectively interpret the scientific evidence" (Doretti and Snow 2003). The ultimate goals of these efforts are to identify and repatriate the remains of victims, to interpret trauma and determine the cause and manner of death, and to maintain an accurate historical record through documentation of the evidence (Doretti and Snow 2003). Within the sphere of a humanitarian response, many anthropologists believe that another principle objective of the forensic investigation should be to provide direct care to the community through family assistance and to pursue truth, justice, and the restoration of human dignity to those affected (Kimmerle 2014; Doretti and Burrell 2007). Within this context, Baraybar and Blackwell (2014) argue that, "Forensic investigators can contribute substantially to advocacy supporting human rights against impunity and exclusion, transcending the strict scientific sphere."

As intermediaries between the scientific investigation and the affected communities, broadly trained forensic anthropologists play a central role in this advocacy and the pursuit of truth and justice through objective examination and expert witness testimony, compassionate communication of the investigative findings to the families and affected communities, and the public dissemination of the scientific findings (Kimmerle 2014). Within the humanitarian context, these scientific findings provide physical evidence that can corroborate witness testimonies and community history and can advocate for justice and the rights and dignity of the survivors and their family members. As the majority of humanitarian crises and human rights violations are often experienced by the most vulnerable and marginalized communities, public dissemination of the physical evidence and resulting advocacy may be the only validation and justice they ever receive.

As has been the case historically during human rights investigations and humanitarian disasters, forensic anthropologists are uniquely positioned to provide a broad and effective response to the USA-Mexico border crisis. Forensic anthropologists working within medical examiners' offices; university professors running large-scale research, recovery, and identification efforts; as well as anthropologists working within local and international nonprofit organizations bring together diverse specializations to the investigation of migrant deaths. The identification of a heterogeneous group of victims united by the act of undocumented migration relies on investigating the biological characteristics of a diverse

Hispanic population (Spradley et al. 2016; Baker 2015; Spradley 2014), combining context and physical evidence to distinguish migrant remains (Soler et al. 2014; Anderson and Parks 2008; Birkby et al. 2008), knowledge of the biological and social markers of marginalization of migrants (Beatrice and Soler 2016; Reineke 2016), and an understanding and coordination of approaches to the crisis in different jurisdictions (Anderson and Spradley 2016; Reineke and Anderson 2016). A holistic anthropological approach with a population-level focus is critical to understanding patterns common to migrants as a group—patterns that ultimately facilitate the identification process and provide insight into the experience of marginalization and migration itself.

In the following sections, we define the surge in migrant deaths during the past two decades as a humanitarian crisis and briefly outline the complexities of forensic work within a vulnerable and marginalized community. We discuss the achievements of forensic anthropologists in Arizona to demonstrate how practitioners have expanded beyond the traditional scope of forensic anthropology in the medicolegal context. In this setting, forensic anthropologists work not only to identify individuals, interpret skeletal trauma, and provide direct family assistance but also to contribute a scientific truth about migrants' status as a marginalized and vulnerable community impacted by this large-scale humanitarian crisis.

## Migrant Fatalities at the USA-Mexico Border: A Humanitarian Crisis in Our Midst

Nongovernmental and international organizations and academic researchers have long argued that the considerable number of migrant deaths along the USA-Mexico border represents a humanitarian crisis (De La Torre 2016; American Public Health Association 2014; Jimenez 2009). Although a complex variety of factors influence undocumented migration, many individuals crossing the USA-Mexico border consciously risk their lives to flee impoverished and exceedingly violent conditions in their home countries (Franklin 2014; Gonzalez-Barrera et al. 2014). Academic research and policy reports demonstrate that increased migration from Mexico starting in the 1990s and 2000s was initially correlated with the passage of NAFTA and the collapse of local farming economies and extensive unemployment (Wise 2010; Jimenez 2009; García-Zamora 2009). While poverty and established family connections in the USA continue to influence migration, there has also been a more recent influx of both Mexican and Central American migrants—including many women and children—fleeing widespread gang and drug violence (Palmer 2015; Velez and Boehner 2014). Factors such as impoverishment and violence, coupled with the acute dangers of crossing the USA-Mexico border and continued marginalization once settled within the USA, accentuate the vulnerable position of migrants and their families (de León 2015; Holmes 2013; Abrego 2011).

US Border Patrol statistics indicate that more than 6,000 migrants have perished while attempting to cross the USA-Mexico border between 1997 and 2013

(U.S. Border Patrol 2014). This number is a gross underestimate as many deaths have not been accurately categorized as border crossing fatalities and as the remains of many more individuals have not been recovered from the vast, isolated desert and ranchland along our southern border (Martínez et al. 2013, 2014; Jimenez 2009; United States Government Accountability Office 2006; Rubio-Goldsmith et al. 2006). Furthermore, the rate of migrant fatalities has continued to increase despite an overall decrease in undocumented migration over the last several years (Martínez et al. 2013, 2014; Kovic 2013; Massey 2012; Passel et al. 2012). According to Martinez et al. (2013), the approximate death rate of undocumented border crossers in the Tucson Sector (southern Arizona) has steadily increased from 11.5 fatalities per 100,000 border patrol apprehensions in 2000 to a startling 142.5 fatalities per 100,000 apprehensions in 2012. Migrant death rates have also increased significantly in Texas from 30.45 fatalities per 100,000 border patrol apprehensions in 2000 to 152.25 fatalities per 100,000 apprehensions in 2012 (Kovic 2013).

This surge in the rate of border crossing deaths has been correlated with changes in US Border Patrol policy in the mid-1990s, which effectively funneled migrants away from populated centers of crossing into more remote and perilous terrain in the Arizona and Texas deserts (de León 2015; Rubio-Goldsmith 2006). This funneling pushed migrants to cross greater distances over a desolate landscape without access to food, water, and shelter against the harsh desert environment. As a result, migrants began dying overwhelmingly from preventable causes, such as environmental exposure, dehydration, drowning, or contact with desert wildlife (Parks et al. 2016; Martínez et al. 2013, 2014). Furthermore, the number of individuals dying from heat-related deaths along the Tucson Sector of the border significantly increased from approximately 39.2% of deaths from 1990 to 1999 to 61.4% of deaths from 2000 to 2006, suggesting a relationship between the changing patterns of border crossing and cause of death among undocumented border crossers (Rubio-Goldsmith 2006).

A direct consequence of migrant deaths in the remote desert is the large number of missing persons. As of 2017, The Colibrí Center for Human Rights, housed at the Pima County Office of the Medical Examiner (PCOME), had collected missing person reports for at least 2118 individuals who disappeared while crossing the USA-Mexico border into Arizona and Texas (Reineke et al. 2017). Independently, the Argentine Forensic Anthropology Team (EAAF) Border Project maintains approximately 929 missing person reports and hundreds of DNA family reference samples for individuals from El Salvador, Honduras, and Chiapas, Mexico, who went missing while crossing through Mexico or the USA (Reineke et al. 2017). The South Texas Human Rights Center maintains an additional 285 missing persons reports (Reineke et al. 2017). Despite the tremendous number of reports collectively maintained by these NGOs as well as by foreign consulates, the current record of missing persons does not account for individuals who were never recorded as missing. In many instances, a report is not filed either because the family does not know where to report someone as missing, their request to file a report was denied by US law enforcement agencies due to jurisdictional issues, or the family fears deportation, retaliation from smugglers, and/or government corruption.

For all the individuals reported as missing, there are a comparable number of unidentified individuals buried as "unknowns" in county public cemeteries along the southwest border. According to Hinkes (2008), as of 2003 roughly 20% of the hundreds of undocumented migrants in California had not been identified. Approximately 35% of the nearly 2,500 undocumented border crossers examined at the PCOME remained unidentified as of 2015. Lastly, in Texas, at least 36% of the 147 migrants recovered in Brooks County from 2010 to 2012 remain unidentified (Kovic 2013). Even more alarming, Kovic (2013) estimates that the true number of properly identified individuals is likely much lower, as some initial identifications were conducted without scientific merit, utilizing driver's licenses and personal effects to establish a purported identity.

The vast number of unidentified remains and missing person's reports amplifies the urgency by leaving families without answers about what happened to their loved ones. In this way, "the survivors are victims too" (Burns 1998). As with the Madres de la Plaza de Mayo searching for their disappeared sons and daughters after the "Dirty War" in Argentina, the families of missing undocumented migrants are searching in vain for their own disappeared. These families

> are not 'bereaved,' they are not 'mourning,', and they are not 'grieving,' as each of these implies a confirmed loss…Relatives of the missing remain in limbo, their status mimicking that of the missing person. The only cure for their condition is seeing the person in flesh and bone. The search for this cure becomes all-consuming (Reineke 2016: 136).

Time does not lessen this pain and the search for the disappeared becomes increasingly more desperate the longer the individual has been missing and the family receives no answer as to what happened to them.

Understandably, the main objective of forensic scientists working along the USA-Mexico border has been the recovery, identification, and repatriation of unidentified remains, as well as the determination of cause and manner of death. However, the scope and gravity of the migrant death crisis, as well as the vulnerable position of the affected communities, dictate the need to expand beyond the traditional sphere of forensic investigations within the medicolegal system. Few truly understand the depth of the problem of undocumented migration, including the reasons people cross, the number of preventable deaths, and the incredible difficulty migrant families have in recovering their missing loved ones. Using a broad skillset, forensic anthropologists can address this crisis not only through efforts to identify and return the missing but also by providing evidence of the systematic denial of access to basic resources (e.g., income, adequate nutrition, health care) experienced by many of the victims during life. In the following section, we discuss recent research and approaches adopted by the PCOME that work toward the traditional medicolegal goals and simultaneously document some of the important causes and consequences of the crisis.

## Expanding the Role of Forensic Anthropology: Migrant Death Investigation in Southern Arizona

Over the last two decades, the PCOME, located in Tucson, Arizona, has contended with the examination of an overwhelming number of undocumented border crossers dying in the southern Arizona desert. Because the deaths at the border represent a large-scale, ongoing humanitarian crisis and because of the difficulties in identifying individuals from a heavily marginalized migrant population, the PCOME has had to adapt from the typical individual-based medicolegal case approach to a more multidisciplinary and community-wide humanitarian-based approach. Reineke and Anderson (2016) explain that,

> Migrants' lived experience of social marginalization impacts the work of investigators at the PCOME, who struggle without consistent access to missing person's data, investigation experience from local law enforcement, clues based on migrants' personal effects, and other assists that are available in typical medico-legal contexts within the US.

In addition, the lack of adequate antemortem records or a centralized nationwide DNA database accessible to the families of undocumented migrants further complicates the identification process. Family members living abroad or undocumented in the USA are less likely to approach US law enforcement and thus cannot get their missing person reports or DNA reference samples into the national databases accessible to US medical examiners' offices.

In response to these complications, anthropologists at the PCOME have taken on more expansive roles in the investigative process. Such roles include, but are not limited to, directly examining the physical bodies, washing and cataloguing the clothing and personal effects, following up on investigative leads, working directly with various organizations and families to collect antemortem information, and making comparisons and scientific identifications of missing persons and unidentified remains. Due to the extensive number of cases of unidentified and missing migrants, anthropologists engaged in these activities are challenged daily by the evidence of human suffering they see not only in the physical remains but also in the intimate stories associated with the personal effects and through communication with families searching for their loved ones.

As a result, much of the research and multidisciplinary approaches implemented at the PCOME both respond to the complexities of identification and the death investigation and scientifically document the humanitarian disaster and speak to the marginalization of migrants dying along the border. While unusual within a medicolegal framework, these contextually minded advancements were necessary given the nature of the crisis and are more aligned with the holistic anthropological approaches typically employed within a human rights framework. Such advances at the PCOME include the "UBC Profile" and the "Biocultural Profile," which are biosocial approaches that use a combination of biological, socioeconomic, and cultural features to help distinguish the remains of undocumented migrants (Soler et al. 2014; Reineke 2016; Reineke and Anderson 2010, 2016). The UBC Profile incorporates the geographic location of recovery, personal effects, biological features of ancestry, and cultural accoutrements (Anderson 2008; Anderson and Parks 2008; Birkby et al. 2008). The Biocultural Profile focuses on the biological features of the UBC Profile and is defined as "the manifestation of cultural and socioeconomic factors on the physical body, either incorporated into one's biology or applied as semi permanent modifications observed on one's remains" (Soler et al. 2014). Among undocumented migrants examined at the PCOME, these features include poor oral health, short stature, skeletal indicators of stress, culturally relevant tattoos, and cosmetic dental restorations (Beatrice and Soler 2016; Reineke and Soler 2013; Anderson et al. 2009; Birkby et al. 2008). While the primary purpose of the biosocial approach at the PCOME was to aid investigators in identifying the remains of probable undocumented border crossers, a secondary outcome was the ability to more accurately count the number of deceased migrants recovered from southern Arizona (Anderson 2008). This scientific data provides irrefutable evidence of the vast number of people dying along the Arizona border, which can help inform policy decisions.

As the biosocial approach was researched and implemented, it became increasingly clear that a majority of the features used to identify the remains of undocumented migrants, such as recovery from a remote desert region, short stature, poor oral health, and poorly set antemortem fractures, along with handwritten letters, photographs, and crumpled pieces of paper with names and phone numbers, were manifestations of migrants' marginality (Reineke 2016; Reineke and Anderson 2010, 2016; Anderson et al. 2009; Anderson 2008). Consequently, a third outcome of the biosocial approach at the PCOME was the documentation of poverty and vulnerability recognized in the associated personal effects and embodied in the physical remains of individuals dying along the Arizona border (Soler et al. 2014; Soler et al. forthcoming, 2018; Beatrice and Soler 2016; Martínez et al. 2013, 2014; Reineke and Anderson 2010). Thus, a recognition of the biological effects of structural violence became another important aspect of the forensic anthropological examination and identification of undocumented migrants.

First defined by Johan Galtung, structural violence is "indirect violence built into repressive social orders creating enormous differences between potential and actual human self-realization" (Galtung 1975). As Paul Farmer argues, structural violence implies that "human life may be differentially valued, with some lives worth more than others" (Farmer 2010). In other words, structural violence refers to the institutional barriers that restrict access to basic human necessities and prevent specific individuals from reaching their full physical or socioeconomic potential. Particular subsets of populations are typically more affected by structural violence based on gender, race, culture, or socioeconomic status and thus are more susceptible to discrimination, violence, disease, infection, malnutrition, environmental toxins, and death (Quesada et al. 2011; Farmer 2005).

Structural violence in deceased undocumented migrants was first discussed by Martinez et al. (2013, 2014) in an analysis of the death rate and cause and manner of death in individuals who died while clandestinely crossing the border. They argue that the increased death rate in undocumented border crossers, as well as the untimely and unnatural death of young, vibrant migrant individuals, is a direct manifestation of the lack of value attributed to migrant lives. Anthropological research that documents the biological effects of marginalization in the human skeleton furthers this argument by demonstrating that the structural violence experienced by undocumented migrants occurs throughout the life course and is not solely related to the circumstance of death (Soler et al. forthcoming, 2018).

At the PCOME, practitioners beginning with Dr. Walter Birkby have utilized patterns of health-related skeletal and dental conditions (e.g., short stature, carious lesions, abscesses, antemortem tooth loss) along with other biological and cultural variables to distinguish the remains of foreign national Hispanics from those born in the USA (Soler et al. 2014; Anderson et al. 2009; Birkby et al. 2008). Building on these efforts, Beatrice and Soler (2016) have demonstrated that certain skeletal indicators of stress such as linear enamel hypoplasias (LEH), orbital lesions (OL), and porotic hyperostosis (PH) appear more frequently in undocumented migrants crossing into southern Arizona than in USA-born individuals from medical examiner and documented collections. Beatrice and Soler (2016) used odds ratios to demonstrate that the prevalence rates of LEH, OL, and PH were approximately 3.01, 5.98, and 7.91 times greater, respectively, in migrants examined at the PCOME than in an American comparative sample. Furthermore, and most startling, the prevalence rates of LEH (30.4%), OL (10.3%), and PH (64.7%) seen in undocumented border crossers in southern Arizona are similar to and, in some cases, greater than those recorded by bioarchaeologists in historic and prehistoric populations.

These data indicate that skeletal stress indicators should be included in criteria used to identify undocumented migrants in this context on a case-by-case basis. Equally important, however, is that the data reveal commonalities in life experiences among the community of individuals who ultimately attempt to cross the USA-Mexico border into southern Arizona. The prevalence rates of LEH and porotic cranial lesions in this group of migrants strongly suggest that they are often affected by chronic nutritional deficiencies and acute infections during childhood. Furthermore, examples of active and partially healed porotic cranial lesions in adolescents and young adults demonstrate that these forms of physiological disruption are, at least occasionally, not limited to childhood.

In this way, methods initially aimed at distinguishing UBCs from American-born individuals can be applied by forensic anthropologists to understand migrant lives and deaths in a broader humanitarian framework. Although it may not always be possible to identify the proximate causes of conditions such as porotic hyperostosis (e.g., a specific micronutrient deficiency, parasitic infection, or a combination of factors), their frequent appearance among migrants in southern Arizona supports a large body of interdisciplinary research that ultimately connects skeletal and dental evidence of physiological disruption to structural factors such as social marginalization and poverty (see, e.g., Goodman et al. 1987, 1991; Goodman and Rose 1991; Chaves et al. 2007). Because those factors limit access to adequate housing and sanitation, nutrition, health care, and education, skeletal indicators of stress in the remains of migrants represent embodied structural violence that is visible to careful practitioners. In broad terms, this means that forensic anthropologists are able to speak—at least to some degree—about the ways in which structural forces affect the life histories of vulnerable individuals.

## Structural Violence and Humanitarian Forensic Science

The anthropological response to migrant deaths in southern Arizona illustrates the importance of holistic approaches to addressing a humanitarian crisis. It also raises important questions about the roles of forensic scientists working in such contexts. The fact that structural violence has biological consequences observable in human skeletal remains means that forensic anthropologists with training in the recognition of pathological conditions are exceptionally well positioned to document and call attention to the vulnerability of migrants. However, can forensic anthropologists remain objective when the reconstruction of migrants' life and death histories continually affirms their status as victims of a human rights crisis? Should forensic anthropologists avoid recording skeletal evidence of structural violence altogether because doing so leans toward advocacy?

We argue that although reporting on structural violence may be atypical of anthropological practice within a traditional medicolegal framework, it is necessary in order to fulfill the obligations of forensic investigators working in a humanitarian crisis context. In the case of migrant deaths in southern Arizona, documenting the impact of poor living conditions on human biology and explaining the connection with structural violence are vital elements in the pursuit of truth, dignity, and justice for deceased migrants, as well as their families and communities. In the absence of this data, forensic scientists would be unable to provide a complete account of the circumstances of individuals whose quality of life was diminished by repressive structural forces and who, in death, became victims of a human rights crisis. The holistic examination of the physical remains of undocumented migrants thus provides a scientific truth about how they lived and died, and as Kimmerle (2014) has argued, "truth itself is justice."

The interpretations of forensic anthropologists engaged in this work are driven by standardized recording techniques and statistical analysis of the prevalence of skeletal lesions. By speaking about the data, anthropologists do not compromise their position as objective scientists. The function of scientific research is to discover and document information arising from objective data. For example, the results generated by Beatrice and Soler (2016) show a statistically significant association between migrant status and the evaluated stress indicators. In the case of porotic hyperostosis, prevalence rates were high enough that to ignore widespread nutritional stress would be to ignore compelling data that scientifically validates the life experience of undocumented migrants. Furthermore, it should be emphasized that forensic anthropologists are likely the only scientists who will recognize such lesions in migrant remains. For this reason, they have a responsibility to report the clear associations revealed through careful analysis of lesion prevalence. While we acknowledge that connecting skeletal pathology and social injustice requires an additional interpretative step, there is no better explanation for the ultimate cause of the suite of skeletal indicators of stress that appear so frequently in the remains of undocumented migrants. Anthropologists investigating health and stress in historic and prehistoric skeletal samples have recently adopted this framework (Martin and Harrod 2015; Klaus 2012). The results of this approach for migrants—a living group of people with known socioeconomic conditions—are much more straightforward. Forensic anthropologists recording embodied structural violence are documenting the physical evidence of migrants' marginalized status.

As discussed previously, one of the differences between forensic anthropology conducted in a traditional medicolegal setting and in a humanitarian crisis context is that the latter often allows practitioners to evaluate and disseminate information on the effects of forces such as structural violence on a group or community as opposed to an individual. In the case of migrant deaths, this perspective elucidates one of the reasons for which individuals from sending communities risk crossing the border clandestinely in the first place. For example, undocumented migrants crossing into southern Arizona are far from a homogenous group of people. While most originate from Mexico (Martinez et al. 2013, 2014), the specific groups of people and the geography of sending regions have changed over time. Nevertheless, a common factor driving outmigration has been a lack of local economic opportunity (DeLuca et al. 2010; Weeks et al. 2009). The addition of biological data on structural violence in migrants demonstrates that impoverishment is more than just a life encumbrance—it impairs physical bodies and reduces human potential. In this way, forensic anthropologists reconstructing life events recorded in migrant remains can assist other researchers, humanitarian organizations, and policy makers in developing a more precise understanding of the factors precipitating the crisis of migrant deaths.

Forensic anthropologists engaged in humanitarian efforts have a broad set of obligations that includes using objective, scientific evidence to provide a path toward reconciliation and justice for victims' families and communities. In the investigation of migrant deaths, documenting embodied life stresses is an important part of this process. By recording and publishing these data, forensic anthropologists can reveal evidence of systematic, indirect violence committed against social groups sending migrants to the USA. The results of this type of analysis augment traditional roles in recovery and personal identification and support the human rights of a vulnerable group of people.

## Conclusion

The biosocial approach employed by forensic practitioners at the PCOME to investigate border crossing deaths in southern Arizona draws from both medicolegal and humanitarian perspectives. The unique conditions of the migrant death crisis dictate that efforts to distinguish migrant remains utilize biological features suggestive of marginalized status, among other socioeconomic and cultural variables. In this paper, we have highlighted how one group of biological features—skeletal indicators of stress such as porotic cranial lesions and enamel hypoplasias—provides insight into migrants' life histories. While the prevalence rates of these conditions strongly suggest their ultimate cause is structural violence enacted on communities that send migrants, raising this point may be viewed as outside the usual role of a forensic scientist. However, we do not believe that reporting this information is in contradiction with impartial forensic science. Especially in a humanitarian crisis context, it offers instead a new avenue of investigation. As Doretti and Burrell (2007) point out, negotiations over the roles of anthropologists working in these contexts "...both define the limits of forensic anthropology as an engaged practice in the field of human rights and push at its boundaries, opening new arenas and new possibilities." The forensic anthropological examination of structural violence not only offers a way to assist in the identification and repatriation of undocumented border crossers but also provides objective physical evidence of preventable suffering in migrants.

We argue that practitioners who recognize skeletal indicators of stress and other biological indicators of marginality in migrant remains have an obligation to record and disseminate that information. Failing to do so would result in a loss of data that could be used to provide a complete account of migrants' life and death histories. Those details may also be crucial to reconstructing histories of systematic oppression on the community level. Furthermore, we agree with Baraybar and Blackwell's (2014) assertion that anthropological responses to human rights issues can be proactive by raising awareness of "the causes and not just the consequences of marginalization and exclusion." Drawing attention to embodied structural violence helps elucidate the causes of the migrant death crisis because it provides biological evidence of poor living conditions that influence undocumented migration. Improvements in the socioeconomic circumstances of marginalized groups are more likely if information on current conditions is well documented and made available to a broader public. Forensic anthropologists are among the few scientific investigators who can contribute this service to migrant sending communities.

## References


Abrego, L. J. (2011). Legal consciousness of undocumented Latinos: Fear and stigma as barriers to claims-making for first and 1.5 generation immigrants. *Law & Society Review, 45*(2), 337–370.

American Public Health Association (2014). Border crossing deaths: A public health crisis along the US-Mexico border. Retrieved from https://www.apha.org/policies-and-advocacy/public-health-policy-statements/policy-database/2014/07/24/08/56/border-crossing-deaths-a-public-health-crisis-along-the-us-mexico-border.

Anderson, B. E. (2008). Identifying the dead: Methods utilized by the Pima County (Arizona) Office of the Medical Examiner for undocumented border crossers: 2001–2006. *Journal of Forensic Sciences, 53*(1), 8–15.

Anderson, B. E., & Parks, B. O. (2008). Symposium on border crossing deaths: Introduction. *Journal of Forensic Sciences, 53*(1), 6–7.

Anderson, B. E., Smith, T. R., Birkby, W. H., Fenton, T. W., Hurst, C. V., & Gordon, C. C. (2009). Differentiating between foreign national Hispanics and US Hispanics in the southwest: The influence of socioeconomic status on dental health and stature. Proceedings of the 61st Annual Scientific Meeting of the American Academy of Forensic Sciences, Denver, Feb 16–21, 2009.

Anderson, B. E., & Spradley, M. K. (2016). The role of the anthropologist in the identification of migrant remains in the American Southwest. *Academic Forensic Pathology, 6*(3), 432–438.

Baker, L. E. (2015). Identification of deceased unauthorized border crossers in the United States. In G. E. Berg & S. Ta'ala (Eds.), *Biological affinity in forensic identification of human skeletal remains* (pp. 271–286). Boca Raton: CRC Press.
Baraybar, J. P., & Blackwell, R. (2014). Where are they? Missing, forensics, and memory. *Annals of Anthropological Practice, 38*(1), 22–42.
Beatrice, J. S., & Soler, A. (2016). Skeletal indicators of stress: A component of the biocultural profile of undocumented migrants in southern Arizona. *Journal of Forensic Sciences, 61*(5), 1164–1172.
Birkby, W. H., Fenton, T. W., & Anderson, B. E. (2008). Identifying southwest Hispanics using nonmetric traits and the cultural profile. *Journal of Forensic Sciences, 53*(1), 29–33.
Burns, K. R. (1998). Forensic anthropology and human rights issues. In K. Reichs (Ed.), *Forensic osteology: Advances in the identification of human remains* (2nd ed., pp. 63–85). Springfield: Charles C. Thomas.
Burns, K. R. (1999). *Forensic anthropology training manual*. Upper Saddle River: Prentice Hall.
Chaves, A. M., Rosenblatt, A., & Bazerra Oliveira, O. F. (2007). Enamel defects and its relation to life course events in primary dentition of Brazilian children: A longitudinal study. *Community Dental Health, 24*, 31–36.
De La Torre, M. (2016). *The U.S. immigration crisis: Toward an ethics of place*. Eugene: Cascade Books.
de León, J. (2015). *The land of open graves: Living and dying on the migrant trail*. Oakland: University of California Press.
DeLuca, L. A., McEwen, M. M., & Keim, S. M. (2010). United States-Mexico border crossing: Experiences and risk perceptions of undocumented male immigrants. *Journal of Immigrant and Minority Health, 12*(1), 113–123.
Doretti, M., & Burrell, J. (2007). Gray spaces and endless negotiations: Forensic anthropology and human rights. In R. Fox & L. Field (Eds.), *Anthropology put to work* (pp. 45–64). New York: Berg Publishers.
Doretti, M., & Snow, C. C. (2003). Forensic anthropology and human rights: The Argentine experience. In D. W. Steadman (Ed.), *Hard evidence: Case studies in forensic anthropology* (pp. 303–320). Upper Saddle River: Prentice Hall.
Farmer, P. (2005). *Pathologies of power: Health, human rights, and the new war on the poor*. Berkeley: University of California Press.
Farmer, P. (2010). Introduction to part III. In H. Saussy (Ed.), *Partner to the poor: A Paul Farmer reader* (pp. 293–297). Berkeley: University of California Press.
Fondebrider, L. (2004). *Uncovering evidence: The forensic sciences in human rights*. Minneapolis: The Center for Victims of Torture.
Franklin, R. (2014). Crossing the U.S./Mexico border: Push and pull factors for migration. *Righting Wrongs: A Journal of Human Rights, 4*(2), 1–23.
Galtung, J. (1975). *Peace: Research, education, action. Essays in peace research*. Copenhagen: Christian Ejlers.
García-Zamora, R. (2009). Migration under NAFTA: Exporting goods and people. In K. P. Gallagher, E. D. Peters, & T. A. Wise (Eds.), *The future of north American trade policy: Lessons from NAFTA (79–83). Report of the Frederick S. Pardee Center for the Study of the longer-range future*. Boston: Boston University.
Gonzalez-Barrera, A., Krogstad, J. M., & Lopez, M. H. (2014). *Violence, poverty is driving migrants to flee central America to U.S.* Washington, DC: Pew Research Center.
Goodman, A. H., Allen, L. H., Hernandez, G. P., Amador, A., Arriola, L. V., Chávez, A., & Pelto, G. H. (1987). Prevalence and age at development of enamel hypoplasias in Mexican children. *American Journal of Physical Anthropology, 72*, 7–19.
Goodman, A. H., Martinez, C., & Chávez, A. (1991). Nutritional supplementation and the development of linear enamel hypoplasias in children from Tezonteopan, Mexico. *American Journal of Clinical Nutrition, 53*, 773–781.

Goodman, A. H., & Rose, J. C. (1991). Dental enamel hypoplasias as indicators of nutritional status. In M. A. Kelley & C. S. Larsen (Eds.), *Advances in dental anthropology* (pp. 279–293). New York: Wiley-Liss.

Hinkes, M. J. (2008). Migrant deaths along the California-Mexico border: an anthropological perspective. *Journal of Forensic Sciences, 53*(1), 16–20.

Holmes, S. M. (2013). *Fresh fruit, broken bodies: Migrant farmworkers in the United States (California series in public anthropology)*. Berkeley: University of California Press.

Jimenez, M. (2009). *Humanitarian crisis: migrant deaths at the U.S.-Mexico border*. San Diego: ACLU of San Diego & Imperial Counties and Mexico's National Commission of Human Rights.

Kimmerle, E. H. (2014). Forensic anthropology in long-term investigations: 100 cold years. *Annals of Anthropological Practice, 38*(1), 7–21.

Klaus, H. D. (2012). The bioarchaeology of structural violence: A theoretical model and a case study. In D. L. Martin, R. P. Harrod, & V. R. Pérez (Eds.), *The bioarchaeology of violence* (pp. 29–62). Gainesville: University Press of Florida.

Komar, D. A., & Buikstra, J. E. (2008). *Forensic anthropology: Contemporary theory and practice*. New York: Oxford University Press.

Kovic, C. (2013). *Searching for the living, the dead, and the new disappeared on the migrant trail in Texas: Preliminary report on migrant deaths in south Texas*. Houston United.

Martin, D. L., & Harrod, R. P. (2015). Bioarchaeological contributions to the study of violence. *Yearbook of Physical Anthropology, 156*, 116–145.

Martinez, D. E., Reineke, R. C., Rubio-Goldsmith, R., Anderson, B. E., Hess, G. L., & Parks, B. O. (2013). *A continued humanitarian crisis at the border: Undocumented border crosser deaths recorded by the Pima County Office of the Medical Examiner, 1990–2012*. Tucson: The Binational Migration Institute and The University of Arizona.

Martinez, D. E., Reineke, R. C., Rubio-Goldsmith, R., & Parks, B. O. (2014). Structural violence and migrant deaths in southern Arizona: Data from the Pima County Office of the Medical Examiner, 1990–2013. *Journal on Migration and Human Security, 2*(4), 257–286.

Massey, D. S. (2012). *Immigration and the great recession*. Stanford: Stanford Center on Poverty and Inequality.

Palmer, C. (2015). Drug trafficking, gang violence, and the U.S. immigration crisis. *Michigan Journal of Public Affairs, 12*, 56–70.

Parks, B. O., Peters, E. D., Porterfield, C., Winston, D., & Anderson, B. E. (2016). Border migrant deaths and the Pima County Medical Examiner's Office. In R. Rubio-Goldsmith, C. Fernandez, J. K. Finch, & A. Masterson-Algar (Eds.), *Migrant deaths in the Arizona desert: La vida no vale nada* (pp. 120–131). Tucson: The University of Arizona Press.

Passel, J., Cohn, D., & Gonzalez-Barrera, A. (2012). *Net migration from Mexico falls to zero- and perhaps less*. Washington, DC: Pew Research Center.

Quesada, J., Hart, L. K., & Bourgois, P. (2011). Structural vulnerability and health: Latino migrant laborers in the United States. *Medical Anthropology, 30*, 339–362.

Reineke, R. C. (2016). Los desaparecidos de la frontera (The disappeared on the border). In R. Rubio-Goldsmith, C. Fernández, J. K. Finch, & A. Masterson-Algar (Eds.), *Migrant deaths in the Arizona desert: La vida no vale nada* (pp. 132–152). Tucson: The University of Arizona Press.

Reineke, R. C., & Anderson, B. E. (2010). Sociocultural factors in the identification of undocumented migrants. Poster presented at the 62nd annual meeting of the American Academy of Forensic Sciences, Seattle, Feb 22–27, 2010.

Reineke, R. C., & Anderson, B. E. (2016). Missing in the US-Mexico borderlands. In D. Congram (Ed.), *Missing persons: Multidisciplinary perspectives on the disappeared* (pp. 249–268). Toronto: Canadian Scholars' Press.

Reineke, R.C., Osorno Solís, C.E., Doretti, M., Daniell, R., Strand, R., & Halstead, C. (2017). Missing migrant data managed by the Forensic Border Coalition (FBC). Paper presented at the 69th annual scientific meeting of the American Academy of Forensic Sciences, New Orleans, Feb 13–18, 2017.

Reineke R. C., & Soler, A. (2013). Dental ornamentation among Southwest Hispanic border crossers at the Pima County Office of the Medical Examiner. Paper presented at the 65th Annual Meeting of the American Academy of Forensic Sciences, Washington, DC.

Rubio-Goldsmith, R., McCormick, M., Martinez, D., & Duarte, I. M. (2006). *The 'funnel effect' & recovered bodies of unauthorized migrants processed by the Pima County Office of the Medical Examiner, 1990–2005. Report submitted to the Pima County Board of Supervisors*. Tucson: The Binational Migration Institute.

Soler, A., Reineke, R. C., Beatrice, J. S., & Anderson, B. E. (2014). An integrated approach to the identification of human remains: The biocultural profile of undocumented migrants. Paper presented at the 66th annual scientific meeting of the American Academy of Forensic Sciences, Seattle, Feb 17–22, 2014.

Soler, A., Reineke, R. C., Beatrice, J. S., & Anderson, B. E. (forthcoming, 2018). Etched in bone: Embodied suffering in the remains of undocumented migrants. In: T. Sheridan, & R. McGuire (Eds.), *The border and its bodies: The corporeality of risk at the U.S.-Mexico borderlands*. Tucson: The University of Arizona Press.

Spradley, M. K. (2014). Toward estimating geographic origin of migrant remains along the United States-Mexico border. *Annals of Anthropological Practice, 38*(1), 101–110.

Spradley, M. K., Stull, K. E., & Hefner, J. T. (2016). Craniofacial secular change in recent Mexican migrants. *Human Biology, 88*(1), 15–29.

United States Border Patrol. (2014). *Sector profile-fiscal year 2013 (Oct 1st through Sept. 30)*. Washington, DC: United States Border Patrol.

United States Government Accountability Office. (2006). Illegal immigration: Border crossing deaths have doubled since 1995; Border Patrol's efforts to prevent deaths have not been fully evaluated. GAO-06-770.

Velez, L., & Boehner, N. (2014). *Children on the run: Unaccompanied children leaving Central America and Mexico and the need for international protection*. Retrieved from http://www.unhcrwashington.org/sites/default/files/UAC_UNHCR_Children%20on%2 0the%20Run_Full%20Report.pdf.

Weeks, J. R., Stoler, J., & Jankowski, P. (2009). Who's crossing the border: New data on undocumented immigrants in the United States. *Population, Space, and Place, 17*(1), 1–26.

Wise, T. A. (2010). *Agricultural dumping under NAFTA: Estimating the costs of U.S. agricultural policies to Mexican producers, Report of the Woodrow Wilson International Center for Scholars*. Washington, DC: Woodrow Wilson International Center for Scholars. Retrieved from http://www.ase.tufts.edu/gdae/Pubs/rp/AgricDumpingWoodrowWilsonCenter.pdf.

# Chapter 10
# Identifying Difference: Forensic Methods and the Uneven Playing Field of Repatriation

**Eric J. Bartelink**

The identification of the dead is a key function of medical examiner and coroner's offices throughout the United States. This is important for documenting mortality statistics (tabulating cause and manner of death and demographics of the dead), for investigating whether a homicide has taken place, to facilitate legal paperwork (e.g., death benefits, wills, estates), and most importantly to provide closure to relatives and friends of the deceased. While society clearly recognizes the importance of identification of the dead to the medicolegal system and the need for closure, the reality is that there is tremendous variation in the range of identification techniques used and the amount of effort employed in identifying the dead. In the United States, standard identification modalities include visual identification by family members, circumstantial evidence, and scientific methods such as comparisons of fingerprints, dental and medical records, and DNA profiles. Well-funded jurisdictions, especially those with a centralized regional medical examiner's office, often have the resources available to successfully conduct scientifically based personal identifications. In areas where an elected coroner or justice of the peace are established, there tends to be more variation in the range of scientific modalities utilized in identifications, with a greater emphasis on visual identifications, circumstantial evidence, fingerprints, and dental records. These practices may reflect a lack of scientific experts in the local area, a lack of awareness by investigators of other areas of scientific expertise, or a reluctance to utilize more expensive identification methods. Regardless of which type of medicolegal system is followed for a death investigation, there is a finite amount of financial resources and time available to identify the dead.

Another (often unspoken) layer to this issue relates to the demographics of the deceased and the context in which they are found. For example, a law enforcement agency often will provide more financial and personnel resources for a death

E.J. Bartelink (✉)
California State University, Chico, CA, USA
e-mail: ebartelink@csuchico.edu



K.E. Latham, A.J. O'Daniel (eds.), *Sociopolitics of Migrant Death and Repatriation*, Bioarchaeology and Social Theory,
DOI 10.1007/978-3-319-61866-1_10

investigation or missing persons case if it has garnered significant media attention (e.g., celebrities, politicians, notable members of a community, members of service, victims of terrorism, etc.) than they will if the decedent is believed to belong to a socially marginalized or otherwise high-risk segment of the population (e.g., drug addicts, transient and homeless individuals, undocumented workers, foreigners from non-western countries, etc.) (Morewitz 2016; Morewitz and Sturdy Colls 2016). This notion is antithetical to federal and state laws that regulate identification of the dead and remains largely as an invisible process to the public. However, this is the reality in practice in many jurisdictions as investigators respond to public pressure by family and community members regarding the death of an important individual or in a case that has otherwise garnered significant media attention (Morewitz 2016; Morewitz and Sturdy Colls 2016). Further, law enforcement agencies must use discretion in deciding how to allocate limited resources, which often means placing a lower priority on missing persons cases and decedents who derive from high-risk or marginalized populations (Kim et al. 2016). A large proportion of the more than 4,400 unidentified dead from medical examiner and coroner's offices each year reflect individuals from these marginalized communities (Quinet 2007). Identification of these individuals is complicated by the fact that they often do not carry identification, are often found in outdoor contexts such as homeless camps and abandoned buildings (as opposed to a residence, vehicle, or hospital), are often found in areas where they have few or no ties to the local community, and are often discovered long after death (e.g., as decomposed, mummified, or skeletonized remains). This disparity in resource allocation (i.e., time, effort, and expense for a death investigation and personal identification) provided to a decedent from a marginalized segment of society versus a higher profile decedent can be characterized as *inequality in death and identification*. This phrase reflects the reality that law enforcement often invest more resources in some cases over others based on a variety of factors, including the socioeconomic status of the dead and the context in which they are found (Morewitz 2016; Morewitz and Sturdy Colls 2016; Paulozzi et al. 2008). *Inequality in death and identification* thus not only reflects who the decedent is (e.g., a celebrity versus a transient or an undocumented person); it also reflects the practices and limitations of the medicolegal authorities in the jurisdiction where the death occurs. Despite the best efforts of medicolegal agencies (even those with adequate financial resources and dedicated investigators), some deceased individuals will never be identified.

## Legal and Moral Reasons for Identification

Identification of the dead fulfills several legal and moral obligations. As mentioned above, identification aids in the documentation of mortality statistics which are analyzed for comparative purposes to understand temporal and regional variation in causes and manners of death. These data are important sources of epidemiological information, which, in turn, are used to influence public policy. For example, an increase in the homicide rate may be used as evidence for the need to hire additional police officers in a specific jurisdiction, whereas an increase in the suicide rate may be used to argue for the need for more mental health facilities within a city. Further, identification of the dead is critical for settling wills and estates and for relatives to claim death benefits; thus, identification and the issuing of a death certificate can relieve financial strain on dependent relatives of the decedent (Morewitz 2016). On the other hand, identification also has a strong moral component—that is, to provide closure to the loved ones of the deceased (Holmes 2016). Knowing that a missing loved one is deceased and what happened to them are important steps for families seeking closure (Holmes 2008, 2016). Families of the missing often live in a state of limbo as there is constant worrying about whether or not the missing relative is dead or alive (Holmes 2008, 2016). Identification of the dead also provides a sense of closure by allowing family members of the deceased to honor and mourn the dead, something that is very difficult in the absence of confirmation of the death. In the context of the United States, this will especially apply to individuals marginalized by society, such as the homeless and undocumented individuals, who are the most difficult to identify for the aforementioned reasons.

## Inequality in Death and Identification

In the United States, *inequality in death and identification* is most apparent when it comes to the thousands of undocumented border crossers (UBCs) who have perished along the 2,000 mile stretch of the US-Mexico border. Over the past three decades, a series of border security policies has resulted in the increasing militarization of the border, including "Operation Hold the Line" (aka, "Operation Blockade") in El Paso, Texas, in 1993; "Operation Gatekeeper" in San Diego, California, in 1994; "Operation Safeguard" in 1995 in southern Arizona; and "Operation Rio Grande" in south Texas in 1997 (Martínez et al. 2014). The cumulative effect of these "prevention through deterrence" policies has been a decline in the apprehension rate of UBCs. However, the UBC death rate has shown a dramatic increase in Arizona and Texas, with most deaths occurring due to dehydration, heat stroke, and exposure (De León 2015; Martínez et al. 2014; Reineke and Martínez 2014). This apparent contradiction indicates that while increased border security and policies focused on deterrence have significantly reduced migration into the United States from Latin American countries, this has created a "funnel effect" where individuals attempt to cross the border through extremely harsh desert terrain in remote locations (De León 2015; Martínez et al. 2014; Reineke and Martínez 2014; Rose 2012). In southern Arizona, more than 2,700 UBC deaths have been recorded, approximately 30% of which remain unidentified (De León 2015). Estimates of the total number of UBC deaths since 1998 on the US side of the border vary from about 5,000 to over 7,500 (Jimenez 2009).

In 2012, UBC deaths along the southern Texas border surpassed that of southern Arizona, with 271 recorded deaths, a 73% increase over 2011 (Kovic 2013). The majority of these deaths occurred approximately 70 miles north of the border in the vicinity of the Falfurrias Border Patrol Checkpoint in Brooks County, located within the Rio Grande Valley sector of Texas (Kovic 2013). UBC deaths commonly occur on privately owned ranch land as individuals attempt to bypass the border checkpoint and become disoriented in the harsh terrain of a nearly featureless landscape. These reported UBC death rates should be viewed as minimum estimates since they only reflect remains that have been located and also do not include deaths that occurred on the Mexican side of the border (Kovic 2013). Border patrol statistics from 2011 further indicate that roughly 75% of unauthorized border crossings occurred in Arizona and Texas, the two states comprising the majority of UBC deaths (Baker 2014).

The high volume of UBC deaths has created an unprecedented identification effort, especially in southern Arizona and south Texas. The remains of deceased UBCs often lack documentation (e.g., ID cards) and when discovered are often significantly decomposed or skeletonized due to the extremely hot and arid environment (Baker 2014). In addition, UBCs are often not reported as missing persons by family or friends who reside in the United States. Traditional identification modalities, such as fingerprint records, dental records, and medical records are often unavailable or nonexistent, significantly limiting their use. DNA testing has also been a challenge since it is difficult to obtain family reference sample DNA from foreign nationals or from undocumented family members living within the United States. Unfortunately, current laws requiring that law enforcement collect family reference samples have created a further deterrent for DNA-based identifications. Until recently, the majority of deceased UBCs from south Texas were buried as unidentified remains in the Sacred Heart Cemetery in Falfurrias without the mandatory DNA testing being conducted as required by Texas State Law (Kovic 2013). Lack of financial resources and personnel during this rise in migrant deaths in Brooks County also appear to be important factors hindering identification of UBCs. However, in 2014, the University of North Texas Center for Human Identification began to receive samples of unidentified UBCs for DNA testing.

## Identification Efforts of UBC Remains from South Texas

In 2013, Drs. Krista Latham (University of Indianapolis) and Lori Baker (Baylor University) began a large-scale effort to exhume and identify deceased border crossers buried at the Falfurrias Sacred Heart Cemetery in Brooks County. Three seasons of excavation have been conducted between 2013 and 2017, and the exhumed remains are currently held at Texas State University (in San Marcos) for skeletal analysis, DNA and stable isotope sampling, and temporary curation under the supervision of Drs. Kate Spradley and Timothy Gocha. This collaboration between Texas State University, the University of Indianapolis, and Baylor University has resulted in a concerted effort to identify these deceased migrants and to repatriate them to family members. In addition, these institutions have worked closely with law enforcement, numerous NGOs (e.g., the South Texas Human Rights Center, the Argentine Forensic Anthropology Team, the Colíbri Center for Human Rights, etc.), the University of North Texas Center for Human Identification, the California State University Human Identification Laboratory, and also private DNA laboratories such as Bode Cellmark Forensics to facilitate identifications. This unprecedented identification effort, appropriately called "Operation Identification," represents a model more akin to a "grassroots" forensic science effort than one based on medicolegal infrastructure given that the identification effort is largely being guided by scientists instead of law enforcement. The *inequality in death and identification* in the Brooks County case has only been partially circumvented through the dedication of the forensic community to this massive identification problem. While Operation Identification has succeeded where local, state, and federal agencies have failed, numerous barriers to identify UBCs continue.

## Stable Isotope Analysis as an Investigative Tool for Identifying Border Crossers

As discussed above, most traditional identification modalities such as fingerprints and dental records are of limited use for identifying deceased UBCs in south Texas. DNA testing and personal effects have provided some of the most useful information for identification, facilitated by recent submissions of DNA samples for testing and through the posting of photographs of clothing and personal effects on missing persons websites such as the National Missing and Unidentified Persons System or NamUs (https://namus.gov/). These lines of evidence have already been successful in the identification of a number of UBCs from Brooks County.

Stable isotope analysis (SIA) has been recently added to the repertoire of techniques that can provide investigative leads toward the identification of human remains. Stable isotopes measured in human tissues act as chemical tracers that record inputs from consumed foods, imbibed water, and pollutants in the environment. By measuring isotope ratios in various tissues of the body that form over different intervals of the lifespan (e.g., hair, nails, bones, and teeth), analysts can generate dietary profiles, can provide predictions regarding a person's region of origin, and can track a decedent's migration history. Recent applications of SIA have focused on the analysis of isotopes of the bio-elements hydrogen (H), carbon (C), nitrogen (N), oxygen (O), and sulfur (S) as well as the geo-elements of strontium (Sr) and lead (Pb) in human remains. The following is a very brief and nontechnical discussion of the use of SIA for predicting region of origin and migration history of unidentified remains. The interested reader should refer to more technical reviews of these forensic applications of SIA (see Bartelink et al. 2014a, b, 2016; Cerling et al. 2016; Chesson et al. 2014; Ehleringer et al. 2007, 2010; Meier-Augenstein 2007, 2010).

Stable isotopes are atoms of an element that contain the same number of protons but a different number of neutrons (Fry 2006). Thus, stable isotopes of the same element have different atomic weights (due to the slight differences in mass) and travel at different rates in chemical reactions. Stable isotopes for a given element (e.g., C) are measured as the ratio of the "heavy" isotope to the "light" isotope (e.g., $^{13}C/^{12}C$) in human tissues, which are compared to ratios measured in international standards. Stable isotope ratios of bio-elements (e.g., HCNOS) are measured using isotope ratio mass spectrometry (IRMS) and are reported in parts per 1,000 difference relative to the standard (in per mil, expressed as ‰). Once converted to a per mil value, the delta symbol (δ) is used to report the value (e.g., $\delta^{13}C$). For geo-elements (e.g., Sr and Pb), the raw ratios are typically used since values are often meaningful to several decimal places.

Carbon and nitrogen isotopes act as dietary tracers in ecosystems and can be measured in hair, nails, bone, and dentinal (tooth) collagen (Chesson et al. 2014; Valenzuela et al. 2011; Ehleringer et al. 2007, 2010; Meier-Augenstein 2007, 2010). In addition, carbon isotopes can be measured in bone and tooth bioapatite. Carbon isotope values vary in plants (and the animals that eat them) based on the specific photosynthetic pathway the plant evolved to use for metabolism. The majority of the earth's vegetation (~95%) is classified as $C_3$ plants, which include foodstuffs such as fruits, vegetables, beans, and grains. Less than 5% of plants are classified as $C_4$, and these include cultigens such as corn, sugar, amaranth, millet, and sorghum. Due to differences in these photosynthetic pathways, $C_4$ plants show significantly higher $\delta^{13}C$ values than $C_3$ plants, which are incorporated into the tissues of human consumers. Seafood derives its carbon from dissolved bicarbonate in the ocean, which results in elevated values similar to $C_4$ resources in human consumers. Thus carbon isotopes can provide useful information regarding culturally or regionally specific dietary practices (Hülsemann et al. 2015; Bartelink et al. 2014a; Valenzuela et al. 2011). In the case of UBCs, they demonstrate significantly higher $\delta^{13}C$ values than US Americans due to their heavy reliance on corn products in their diet. In contrast to carbon isotopes, nitrogen isotopes (reported as $\delta^{15}N$) provide information on trophic level, with a 2–4‰ stepwise increase for each level of the food chain. Thus, consumers of meat will have higher $\delta^{15}N$ values than that of vegetarians and vegans. Finally, sulfur isotopes (reported as $\delta^{34}S$) provide a record of the source of food resources grown on the local landscape and thus also can reflect information on the local geology where plants are grown.

Oxygen and hydrogen isotopes both track meteoric precipitation and are incorporated into human tissues through drinking water. Oxygen and hydrogen isotope values (reported as $\delta^{18}O$ and $\delta^{2}H$, respectively) decrease in cloud vapor and precipitation as a cloud rains out over the landscape and are influenced by temperature, distance from large bodies of water, aridity, and altitude (Chesson et al. 2014; Ehleringer et al. 2007, 2010). Thus, $\delta^{18}O$ and $\delta^{2}H$ in human tissues strongly correlate with the sources of drinking water. Hydrogen isotopes in hair and nails can exchange with hydrogen in the atmosphere, which can complicate region of origin predictions. However, because hydrogen isotope values can be predicted using oxygen isotope values, the latter are often used to make predictions regarding migration history or region of origin from human tissues. $\delta^{18}O$ values of serially growing tissues, such as hair and nails, can provide information regarding recent travel history of an unidentified individual, whereas $\delta^{18}O$ values based on the bioapatite of bone or tooth mineral provide information regarding the region of origin or birthplace. In contrast, strontium isotopes (reported as $^{87}Sr/^{87}Sr$) are incorporated into the bones and teeth through the diet and reflect the geological signature where food was grown. Strontium substitutes for calcium in the skeleton, and trace amounts can be measured in the bones and teeth using mass spectrometry. Finally lead isotopes (reported as $^{207}Pb/^{206}Pb/^{204}Pb$) are incorporated into the bones and teeth from pollutants in the environment (also substituting for calcium in the skeleton) and thus may also reflect a local signature. Once measured in human tissues, oxygen and strontium isotope values can be plotted on maps using GIS. These plots show possible locations where these values could have derived from on the landscape (based on geological Sr and O water signatures) and are referred to as "isoscapes."

## Case Studies

Over the past decade, SIA has become a more commonly utilized method used as an investigative tool in missing persons cases (Cerling et al. 2016; Bartelink et al. 2014a, b, 2016; Chesson et al. 2014; Ehleringer et al. 2007, 2010; Meier-Augenstein 2007, 2010). Since 2008, the Human Identification Laboratory (HIL) at California State University, Chico (CSU, Chico), has provided forensic stable isotope services to local and federal law enforcement agencies as well as the Department of Defense (Bartelink et al. 2014a, 2016). For law enforcement cases, the HIL has processed numerous samples for stable isotope analyses and has provided analytical data reports, most of which were funded by the requested agencies. Mass spectrometry fees for these cases typically vary between \$100 and \$1,200 depending on the number of tissues analyzed (e.g., bone, tooth, and hair), the number of different isotopes measured, and the mass spectrometry facility used. The HIL currently only charges law enforcement agencies for the mass spectrometry fees incurred at external isotope laboratory facilities; all sample preparation is volunteered time, and all supplies and chemicals are covered through HIL forensic case funds to help promote the educational mission of the university. Two case studies are provided below to highlight the application of SIA as an investigative tool for identifying unknown decedents and also to demonstrate the disparity in funding available to conduct these analyses for a typical case from northern California versus a UBC case from south Texas. The first case study focuses on unidentified human remains discovered in a remote area of Tulare County, California, and the second case study focuses on unidentified remains discovered in Brooks County, Texas.

The case from Tulare County was received in 2016 by the HIL at CSU, Chico. The biological profile was consistent with a young to middle-aged Hispanic male. Following the examination by one of the lab's forensic anthropologists, permission was granted by the Tulare County Sheriff's Office to conduct SIA analysis on a sample of bone and on the right first maxillary premolar. The sheriff's office agreed to pay for the mass spectrometry fees for stable isotope analysis, and the HIL staff agreed to volunteer their time for sample preparation and for the writing of the technical report. Bone collagen carbon and nitrogen isotope values ($\delta^{13}C = -14.9‰$; $\delta^{15}N$ value = +10.3‰) are consistent with a diet composed of both $C_3$-terrestrial and $C_4$ resources, and the $\delta^{13}C$ value falls just slightly out of the 95% confidence interval for hair keratin samples of US Americans reported in Valenzuela et al. (2011:862). This finding is also supported by the bioapatite $\delta^{13}C$ value of −10.5‰. The $\delta^{15}N$ value is consistent with terrestrial meat consumption.

Strontium and oxygen isotope data based on tooth enamel bioapatite provide region of origin predictions (i.e., an isoscape) for several areas within the United States (Fig. 10.1). The lighter gray highlighted areas indicate locations where the individual may have obtained his food (based on strontium isotopes). The darker gray highlighted areas indicate locations where the individual may have obtained his drinking water (based on oxygen isotopes). The areas highlighted in red indicate regions of overlap in both oxygen and strontium and thus represent the most likely possible childhood regions of origin for the decedent. For California, these areas include portions of the northern one-third of California, as well as the counties of

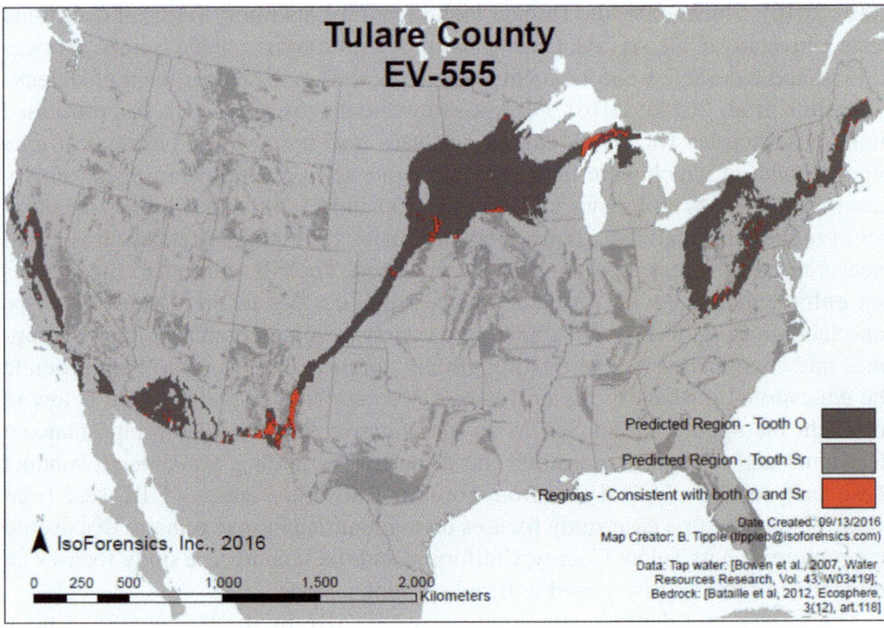


**Fig. 10.1** Region of origin prediction map for the Tulare County case using isotopic data from both oxygen and strontium isotopes of tooth enamel. Oxygen isotope data are predicted from tap water reference data

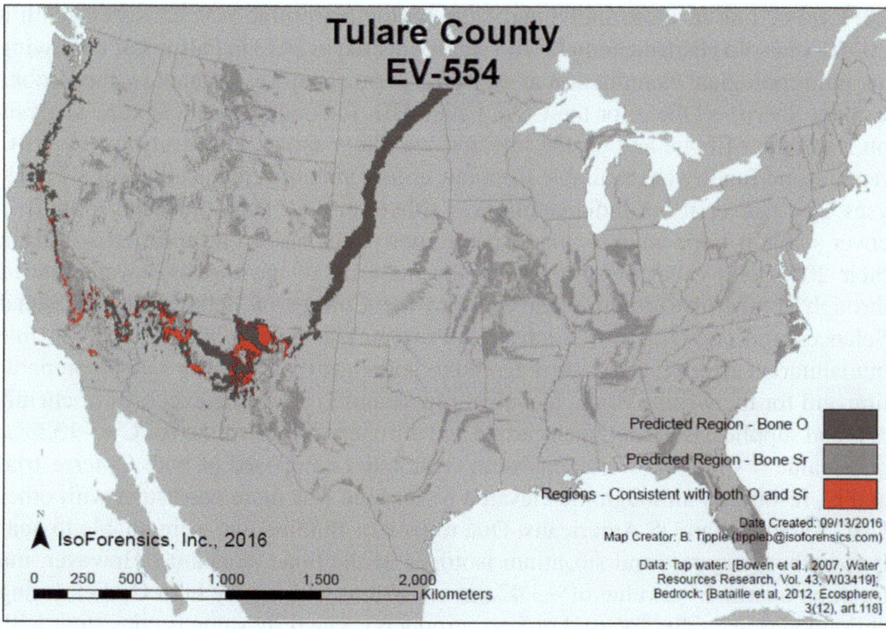


**Fig. 10.2** Region of origin predictive map for the Tulare County case using isotopic data from both oxygen and strontium isotopes of bone bioapatite. Oxygen isotope data are predicted from tap water reference data

Santa Clara, Fresno, and Santa Barbara. Outside of California, this could include areas of the Southwest, the Midwest, and the Northeast. Based on these isotope values, it is possible that the decedent may have grown up around the general area near where his body was discovered.

Strontium and oxygen isotope data based on bone bioapatite also provide region of origin predictions (i.e., an isoscape) for several areas within the United States (Fig. 10.2). For California, these areas include portions of the Sierra Nevada region of central and southern California, as well as even more southern and southeastern areas of the state. Outside of California, this could include areas of southern Oregon, southern Nevada, northern Arizona, and northern New Mexico. Based on these isotope values, it is possible that the decedent lived the last several years of his life in an area close to where his body was discovered. The decedent was later identified as a 29-year-old Hispanic male missing from Fresno County, California (adjacent to Tulare County). The remains were found approximately 110 miles away from the decedent's place of residence. The tooth enamel and bone bioapatite prediction maps based on the strontium and oxygen isotope values include his known place of residence in Fresno County.

In 2014, samples from 12 Brooks County cases were submitted to the CSU, Chico HIL, via the University of Indianapolis Archeology and Forensics Laboratory

(AFL). For one of these individuals, the biological profile was consistent with a 30–50-year-old Hispanic female who was recovered in 2013 in Falfurrias. Following an anthropological examination at the AFL, permission was granted by the Brooks County Sheriff's Office for the CSU, Chico HIL to conduct stable isotope analysis on a sample of bone and on the left first maxillary molar. However, for the UBC remains, no funds were available from law enforcement to conduct the isotope analyses. The University of Indianapolis was able to provide some financial support to cover stable isotope analysis mass spectrometry fees based on funds leftover from their 2013 field excavation; however, the majority of the expenses were funded through competitive grants received from the College of Behavioral and Social Sciences and the Office of Sponsored Programs at CSU, Chico. To aid in this humanitarian effort, the HIL staff agreed to volunteer their time for sample preparation and for the writing of the technical report and to cover the expenses of chemicals and supplies. Bone collagen carbon and nitrogen isotope values ($\delta^{13}C = -13.5‰$; $\delta^{15}N$ value = +10.7‰) were consistent with a diet composed of both $C_3$-terrestrial and $C_4$ resources, although the elevated $\delta^{13}C$ value was more consistent with other UBC remains than US Americans. Due to lack of funding, we were unable to analyze carbon, oxygen, and strontium isotopes of the bone bioapatite. However, the tooth bioapatite $\delta^{13}C$ value of −3.4‰ is consistent with a very high $C_4$ diet during childhood (e.g., a diet focused on corn products). The $\delta^{15}N$ value is consistent with terrestrial meat consumption.

Oxygen isotope data based on tooth enamel bioapatite provided region of origin predictions for several areas within the southern, eastern, and midwestern areas of the United States, as well as numerous areas within Latin America (Fig. 10.3). The dark gray highlighted areas indicate locations where the individual may have obtained her drinking water (based on oxygen isotopes). Unfortunately, due to the lack of tap water reference data from Latin American countries, predictions need to be made using precipitation water maps that have lower levels of resolution. Further, the strontium value cannot be plotted on the map using GIS because geological strontium baseline maps do not currently exist for this region. One option is to compare the strontium isotope value for the UBC case to bioarchaeological data sets to identify possible locations that are consistent with the measured tooth strontium value. The strontium isotope value for the UBC case ($^{87}Sr/^{87}Sr = 0.70795$) is most consistent with the northern and southern lowlands of Guatemala when compared with data on the ancient Maya (Price et al. 2015; Hodell et al. 2004; Wright 2005). Further, the oxygen isotope data also include Guatemala in the prediction. Based on these isotope signatures, Guatemala cannot be excluded as a likely place of origin for the decedent. However, other places in Latin America should not be ruled out as not all areas have been thoroughly characterized in bioarchaeological and geological studies. The remains were recently positively identified as a Guatemalan female national through DNA comparisons with family reference samples.

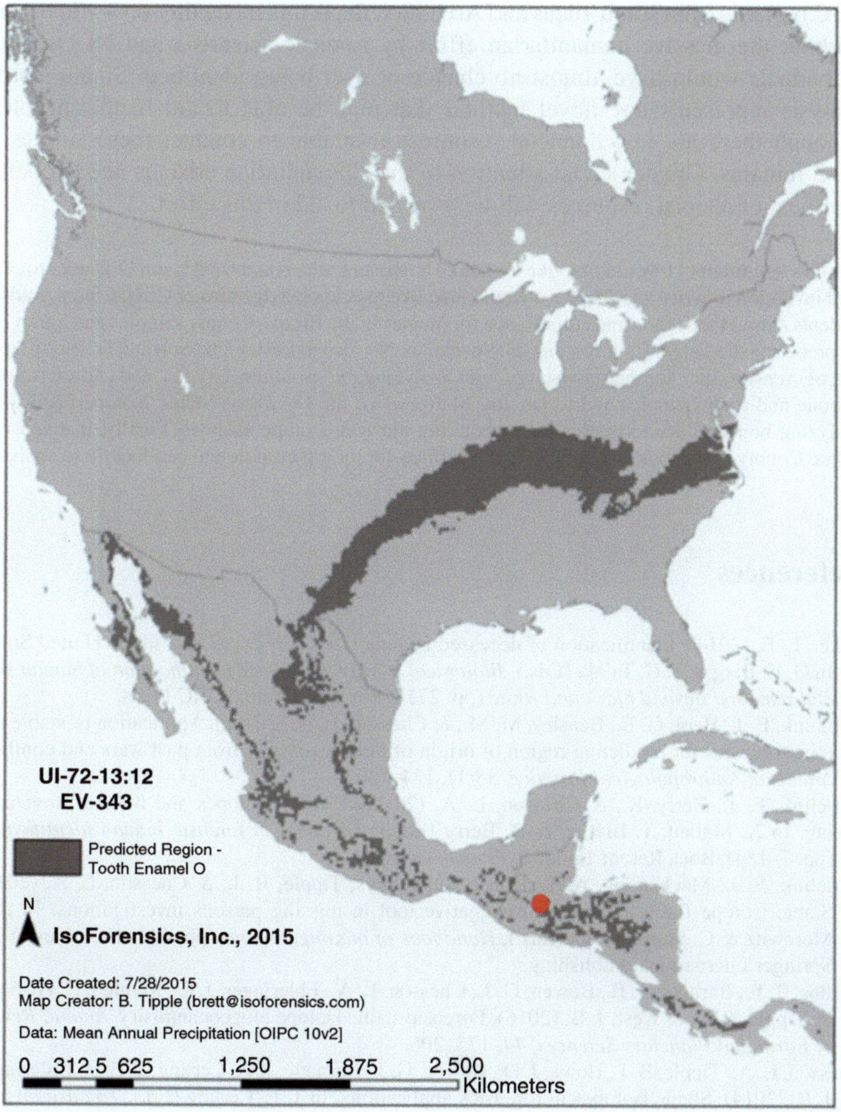


**Fig. 10.3** Region of origin predictive map for Brooks County UBC remains using isotopic data from oxygen isotopes of tooth enamel. Oxygen isotope data are predicted from precipitation water reference data

## Conclusions

*Inequality in death and identification* is a reality for the thousands of unidentified remains found each year in the United States, especially for decedents from marginalized segments of society. The large-scale identification effort for the unidentified

UBC remains from south Texas and Arizona reflects this inequality on a grand scale. Without the massive humanitarian effort by forensic scientists and NGOs, these individuals would have almost no chance of ever being identified. Stable isotope analysis represents one novel method that may be able to aid in this problem, although there are few financial resources available to conduct these studies on UBC remains. Greater social attention to this humanitarian crisis is needed before significant financial resources will be provided to aid in this effort.

**Acknowledgments** I would first like to thank Dr. Krista Latham and Dr. Alyson O'Daniel for their kind invitation to write this chapter. I would also like to acknowledge former CSU, Chico, graduate students Amy MacKinnon and Julia Prince for preparing the Brooks County samples and Sarah Hall for preparing the Tulare County samples. Special thanks also to Lesley Chesson and Dr. Brett Tipple of IsoForensics, Inc., for their assistance with analyzing the strontium, oxygen, and carbon isotopes of bone and tooth samples and to Dr. Joy Matthews of the UC Davis Stable Isotope Facility for analyzing bone collagen samples for carbon and nitrogen isotope analysis. Finally, thanks to the Tulare County and Brooks County Sheriff's Offices for their permission to conduct these analyses.

## References

Baker, L. E. (2014). Identification of deceased unauthorized border crossers in the United States. In G. E. Berg & S. C. Ta'ala (Eds.), *Biological affinity in forensic identification of human skeletal remains: Beyond black and white* (pp. 271–285). Boca Raton: CRC Press.

Bartelink, E. J., Berg, G. E., Beasley, M. M., & Chesson, L. A. (2014a). Application of stable isotope forensics for predicting region of origin of human remains from past wars and conflicts. *Annals of Anthropological Practice, 38*(1), 124–136.

Bartelink, E. J., Berry, R., & Chesson, L. A. (2014b). Stable isotopes and human provenancing. In X. Mallett, T. Blythe, & R. Berry (Eds.), *Advances in forensic human identification* (pp. 7–184). Boca Raton: Taylor & Francis Group.

Bartelink, E. J., MacKinnon, A. T., Prince-Buitenhuys, Tipple, B. J., & Chesson, L. A. (2016). Stable isotope forensics as an investigative tool in missing persons investigations. In S. J. Morewitz & C. Sturdy Colls (Eds.), *Handbook of missing persons* (pp. 443–462). New York: Springer International Publishing.

Cerling, T. E., Barnette, J. E., Bowen, G. J., Chesson, L. A., Ehleringer, J. R., Remien, C. H., Shea, P., Tipple, B. J., & West, J. B. (2016). Forensic stable isotope biogeochemistry. *Annual Review of Earth and Planetary Sciences, 44*, 175–206.

Chesson, L. A., Tipple, B. J., Howa, J. D., Bowen, G. J., Barnette, J. E., Cerling, T. E., & Ehleringer, J. R. (2014). Stable isotopes in forensics applications. In T. E. Cerling (Ed.), *Treatise on geochemistry* (2nd ed., pp. 285–317). New York: Elsevier.

De León, J. (2015). *The land of open graves: Living and dying on the migrant trail*. Berkeley: University of California Press.

Ehleringer, J. R., Cerling, T. E., & West, J. B. (2007). Forensic science applications of stable isotope ratios. In R. D. Blackledge (Ed.), *Forensic analysis on the cutting edge: New methods for trace evidence analysis* (pp. 399–422). San Diego: Wiley.

Ehleringer, J. R., Thompson, A. H., Podlesak, D., Bowen, G. J., Chesson, L. A., Cerling, T. E., Park, T., Dostie, P., & Schwarcz, H. (2010). A framework for the incorporation of isotopes and isoscapes in geospatial forensic investigations. In J. B. West, G. J. Bowen, T. E. Dawson, & K. P. Tu (Eds.), *Isoscapes: Understanding movement, pattern, and process on earth through isotope mapping* (pp. 357–387). Dordrecht: Springer.

Fry, B. (2006). *Stable isotope ecology*. New York: Springer Science+Business Media.

Hodell, D. A., Quinn, R. L., Brenner, M., & Kamenov, G. (2004). Spatial variation of strontium isotopes ($^{87}Sr/^{86}Sr$) in the Maya region: A tool for tracking ancient human migration. *Journal of Archaeological Science, 31*(5), 585–601.

Holmes, L. (2008). *Living in limbo: The experiences of, and impacts on, the families of missing people*. London: Missing People.

Holmes, L. (2016). Missing someone: Exploring the experiences of family members. In S. J. Morewitz & C. Sturdy Colls (Eds.), *Handbook of missing persons* (pp. 105–126). New York: Springer International Publishing.

Hülsemann, F., Lehn, C., Schneiders, S., Jackson, G., Hill, S., Rossmann, A., Scheid, N., Dunn, P. J. H., Flenker, U., & Schänzer, W. (2015). Global spatial distributions of nitrogen and carbon stable isotope ratios of modern human hair. *Rapid Communications in Mass Spectrometry, 29*(22), 2111–2121.

Jimenez, M. (2009). *Humanitarian crisis: Migrant deaths at the U.S.-Mexico border*. San Diego: ACLU of San Diego & Imperial Counties and Mexico's National Commission of Human Rights.

Kim, J., Scully, J. L., & Katsanis, S. H. (2016). Ethical challenges in missing persons investigations. In S. J. Morewitz & C. Sturdy Colls (Eds.), *Handbook of missing persons* (pp. 163–175). New York: Springer International Publishing.

Kovic, C. (2013). *Searching for the living, the dead, and the new disappeared on the migrant trail In Texas: Preliminary report on migrant deaths in south Texas*. Austin, Texas: Texas Civil Rights Project. Available from www.texascivilrightsproject.org/5208/migrant-deaths-at-thesouthtexas-border-tcrp-human-rights-report-summer-2013.

Martínez, D. E., Reineke, R. C., Rubio-Goldsmith, R., & Parks, B. O. (2014). Structural violence and migrant deaths in southern Arizona: Data from the Pima County office of the medical examiner, 1990–2013. *Journal on Migration and Human Security, 2*(4), 257–286.

Meier-Augenstein, W. (2007). Stable isotope fingerprinting chemical element "DNA"? In T. Thompson & S. Black (Eds.), *Forensic human identification: An introduction* (pp. 29–53). Boca Raton: Taylor & Francis Group.

Meier-Augenstein, W. (2010). *Stable isotope forensics: An introduction to the forensic applications of stable isotope analysis*. Chichester: Wiley.

Morewitz, S. J. (2016). Missing persons: Forensic sociological factors. In S. J. Morewitz & C. Sturdy Colls (Eds.), *Handbook of missing persons* (pp. 93–104). New York: Springer International Publishing.

Morewitz, S. J., & Sturdy Colls, C. (2016). Missing persons: An introduction. In S. J. Morewitz & C. Sturdy Colls (Eds.), *Handbook of missing persons* (pp. 1–5). New York: Springer International Publishing.

Paulozzi, L. J., Cox, C. S., Williams, D. D., & Nolte, K. B. (2008). John and Jane Doe: The epidemiology of unidentified decedents. *Journal of Forensic Sciences, 53*(4), 922–927.

Price, T. D., Burton, J. H., Fullagar, P. D., Wright, L. E., Buikstra, J. E., & Tiesler, V. (2015). Strontium isotopes and the study of human mobility among the ancient Maya. In A. Cucina (Ed.), *Archaeology and bioarchaeology of population movement among the Prehispanic Maya* (pp. 119–132). New York: Springer International Publishing.

Quinet, K. (2007). The missing missing: Toward a quantification of serial murder victimization in the United States. *Homicide Studies, 11*(4), 319–339.

Reineke, R., & Martínez, D. E. (2014). Migrant deaths in the Americas (United States and Mexico). In T. Brian & F. Laczko (Eds.), *Fatal journeys: Tracking lives lost during migration* (pp. 45–83). Geneva: International Organization for Migration.

Rose, A. (2012). *Showdown in the Sonoran Desert: Religion, law, and the immigration controversy*. Oxford: Oxford University Press.

Valenzuela, L. O., Chesson, L. A., O'Grady, S. P., Cerling, T. E., & Ehleringer, J. R. (2011). Spatial distributions of carbon, nitrogen and sulfur isotope ratios in human hair across the central United States. *Rapid Communications in Mass Spectrometry, 25*(7), 861–868.

Wright, L. E. (2005). Identifying immigrants to Tikal, Guatemala: Defining local variability in strontium isotope ratios of human tooth enamel. *Journal of Archaeological Science, 32*(4), 555–566.

# Chapter 11
# Bodies in Limbo: Issues in Identification and Repatriation of Migrant Remains in South Texas

Timothy P. Gocha, M. Katherine Spradley, and Ryan Strand

## The Migrant Crisis in South Texas and Founding of Operation Identification

Since 2001 more individuals have died along the US/Mexico border than in the September 11th terrorist attacks and Hurricane Katrina – two of the deadliest mass disasters in US history – combined (United States Border Patrol 2017). However, this statistic only takes data from the individuals found in United States into account and does not include data from Mexico or those not found, likely leading to a vast underestimation of the true numbers of deaths. Until recently, the majority of these deaths occurred in Arizona despite the fact that Texas spans 1,254 miles of the total 1,900 miles of the entire US/Mexico border; however, in 2012, Texas surpassed Arizona in migrant deaths, a trend that has continued every year since (Spradley et al. 2016).

The majority of deaths took place in the Rio Grande Valley, and Brooks County in particular represents the epicenter of the migrant death crisis, where 533 unidentified remains were found from 2009 to 2016, peaking at 129 in 2012. Migrants who have successfully crossed the Rio Grande River often head north on US Highway 281 – one of only two major north-south highways in the lower Rio Grande Valley – but then find themselves facing a second border: a Border Patrol checkpoint in

T.P. Gocha (✉)
University of Nevada, Las Vegas, NV, USA
e-mail: timothy.gocha@unlv.edu

M.K. Spradley
Texas State University, San Marcos, TX, USA
e-mail: mks@txstate.edu

R. Strand
South Texas Human Rights Center, Falfurrias, TX, USA
e-mail: sthrc.ryan@gmail.com



K.E. Latham, A.J. O'Daniel (eds.), *Sociopolitics of Migrant Death and Repatriation*, Bioarchaeology and Social Theory,
DOI 10.1007/978-3-319-61866-1_11

Falfurrias, TX. Migrants try to circumvent the checkpoint by hiking around it through private ranchland which is mostly scrub desert. Unfortunately, many individuals are left behind by groups or become lost in the vast land and ultimately perish in the unforgiving terrain. Due to lack of funding and a misinterpretation of the law, for years the unidentified migrants were not sent for autopsy or skeletal analysis, and no DNA samples were collected. Instead they were buried in a local cemetery. Thus, the migrants had no chance of identification, and their families had no chance of ever learning their fate or final disposition.

In response to the humanitarian and human rights crisis in Brooks County, Drs. Krista Latham (University of Indianapolis) and Lori Baker (Baylor University) and their students performed voluntary exhumations of these burials for the purpose of skeletal analysis and DNA sampling in hopes of facilitating positive identifications and returning individuals to their families. The majority of remains, in early to late stages of decomposition, were brought to the Forensic Anthropology Center at Texas State in May of 2013 for processing and analysis to facilitate identifications. This marked the beginning of Operation Identification.

Operation Identification (OpID) aims to facilitate the identification and repatriation of unidentified human remains found within close proximity of the South Texas border through community outreach, forensic anthropological analysis, and collaboration with governmental and nongovernmental organizations. The OpID team works collaboratively with the South Texas Human Rights Center (STHRC), the Argentine Forensic Anthropology Team (EAAF), the Colibrí Center for Human Rights, and the Forensic Border Coalition in order to help further investigations for the missing and unidentified, as well as their families. Since 2013, OpID has received a total of 225 unidentified remains of presumed migrants.

The purpose of this chapter is to outline complexities and intricacies involved within the human rights crisis as it relates to the identification process for migrants that die in Brooks County, Texas. We situate our analysis from the vantage point of OpID, as the authors represent the director (MKS), former manager (TPG), and former missing persons coordinator (RMS) for the project. In an effort to provide a broad overview of complexities of migrant identification and repatriation, we broadly compare the migrant death crisis and response in South Texas to the situation in Arizona. This comparative approach makes clear that the mechanisms of investigation and identification are vastly different along the border in ways that shape the timing and expediency of the work. We further contextualize OpID's work in relation to Texas laws pertaining to unidentified human remains, medicolegal and legal entities that hold jurisdictional author over unidentified human remains, and the major roadblocks to DNA identifications as well as repatriations. Our contextualized approach highlights case studies which demonstrate the complex and intricate nature of identification and repatriation, as well as steps being taken to address these difficulties and move cases forward.

## Different States, Different Investigative Mechanisms

Despite persistent high numbers of migrant deaths in Arizona and the unique complexities that compound migrant death investigations, forensic anthropologists and medical examiners have had great success in identifying the deceased. Between 2001 and 2013, the Pima County Office of the Medical Examiner (PCOME) in Tucson, Arizona, received the remains of 2,203 presumed migrants and was able to successfully identify 1,463 of those individuals (Gocha et al. 2017). This is due, in large part, to the centralized identification efforts in Arizona, where nearly all presumed migrants found in the state are brought to Pima County, one of 15 counties in the state. At the PCOME, the medical examiner, forensic pathologists, and forensic anthropologists all work in one office and are able to easily communicate and collaborate on cases. Consular officials representing common migrant nationalities are also located in Tucson and participate in weekly meetings with forensic investigate staff at the PCOME. Furthermore, the vast majority of migrants in Arizona are from Mexico, allowing staff at the PCOME to work closely with officials from a single foreign government (see Chap. 12 of this volume, for further discussion of work at the PCOME). The situation in Texas, however, is drastically different.

In Texas, efforts to identify remains of presumed migrants are decentralized due to the vast expanse of the state. Texas is comprised of 254 counties, only 14 of which have medical examiner's offices; of these, only one is located on the South Texas border. The other 240 counties in Texas, including the majority of counties along the border, operate under the justice of the peace system. Similar to a coroner's system, justices of the peace are also elected officials charged with the task of overseeing investigations of unexplained deaths and determining cause and manner of death. However, unlike a coroner, a justice of the peace is responsible for performing several duties unrelated to the deaths of individuals, including hearing traffic and other misdemeanor cases punishable by fine only, civil cases with up to$10,000 in controversy, landlord and tenant disputes, and truancy cases, performing magistrate duties, and conducting inquests upon dead bodies (Justice of the Peace 2017). As a result of the large number of tasks assigned by law to the justice of the peace, the task of overseeing death investigations and determining the cause and manner of death is often negatively affected by lack of time and resources.

According to the Texas Code of Criminal Procedure (TCCP), the justice of the peace must conduct an inquest on unidentified human remains. However, an "inquest" is loosely defined as "an investigation into the cause and circumstances of the death of a person, and a determination, made with or without a formal court hearing, as to whether the death was caused by an unlawful act or omission" (TCCP Art. 49.01). Because of this loose definition and along with other laws within Chapter 49 of the TCCP, inquests do not necessarily require an autopsy or additional testing: it is all at the discretion of the justice of the peace, an individual in an elected position that does not require any knowledge of forensic science or medicine. Although the TCCP does not necessarily require an autopsy or additional testing, Chapter 63 (63.056) does require the collection and submission of DNA samples for analysis from all unidentified remains. However, due to a misinterpretation of the law by a county judge, this practice wasn't applied in Brooks County for more than 5 years as local officials were unaware they were required to take and submit DNA samples for analysis (Frey 2015).

Further complexities of addressing migrant deaths in Texas come from the fact that there is a much greater diversity of migrants in Texas than seen in Arizona. Based on data from the South Texas Human Rights Center, approximately 40% of migrants missing in South Texas are from Mexico, while 42% are from Central America, namely, El Salvador, Guatemala, and Honduras; the remaining 18% of cases include South America, the Caribbean, and the United States. In contrast, only ~21% of migrants missing in Arizona are from Central America, while nearly 75% are from Mexico, according to data from the Colibrí Center for Human Rights (Reineke pers. comm. 3/27/17). To make the situation more complicated, the consulate offices of these foreign governments aren't centrally located as they are in Arizona, rather each nation has several offices across the state. While most countries have consular offices along the border itself in McAllen, TX, those offices are typically smaller and underfunded, while the larger, better staffed offices are hundreds of miles away from the border in larger cities such as Austin, Houston, or Dallas.

## Bodies in Limbo

Theoretically, when a set of unidentified remains is found in South Texas, it should be investigated by a medicolegal professional, either a forensic pathologist or forensic anthropologist. DNA samples should be submitted for identification purposes, and once an identification is made, consular representatives from the individuals' home country should work with funeral homes to repatriate the remains. However, due to the circumstances discussed previously in this chapter, including the decentralized nature of this work in Texas, there are many steps in this process where remains might get stuck in a proverbial limbo. Some of these areas are explored in detail below, followed by what is being done to address these issues and improve identification and repatriation efforts of unidentified migrant remains in Texas.

## Discovery, Land Expanse, and Population Density

Exactly how many migrants die each year in South Texas remains a mystery. For one thing, there is no central repository where information on the recovery of unidentified bodies is required to be sent. The statistics compiled by Border Patrol on the number of border deaths are likely the most comprehensive but likely do not include all bodies recovered by local law enforcement and/or funeral homes. Furthermore, the numbers that *do* exist almost certainly underestimate the number of deaths, as they are only counts of the number of remains found; given the landscape in South Texas, it is more than likely that there are countless of individuals who will never be found (see Chap. 6, of this volume).

In contrast to Arizona, where the majority of land – including the Sonoran Desert where many migrants cross – is publicly owned, more than 95% of land in Texas is privately owned. In South Texas, the majority of land are private ranches, which range from a few hundred acres on the small end to nearly a million acres on the large end. The famous King Ranch, for instance, where many deceased migrants have been found, is itself larger than the state of Rhode Island at 825,000 acres. On these vast expanses of private land, migrants can quickly succumb to dehydration and hyperthermia and perish in a remote area rarely visited by other human beings. In the best case scenario, a deceased individual will be found by a ranch hand or hunters on the property and the death reported to the local authorities who will then retrieve the body. However, some of the ranches are so large and parts of them so remote that large tracts of land can go years without a ranch hand or hunter passing through, and in those instances, there may be little left to find of a deceased individual.

The extreme heat of South Texas, particularly in the summertime, can render an individual visually unrecognizable within a day of passing away. Predation by animals and scavenging, particularly by vultures and coyotes, can reduce an individual to almost a completely skeletal state within hours or days. As remains become skeletonized, elements often become scattered by animal activity. Research has demonstrated that vulture activity alone can disperse skeletal elements over an area of nearly 1,000 $ft^2$ (Spradley et al. 2012). Rodents, in particular large rats, have also been known to drag skeletal elements into their large nests, which themselves are sometimes situated within large stands of prickly pear cactus, where they can be a constant source of calcium and a tool to hone their continuously growing incisors. In essence, the rapid skeletonization and dispersal of human remains in the brushland desert of South Texas greatly reduce the chance of an individual being found as time goes on.

Another factor responsible for bodies waiting in limbo to be found is the population density of some areas of South Texas. A comparison of data from Brooks County and neighboring Kenedy County illustrates this difficulty. As mentioned in Chap. 8 (Latham and Strand), from 2009 to 2016, a total of 533 sets of unidentified remains were found in Brooks County, TX – all of them are presumed migrants. The Brooks County Sheriff's Office (BCSO) estimates that for every body found there are five more that are not found (Sheriff Urbino Martinez, 3/30/2017, personal communication). In contrast, far fewer individuals have been found in Kenedy County, despite local officials quoting comparable numbers of migrants passing through their county. While exact numbers are not known, according to data in the National Missing and Unidentified Persons System (NamUs), there have been only 18 unidentified individuals found in Kenedy County from 2009 to 2016.

Brooks County has a land area of 944 $mi^2$ and a population of 7,223 according to the 2010 US census, while Kenedy County is more than twice the size at 1,946 $mi^2$ but has a population of only 416. This makes Kenedy County the fourth least-populous county in the entire United States, and it is likely that this extremely low population plays a role in the low numbers of human remains found there, as there are simply far fewer people to cover the vast expanse of ranchland and discover the deceased. If the number of migrants traveling through and succumbing to the elements in Kenedy County is similar to those in Brooks County, the unfortunate reality is that there are likely hundreds, if not thousands, of unidentified individuals located on private ranchland in Kenedy County that simply haven't been, and likely won't be, discovered.

## Buried in Limbo

When unidentified human remains are found in a Texas county that does not have a medical examiner's office, a justice of the peace is responsible for conducting an inquest on the remains. In most counties in Texas, justices of the peace often work closely or contract with medical examiner's offices elsewhere in the state to ensure the law is properly followed, including the requirement to take a DNA sample. Many counties in South Texas, however, do not actively receive this kind of assistance, often because the counties are far from a medical examiner's office that could assist them. In other cases, a county may lack the funds to pay for contract services with a medical examiner. This was the case for Brooks County, who historically contracted with the Nueces County Medical Examiner's Office to analyze unidentified remains. In 2007, however, a county judge ordered this work shifted to a family-owned funeral home in South Texas where a local family doctor could provide autopsy services. The funeral home staff, none of whom were trained in scientific methods of identification, along with the doctor who was not a forensic pathologist, were ultimately responsible for trying to make identifications of deceased migrants. Conversations with the funeral home staff indicate that many identifications were made solely based on identification cards and/or phone numbers written on clothes or paper found in proximity to skeletal remains. In an extreme scenario, identifications were made based on the relative size of crania found at a scene. If, however, the funeral home did not make an identification, through whatever means, the remains would be returned to Brooks County and buried in Sacred Heart Cemetery in Falfurrias. Unfortunately, neither maps nor lists of the unidentified buried were kept (Srikrishnan and Hennessy-Fiske 2014). Once buried, an unidentified individual's only hope for identification was and is to be exhumed and scientifically examined.

As detailed by Latham and Strand (see Chap. 8 of this volume), exhumations at Sacred Heart were undertaken by Baylor University and the University of Indianapolis in 2013 and 2014, unearthing more than 100 unidentified remains. In January 2017, further exhumations were undertaken by Texas State University and the University of Indianapolis, where an additional two dozen individuals were exhumed. During these latest exhumations, anthropologists first exhumed burials with grave markers indicating the remains were unknown, though additional efforts focused on an area of the cemetery that was seemingly empty and had no grave markers. This was due to new information from the cemetery groundskeeper, who informed the anthropologists that even though this corner was empty it once had three grave markers indicating unidentified individuals were buried there, but they had become dislodged by a lawn mower and never replaced. After the area was excavated, anthropologists found not three bodies, as the groundskeeper indicated there would be, but eight unidentified bodies. Because no formal records are kept of where unidentified individuals are buried, without local knowledge such as this, those unidentified individuals could have been forever buried and remained unidentified. Unfortunately, the lack of record keeping for where unidentified and presumed migrant remains are buried, as well as the loss of grave markers, is not unique to Brooks County and extends across South Texas.

## The Cost of DNA Analysis

Once the skeletal remains of an unidentified individual have been recovered and/or exhumed, it is the task of the forensic anthropologist to study the skeletal remains and construct a biological profile. Anthropologists with OpID will then enter this demographic information, along with any and all case background, including images/descriptions of all personal effects, into the National Missing and Unidentified Persons System (NamUs, www.namus.gov), as well as write an anthropological report detailing all of this information. Next anthropologists will take a sample of bone from the unidentified individual and submit it for DNA analysis as required of all unidentified remains, as per Chapter 63 of the Texas Code of Criminal Procedures. Specifically, OpID sends DNA samples for every case analyzed to University of North Texas Center for Human Identification (UNTCHI), one of only four DNA labs in the United States which uploads case information into the Combined DNA Index System (CODIS). Once in CODIS, the DNA sequence information from unidentified human remains is compared to known DNA sequence information from criminal offender databases, family reference DNA samples for those who are missing loved ones, as well referenced against other unidentified remains samples in case two or more partial recoveries occurred for the same unidentified set of remains. However, family reference DNA is never compared against the criminal offender database.

Fortunately for anthropologists of limited means, UNTCHI is funded through the state of Texas and the federal government, making DNA analysis free of charge. The major cost to OpID, then, is usually in terms of time. Because their services are federally subsidized and are thus in high demand, there is a backlog of samples to be analyzed. For all DNA samples submitted by OpID to UNTCHI between 2014 and 2016, the average turnaround time for processing/sequencing from a sample was just under 7 months, during which time there is little else that can be done to move a case forward toward identification.

While the services provided by UNTCHI allow DNA information from unidentified persons cases to get into CODIS at no charge, there are difficulties in comparing this DNA information to appropriate family reference DNA samples. CODIS is controlled by the Federal Bureau of Investigation which has strict regulations for accepting samples. For family reference DNA samples, the sample must be collected in the presence of a medicolegal authority, law enforcement authority, or in the presence of a consular official representing the individual's home country in the United States. For individuals who have perished in South Texas and have no family members in the United States, these requirements are almost impossible to meet. Furthermore, when family members of the deceased *can* get a DNA sample into CODIS, they are essentially required to submit to having their genetic information in a database controlled by the US government. Alternatives to this route of DNA analysis exist with private DNA labs, though this requires monetary resources for processing and collaboration between foreign governments, nongovernmental organizations (NGOs), and scientists (discussed below).

## The Limbo of Identification

Once DNA analysis has either suggested or confirmed an identification hypothesis, the next task is to compare all antemortem, postmortem, circumstantial, and background information regarding the case. Theoretically, the justice of the peace is legally responsible for the inquest over unidentified remains and might be considered responsible for this task, yet these individuals often have no scientific training or investigative experience, not to mention the myriad of responsibilities other than inquests that keep them quite busy. Therefore, out of necessity, anthropologists at OpID have taken over this task of comparing all of this information. Doing so, however, requires hard-to-obtain access to all of the above listed information.

For example, a DNA sample from an unidentified set of remains was submitted to UNTCHI in January of 2016, and genetic analyses were completed in May of that year. One week after the sample was processed and uploaded to CODIS, an association was made with a family reference DNA sample that had been submitted by a sister of the deceased to the Central American consulate in McAllen, TX, in 2012. However, the DNA association between the samples only provided moderate support for the proposed genetic relationship. "Moderate support" indicated that this was a case where antemortem information and circumstances surrounding the last known time and location of the deceased would be crucial to supporting or refuting the identification hypothesis.

It is likely that at the time the family reference DNA sample was submitted, a missing persons report was filed with the consulate's office. This report would have included all of the necessary information. Yet, after contacting the consulate's office and requesting that information, OpID was informed that there were no missing persons report and no record of the DNA sample being taken. A second request for the records yielded no further information. This time the consulate's office asserted that the report couldn't exist because that office didn't open until 2013. A simple check in local media reports from years past clearly shows the office opened in

2011. Unfortunately, this type of occurrence is not isolated but is symptomatic of consulate's offices that are understaffed, overworked, and have high turnover, all factors which can lead to poor record keeping and poor institutional memory. The consulate's office informed OpID they would try to track down the family and conduct a missing persons intake to collect the necessary information to compare to the postmortem findings. As of March 2017, this information still has not been received, meaning the identification of these remains is completely stalled.

If antemortem information is available and consistent with the postmortem findings from a set of skeletal remains, the next step in the identification process is to have the identification legally recognized by the appropriate justice of the peace who has jurisdiction over the remains. Anthropologists at OpID help facilitate this process by synthesizing all information regarding both the missing persons and unidentified persons investigations and comparing all antemortem and postmortem information into a single identification report that is then given to the justice of the peace for their consideration and, should they agree, their signature. However, as aforementioned, justices of the peace have many responsibilities beyond these cases, responsibilities that often involve legal disputes among the living and therefore require more immediate attention. Emails sent and voicemails left can and do go months without response. It is only once an identification is approved by a justice of the peace that the repatriation process begins.

## The Limbo of Repatriation

Theoretically the repatriation of human remains that have been identified is a straightforward process. For remains that are not being investigated by a medical examiner, a justice of the peace signs paperwork legally recognizing the identification, the name is changed on the death certificate, and then the remains are sent back to the individual's home country. The reality on the ground, however, is much less straightforward as it requires the coordinated efforts of family of the deceased, one or more consulate's offices, potentially multiple funeral homes (one handling repatriation, the one that filed the original death certificate), Vital Statistics, and justices of the peace.

One of the first steps in the repatriation process is for the family of the deceased to work with the consular office to select a funeral home to handle the repatriation of their loved one. Often there are many surviving family members making this decision; in a time of grief, this decision is not always easy, and differing opinions can cause delay. In one case, family members of a deceased woman from Mexico disagreed over the funeral home they wanted to repatriate their loved one, resulting in a nearly 2-month break in the process.

Once a funeral home is selected, it is responsible for working to get the name changed on the original death certificate, which would have simply documented "Unknown Remains" along with the date they were recovered. This process requires submission of a death certificate amendment form to the Texas Health and Human

Services Vital Statistics Unit. Part of this form needs to be completed by the funeral home that filed the original death certificate, which is often different from the funeral home handling the repatriation. For the cases exhumed from Brooks County, all of the original death certificates were filed by the private funeral home in South Texas that provided the original "investigation" of the remains. Unfortunately, the funeral home industry is a business, and this funeral home charges $300 to simply fill out part of this form. The cost of this service can cause disagreement between funeral homes and, in turn, egregious delays.

For example, in early July 2012, the family of an El Salvadoran man was contacted by a smuggler, or "coyote," notifying them that their loved one had been left behind in the desert scrub of Brooks County. Three days later, the remains of this individual were found but had begun to decompose and were not visually identifiable. The remains were then transferred to the funeral home in South Texas where no scientific investigation was conducted and no DNA sample was taken. The remains were eventually buried as "unidentified" in Sacred Heart Cemetery. In September 2012, the family of the deceased contacted what is now the Colibrí Center for Human Rights to file a missing persons report. Four days later, a missing persons case was created in the National Missing and Unidentified Persons System (NamUs). A family reference DNA sample was collected by the EAAF in El Salvador in October 2012 and submitted to a private DNA lab not under the jurisdiction of the FBI.

The remains of the individual were exhumed from Sacred Heart in May 2013 by Baylor University and transferred to OpID in June 2013 along with 56 other cases. The remains were analyzed, and an anthropology report was written in March. By June 2014, an unidentified persons case had been created in NamUs. That July, DNA samples from the unidentified remains were submitted to UNTCHI for CODIS inclusion, but a sample was also sent to the private DNA lab based on an identification hypothesis based on personal effects listed in the NamUs missing persons report and the clothing found with the remains. The following August a genetic match report was generated by the private DNA lab, suggesting an association between the family reference samples collected by the EAAF and the unidentified remains sample submitted by OpID.

In September 2014, a report was jointly written by Colibrí, OpID, the EAAF, and Baylor University detailing all of the facts of the case, comparing all antemortem and postmortem information and critically analyzing the genetic results. The report petitioned the justice of the peace to recognize the identification of this young El Salvadoran man. Seven months later, in April 2015, the justice of the peace signed the paperwork legally recognizing the identification. The family and the consulate's office selected a funeral home in Houston, TX, to handle the repatriation of the remains, and in June 2015, the remains were released to the funeral home to await repatriation. As of the writing of this chapter in March 2017, those remains are unfortunately still sitting at the funeral home in Houston, more than 2 years after they were identified and nearly 5 years since their family members lost their loved one.

The proximate cause for this significant and unfortunate delay was, and still is, changing the name on the death certificate to recognize the identity of this El

Salvadoran man. The funeral home in Houston attempted, without collaborating with the funeral home that filed the original death certificate, to submit an application to amend the death certificate to Vital Statistics. Multiple interviews with this funeral home clarified that their application was rejected because they were told it "required too many changes" and that, rather than use the standard application to amend, they needed a court order to mandate the changes of the death certificate. The funeral home next contacted the justice of the peace who had jurisdiction over the remains, but the justice of the peace informed them they did not have the power to produce a court order. The funeral home then sought advice from Vital Statistics on "how a court order works" but claims they were given no clear direction other than to talk to the justice of the peace. The funeral home reportedly asked for further assistance from the justice of the peace but none was received, unfortunately leading to a complete stagnation of the repatriation process for more than a year. When anthropologists at OpID became aware of this situation, they reached out to the funeral home that filed the original death certificate and were assured they were willing to help with the paperwork and had had success in changing previous death certificates, but the funeral home handling the repatriation had to contact them and be willing to pay the $300 fee. This information was relayed to the funeral home in Houston, who assured us multiple times they would contact the funeral home in South Texas, but as of this writing, no contact has been initiated. Anthropologists further appealed to the El Salvadoran consulate to pressure the funeral home to make contact, but with other pressing matters regarding their citizens in this country who are still alive, it doesn't appear any action has been taken.

This case is an unfortunate example of how, without a clear understanding of the processes required by the key players involved, repatriation of individuals already identified can stall. If representatives for all institutions could be brought together and sit in a single room to discuss cases such as these, undoubtedly progress would be made. The hundreds of miles that separate all involved make this impractical, however. Beyond a lack of understanding, there is also the issue that many agencies, such as the justices of the peace and consular offices, have a general lack of resources, both in time and money, to address these issues with their full attention.

## Breaking Out of Limbo

As OpID moves forward with the work of migrant identification, we continuously seek opportunities to advocate for changes that will streamline the process and reduce the chances of unidentified individuals waiting in limbo. One of these steps is participating in searches in the South Texas desert to help recover the unidentified. Recognizing that many individuals who die in Brooks County are likely not found, in 2014, Sheriff Benny Martinez requested assistance from the Texas State Guard in conducting monthly search and recovery operations which have resulted in the recovery of several sets of remains that otherwise might not have been found. However, because the State Guard is a branch of the Texas Military Forces, some ranch owners are reluctant to allow them onto their property. At the request of the Brooks County Sheriff's Office, OpID staff and volunteers began to conduct searches with a sheriff's deputy in the fall of 2016. Not only could these smaller groups of individuals from an academic setting get access to some ranches that the State Guard wasn't granted, we are also trained in skeletal identification, particularly human versus nonhuman, which is a valuable skill in the field. The county has also received funds from the state to help pay for autopsies of unidentified remains found in Brooks. Since fall of 2013, the county has contracted with the Webb County Medical Examiner's Office who provides investigative services and DNA sampling for these recently found cases, helping the county be in compliance with the TCCP.

Efforts have also been taken to enhance exhumation efforts for those unidentified persons who were buried in years past without proper investigative efforts taken at their time of discovery. The exhumation efforts of 2013, 2014, and 2017 were largely volunteer based and without any sponsored funding. This was possible, in large part, thanks to the strong relationships anthropologists have fostered with local law enforcement, NGOs, and citizens of Brooks County. However, since it takes years to establish these relationships, this isn't a sustainable model in moving forward with exhumations in other counties that have buried presumed migrants without identification efforts. To address this, OpID staff recently applied for and were awarded funding through the American Academy of Forensic Sciences Humanitarian and Human Rights Resource Council to fund exhumations in counties other than Brooks for the first time.

While progress has been continuously made at OpID, from its inception until 2016, all efforts in working on these cases were 100% voluntary. Recognizing that this problem was not going away, in 2015, the director of OpID applied for funding through a private foundation as well as the governor's office and received funds enough to hire a full-time postdoctoral associate to manage the project, as well as one full- and one part-time laboratory technician to provide more concentrated efforts. The development of this small but dedicated staff resulted in nearly tripling efforts of case analysis and DNA submission over the previous 3 years. Unfortunately, funding for 2017 has not been renewed at the same level, and moving forward efforts will once again be mostly voluntary.

Operation Identification has also worked on developing and fostering unique collaborations with several NGOs within and outside of Texas to help hasten the identification and repatriation processes. A case study of a recently identified Ecuadoran woman illustrates these collaborations well. Among the clothing and other personal effects for this case was an envelope with a name written on the outside. Inside the envelope was a piece of paper, on one side a child's drawing with the same name as on the envelope and on the other side a hand-written prayer, in Spanish, to Saint Michael the Archangel which specifically mentions Ecuador. A simple Internet search for the name yielded a missing persons flyer for an Ecuadoran woman in her late 20s who had gone missing in Brooks County, TX, and also contact information for the family if anyone had information.

Analysis of the skeletal remains revealed that they belonged to a young woman, in her 20s or 30s, but interestingly had no teeth and wore a full set of dentures. Per

Texas law, a DNA sample was sent to the University of North Texas, but no genetic associations were made in the CODIS database. Anthropologists at OpID reached out to the South Texas Human Rights Center and asked that they make contact with the family of the individual depicted in the missing persons flyer and specifically ask if their loved one, despite being young, wore dentures. After making contact with the family, it was confirmed to the STHRC that indeed the young woman had a full set of dentures. This established a very strong identification hypothesis that needed to be confirmed through genetic analyses.

From talking with the family, the STRHC learned that parents and a child of the missing woman were still living in Ecuador but that several siblings lived in the Northeast United States. Either of these sets of relatives would be suitable for submitting family reference DNA samples – the question then became who would collect the samples and where would they be analyzed. Through NGO contact with the family, it was decided that the family would prefer to not have their genetic material in a database operated by the US government, if an alternative was available. Anthropologists with OpID then began working with the Argentine Forensic Anthropology Team to move this case forward through a private DNA lab.

The Argentine team spoke with the family and conducted a full missing persons intake, and it was decided that team members from the office in New York City would travel to the family and collect DNA samples. These samples were sent to the private DNA lab, along with a sample from the skeletal remains, all of which was paid for by the Argentine Team and their Border Project. A 2-week turnaround was requested for the analysis, and 2 weeks later, genetics confirmed that the remains in OpIDs lab were those of the young Ecuadoran woman. It is only through such unique collaborations with NGOs that this case was able to be moved forward so quickly, especially when an identification through the federal DNA system had not been made.

Our collaboration with the STHRC has also proven invaluable in other areas. As the STHRC is located in Brooks County, they serve as a convenient partner on the ground who can speak to county officials, law enforcement agents, and justices of the peace and, importantly, get documents signed. The STHRC has also helped facilitate meetings with state lawmakers to streamline the repatriation process. Recently the STHRC was able to meet with members of the state legislature to discuss delays in getting name changed on death certificates which in turn were causing delays on repatriation. These lawmakers were able to set up a meeting between the head of Vital Statistics and Dr. Kate Spradley where she was able to elaborate on these difficulties. This has led to an agreement between Vital Statistics and key stakeholders who are working on migrant identifications and repatriations, wherein Vital Statistics will now handle these cases in a direct and expedited manner, rather than simply putting them in the queue with all instances where a death certificate needs to be amended.

Overall, due to the decentralized nature of investigations in Texas, there are many complexities in the identification and repatriation of migrant remains. However, through unique collaborations with local and international NGOs, these cases are moving forward. The unidentified remains of presumed migrants are being found, exhumed, and analyzed quicker now than they were in the past. Furthermore, identifications are being made, and the processes required for repatriation have been simplified, which should allow more individuals to be returned home to their loved ones and laid to rest in accordance with the wishes of their family.

## References

Frey, J. C. (2015). Graves of shame. Texas Observer. https://www.texasobserver.org/illegal-mass-graves-of-migrant-remains-found-in-south-texas/. Accessed 12 Oct 2016.

Gocha, T. P., Spradley, M. K., Strand, R. M., Anderson, B. E., Lusiardo A. (2017). *The role of the anthropologist in the identification and repatriation of deceased migrants along the US-Mexico border*. Presentation at the 69th annual scientific meeting of the American Academy of Forensic Sciences, New Orleans.

Justice of the Peace. (2017). Texas association of counties. https://county.org/texas-county-government/texas-county-officials/Pages/Justice-of-the-Peace.aspx. Accessed 10 Feb 2017.

Spradley, M. K., Hamilton, M. D., & Giordano, A. (2012). Spatial patterning of vulture scavenged human remains. *Forensic Science International, 219*, 57–63.

Spradley, M. K., Reineke, R. C., Doretti, M., Anderson, B. E. (2016). *Death along the United States-Mexico border: A comparative view of policy and practice in Arizona and Texas*. Presentation at the 68th annual scientific meeting of the American Academy of Forensic Sciences, Las Vegas.

Srikrishnan, M., & Hennessy-Fiske, M. (2014). Mass graves of unidentified migrants found in South Texas. Los Angeles Times. http://www.latimes.com/nation/nationnow/la-na-nn-texas-immigrant-graves-20140621-story.html. Accessed 16 Mar 2017.

United States Border Patrol. (2017). U.S. Border Patrol Fiscal Year Southwest border sector deaths. https://www.cbp.gov/sites/default/files/assets/documents/2016-Oct/BP%20Southwest%20Border%20Sector%20Deaths%20FY1998%20-%20FY2016.pdf. Accessed 3 Mar 2017.

# Chapter 12
# Dialog Across States and Agencies: Juggling Ethical Concerns of Forensic Anthropologists North of the US-Mexico Border

**Cate E. Bird and Justin Maiers**

...assigning an identity to a corpse, beyond its worth in humanitarian and legal terms, has a multiplier effect on the entire process. (Fondebrider 2015: 40)

## Introduction

Ethics in forensic science are typically discussed in terms of methodological standards for data collection and interpretation. As expert witnesses, it is our duty to operate with high standards of honesty and professional conduct, avoiding bias, falsification of data/results, and misrepresentation of qualifications. However, the technical and scientific conjuring of "ethics" in our field, with a reliance on methods and clinical distancing of bias, neglects our roles as agents who contribute to specific narratives of the dead. As forensic anthropologists, it is our duty to address ethical concerns regarding identification of unknown decedents, especially when the deceased are believed to come from vulnerable populations. Through a review of unidentified decedents in domestic casework (Bird 2015), it is gravely apparent that persons who die in the United States and remain nameless in death frequently come from the most marginalized groups in society. This includes those whose legal standing is in question, those with lower socioeconomic status, those who lack a cohesive group affiliation, and those with transient or semi-transient lifestyles.

C.E. Bird (✉)
Forensic National Advisor, International Committee of the Red Cross, Republic of Georgia, Tampa, FL, USA,
e-mail: Cate.Bird1@gmail.com

J. Maiers
Human Identification Center, University of Indianapolis, Indianapolis, IN, USA
e-mail: maiersj@uindy.edu



K.E. Latham, A.J. O'Daniel (eds.), *Sociopolitics of Migrant Death and Repatriation*, Bioarchaeology and Social Theory,
DOI 10.1007/978-3-319-61866-1_12

These individuals frequently lack representation and the socioeconomic capital to advocate on their behalf and are frequently stigmatized in society.

Identification of unknown decedents in domestic and international casework serves multiple purposes, including legal and humanitarian goals. In the United States, personal identification of decedents is frequently emphasized for legal reasons (Crossland and Joyce 2015); in particular, it is important to confirm the death of an individual with the State in order to file vital statistics (i.e., death certificate) and to settle legal matters related to wills, inheritance, and insurance policies (Christensen et al. 2014). While these legal functions of identification are important to State functions, identifying unknown decedents also serves humanitarian functions by bringing resolution (although not necessarily closure) to families and friends through naming the deceased, repatriating remains, and permitting proper burial rituals (Juhl and Olsen 2006). Additionally, it is in the interest of public health and safety to identify individuals who are susceptible to particular causes of death (e.g., exposure) in order to mitigate further deaths. However, difficulty arises when there is no tentative name (or name association) for a decedent. The problem of *truly* unknown decedents has beset southern Arizona since 2000, where nearly 900 decedents believed to be foreign nationals remain unidentified.

Identification of truly unknown decedents is rarely the result of one dedicated forensic scientist. Rather, personal identification is frequently the result of a complex process involving investigators, scientists, law enforcement, and/or victim advocates who can each contribute a unique piece to a complicated puzzle. These multiple actors may hold dear their vested interests and distinct approaches, but identification of unknown decedents has a better chance of being resolved when these actors set aside their individual interests and collaborate for a common goal. This collaborative approach is exemplified by an interagency meeting held weekly at the Pima County Office of the Medical Examiner (PCOME). This meeting creates a dialogue among forensic scientists, foreign consulates, US Border Patrol agents, and a nongovernmental organization at the PCOME in order to maximize the potential to identify unknown deceased migrants who die while clandestinely crossing the Arizona desert.

## Background

The Pima County Office of the Medical Examiner (PCOME) located in Tucson, Arizona, serves as the Medical Examiner for three counties in southern Arizona bordering the US-Mexico border (i.e., Pima, Cochise, and Santa Cruz counties) and performs examinations as requested for eight additional counties in Arizona (Fig. 12.1). As such, the PCOME experiences a high case load. In 2015, the PCOME processed 3,171 reported deaths from 11 counties, the majority of which (76.9%) arose from Pima County (PCOME 2015). Pursuant to Arizona Revised Statute §11–593, the PCOME investigates any death within their jurisdiction that is sudden, violent, and unexpected or in which the cause of death is unknown. The PCOME

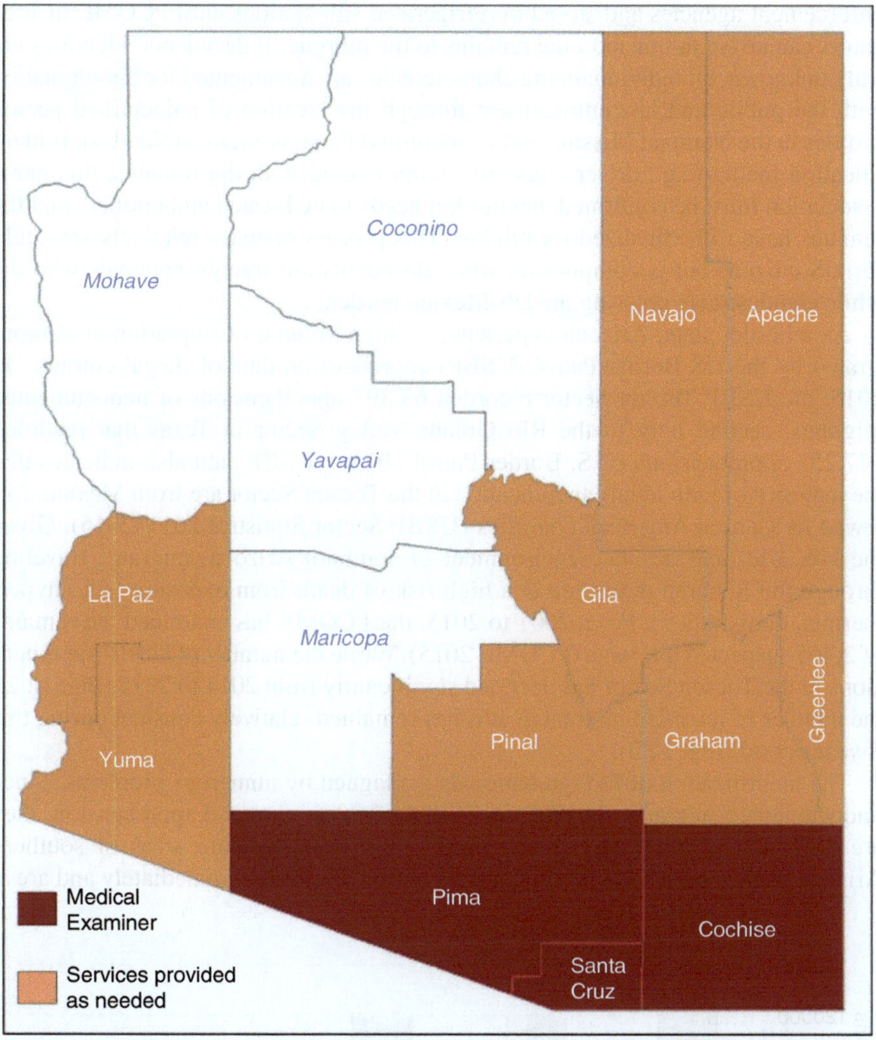


**Fig. 12.1** Map of Arizona counties with counties served by the PCOME highlighted in *red*

also pursues identification of unknown decedents, although this is not a legal obligation of medical examiner offices in the state of Arizona.

From a medicolegal perspective, the processing of unidentified remains is comprised of several major parts, beginning with the discovery of remains and ending with the release of remains for final disposition. In southern Arizona, once human remains are discovered and found to fall under the jurisdiction of the medical examiner, they are recovered and transferred to the morgue facility for postmortem examination. Due to the extensive area that falls under the jurisdiction of the PCOME, decedent remains found in remote areas are frequently recovered by local law enforcement agencies and stored in refrigerated sub-stations until PCOME investigators can arrive to transport the remains to the morgue. If decedents' identities are truly unknown, all individualizing characteristics are documented for dissemination with the public and law enforcement through the creation of unidentified person profiles in the National Missing and Unidentified Persons System (NamUs). If identification media (e.g., driver's license) is discovered with the remains, this name association must be confirmed, next of kin needs to be located and notified, and the remains have to be finalized for release. This process operates relatively smoothly for US citizens but is complicated when decedents are foreign nationals who die while clandestinely crossing the US-Mexico border.

As a border state, Arizona experiences a high volume of migration as demonstrated by the US Border Patrol (USBP) apprehension data of illegal entrants. In 2015, the USBP Tucson Sector recorded 63,397 apprehensions of undocumented migrants, second only to the Rio Grande Valley Sector in Texas that recorded 147,257 apprehensions (U.S. Border Patrol 2015a). USBP data also indicates that the majority of individuals apprehended in the Tucson Sector are from Mexico, followed by Central American countries (USBP Sector Statistics 2011–2015). Given the hot, arid, and desolate environment of southern Arizona, migrants traveling through the Sonoran desert are at a high risk of death from exposure (e.g., hyperthermia, dehydration). From 2001 to 2015, the PCOME has examined the remains of 2,465 suspected migrants (PCOME 2015). While the number of USBP apprehensions in the Tucson Sector has declined significantly from 2011 to 2015 (Fig. 12.2), the number of recorded migrant deaths has remained relatively constant during this 5-year period (Fig. 12.3).

The identification of foreign nationals is plagued by numerous problems. Since undocumented migrants are attempting to avoid detection and apprehension, they are trafficked by foot through the most remote and desolate areas of southern Arizona. If they perish, their remains may not be discovered immediately and are at

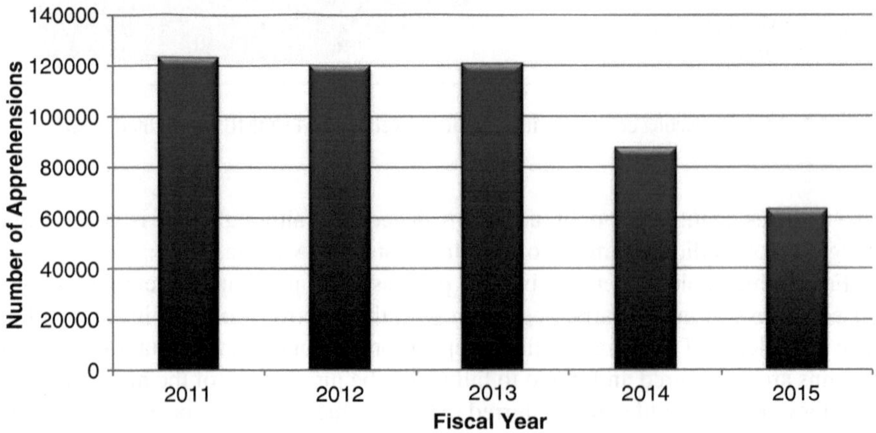


**Fig. 12.2** Apprehension of illegal entrants in the USBP Tucson Sector from 2011 to 2015

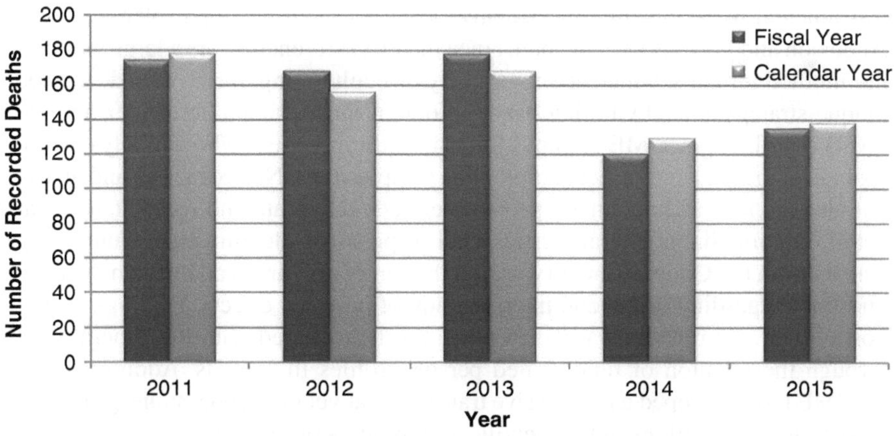


**Fig. 12.3** Recorded death of suspected migrants at the PCOME from 2011 to 2015

risk of advanced rates of decomposition associated with the open air desert environments. In 2015, approximately 86% of migrant remains were noted as decomposed, mummified, or skeletonized (PCOME 2015). As decomposition progresses, traditional identification techniques (e.g., visual recognition, fingerprint analysis, etc.) become impossible to employ as features are lost or obscured. If fingerprints are obtainable, there is no guarantee that they will be helpful for identification. While fingerprint analysis remains a primary method of identification for US citizens who frequently have antemortem fingerprint data in local, state, and national fingerprint databases, the same is not true of migrants, whose fingerprint submissions frequently result in failed or negative hits in US databases. Additional problems include the presence of animal scavengers that prey upon human remains in the open desert and can result in fragmented, incomplete, and scattered remains. Identification media is not consistently found with the remains of migrants, and even when present, it is unknown whether the name association is authentic since many migrants carry false forms of identification media. Furthermore, language and international barriers make communicating with next of kin incredibly difficult. Finally, identification of decedents only occurs when there is reliable antemortem data with which to compare. The "illegal" status of migrants can create havoc for families who are desperate to find their missing loved ones across national boundaries but are unsure of the process of submitting a missing person's report, are averse to approaching law enforcement for fear of deportation, or are turned away by law enforcement due to jurisdictional complications.

Despite these problems, the PCOME has developed a progressive strategy over the last decade to identify unknown migrant decedents who fall within their jurisdiction. First, they recognize that migrants who die while clandestinely crossing the US-Mexico border in southern Arizona are subject to greater risk of death via exposure to the desert environment. Categorizing these individuals as undocumented border crossers (UBCs) through the application of a biocultural profile has been instrumental in establishing investigative leads for identification (Soler et al. 2014; Anderson and Parks 2008). Second, since the PCOME encounters a large number of mummified remains, which are notoriously difficult to fingerprint, they developed a unique strategy for rehydrating hands to obtain fingerprints (Hernandez and Hess 2014). Third, the PCOME employs forensic anthropologists who not only construct biological profiles and resect/submit bone samples for DNA extraction and analysis but also launder and document personal effects, rehydrate and record tattoos, and detail individualizing characteristics vital to personal identification. Cultural specialists from the Colibrí Center (www.colibricenter.org) are available to help answer questions regarding origin and interpretation of personal effects. Findings from the postmortem examinations at the PCOME are then shared with the general public through the creation of unidentified person profiles in NamUs. Additionally, the PCOME has developed a progressive transnational yet grassroots strategy involving numerous organizations in the identification process of migrants.

## Collaboration

Since June 2015, the PCOME has hosted an interagency meeting to share information regarding missing and unidentified deceased migrants. Once a week, the PCOME invites representatives from governmental and nongovernmental agencies to their facility in Tucson, Arizona, to discuss the status of unidentified migrants, to view human remains and associated personal effects recovered during the week, to share information on missing persons, and to discuss investigative leads for identification. This collaboration includes personnel from the PCOME, the Colibrí Center for Human Rights, US Border Patrol, and foreign consulates, each of whom play an important role in the identification of migrants (Figs. 12.4 and 12.5).

**Fig. 12.4** Organizations participating in the interagency meeting to identify deceased migrants in southern Arizona

**Fig. 12.5** Participants in the weekly interagency meeting

As a governmental organization operating at a county level, the PCOME is responsible for (1) establishing the cause and manner of death of decedents and (2) establishing the identity of unknown decedents. In order to perform these tasks, the PCOME employs medicolegal death investigators, forensic pathologists, pathology assistants, and forensic anthropologists (in addition to administrative specialists). Personnel who collaborate during this weekly interagency meeting include investigators, anthropologists, and the morgue supervisor, responsible for sharing postmortem information regarding the decedent and associated personal effects with the other agencies. Human remains discovered during the week are shown to the agencies, as are all clothing and material culture found with the remains. Fingerprint cards and cell phone SIM cards are transferred to US Border Patrol agents for analysis.

The Colibrí Center for Human Rights represents a family advocacy organization dedicated to ending migrant deaths and suffering along the US-Mexico border. This innovative humanitarian organization originated as the Missing Migrant Project (2006) through the partnership of forensic anthropologist, Dr. Bruce Anderson, and cultural anthropologist, Dr. Robin Reineke. Expanding into a nonprofit in 2013, the Colibrí Center serves the vital role of collecting missing persons reports from families of migrants feared deceased while traveling across the US-Mexico border. Families are often more comfortable sharing sensitive information with Colibrí without fear of deportation because they are not affiliated with law enforcement. Antemortem data collected from families is collected in a manner that is directly comparable to postmortem data collected by forensic scientists at the PCOME. Currently, Colibrí maintains more than 2,500 missing person reports of migrants.

The US Border Patrol (USBP) represents an enforcement branch of the US Customs and Border Protection located within the Department of Homeland Security. Established in 1924, their primary mission is to secure US borders between ports of entry and "to detect and prevent the illegal entry of aliens into the United States" (U.S. Border Patrol 2015b). Primary duties of USBP agents include surveillance of border regions, tracking and apprehension of illegal entrants, and collecting intelligence regarding illegal activities (e.g., drug and human smuggling). In March 2016, the USBP formally established the Missing Migrant Initiative to serve as a point of contact for migrants in distress, to dispatch search and rescue teams, to take missing persons reports from migrants' families, and to assist in the identification of deceased migrants. As a collaborator in the interagency weekly meeting at the PCOME, USBP agents run postmortem fingerprints through their apprehension database. Positive fingerprint hits are more prevalent for deceased migrants in the USBP fingerprint database because foreign nationals are often apprehended during previous attempts to clandestinely cross the US-Mexico border. They also employ advanced technology to decrypt cell phones and SIM cards found with deceased migrants in order to provide investigative leads for PCOME medicolegal investigators.

Finally, representatives from several foreign consulates (i.e., Mexican, Salvadoran, Guatemalan, and Honduran Consulates) also attend the weekly interagency meeting at the PCOME. The consulates represent an invaluable piece of this collaboration by taking missing persons reports, maintaining contact and collecting antemortem DNA reference samples from family members in their home countries, paying for expedited 1:1 DNA comparisons when decedents have name associations, confirming next of kin, and helping to arrange repatriation of remains across international borders. The benefit of having the consulates involved in the weekly meeting is that they know exactly which cases have been recovered and can immediately pursue investigative leads, such as comparing decedent information to missing person's reports received from families in their home countries. This meeting also helps bypass bureaucratic delays by permitting direct and regular interaction of agencies and exchange of information in a personal forum.

Each invited agency holds a key piece to this complicated puzzle: the PCOME documents postmortem information from the deceased and disseminates this information for the purposes of identification; Colibrí serves as family advocates and collects missing persons reports in a manner easily comparable to postmortem data; USBP runs postmortem fingerprints through their apprehension database, provides investigative leads using decrypted information from cell phones, and collects missing persons reports; and foreign consulates collect missing persons reports and help expedite the identification process through collecting family reference samples and maintaining contact with next of kin in their home countries. This collaboration has proven invaluable in the identification of deceased migrants, but the process is not without its limitations and ethical issues.

## Discussion

One of the primary issues with including so many diverse parties in the identification process is that each comes with its own stakeholders. As forensic scientists working in a local governmental organization, we play a particular role and are bound by a code of behavior and objectives to the institution. As Luis Fondebrider has studiously observed, forensic experts who perform traditional casework on behalf of the State in domestic contexts are frequently viewed as allies who aid in the investigation, free of political, ethnic, or religious bias that helped create the problem (Fondebrider 2015). The PCOME's primary stakeholders are constituents of Pima, Santa Cruz, and Cochise Counties. While the PCOME is progressive in its approach to deceased migrants, this is not true of every medical examiner or coroner in border regions. Expenditure of resources, time, and expertise must be justified in line with the interests of the county. For example, if a decedent's fingerprints hit in a local fingerprint database to the identity of a foreign national, the county can contend it fulfilled its obligation to "identify" a decedent by listing a name on the death certificate, despite the fact that foreign nationals frequently use aliases when apprehended. The county medical examiner or coroner may choose to not pursue verification of the name by confirming next of kin in the foreign country. In cases such as these, any name regardless of its authenticity may be considered "good enough," especially if an investigator's time could be spent pursuing the identification of other decedents rather than reaching across international borders to find family of the deceased. Institutions control resources and appropriate labor, and those employed by institutions are beholden to the institution's objectives.

This puts anthropologists in a particularly precarious position because our training generally emphasizes an ethics of practice that examines the human condition with a commitment to relieving persistent suffering (Goodman and Leatherman 2001). While forensic anthropologists may state that they adhere to a program of objective science, void of subjectivity in the testing of hypotheses, this simple view of "reading" the bones ignores that the reporting and interpretation of biological information is inherently a political act (Goodman and Leatherman 2001). Forensic anthropologists are often required to make discretionary choices in their allotment of time, energy, and resources dedicated to particular cases. These value-laden choices manifest most notably in medicolegal settings where forensic scientists are faced with limited funding for investigative methods, limited womanpower to perform search and recovery of remains, and limited time to devote to individual cases. For instance, do homicides warrant greater devotion of time and detail than cases of motor vehicle accidents, given that homicides have a greater chance of being tried in a court of law? Should the death of a child receive more attention than the death of an elderly individual? When exhuming unidentified remains from a cemetery, is it better to exhume every grave with meticulous detail if it results in only 20 bodies receiving the chance at being identified, while 40 other bodies remain in the ground, unanalyzed? When partial remains are recovered, how does an anthropologist decide to continue a search for remains when the medical examiner or law enforcement is confident they have recovered enough of the body to establish identity of the decedent and cause and manner of death? When there is only enough money to test five cases for innovative methodologies, such as chemical isotopic analysis to produce identification leads, how does the forensic anthropologist select those 5 cases out of 100? Should forensic anthropologists take the wishes of living relatives of the dead into consideration, especially in cases where families or communities object to exhumations and/or destructive analyses?

Previous researchers (Crossland and Joyce 2015; Winburn 2015; Keenan 2014) have notably challenged the idealistic view of "pure objectivity" in forensic anthropology, maintaining that science is inherently a social process where scientists' values unwittingly affect the representations they create and their subsequent interpretations. To ignore the structural, political, and socioeconomic contexts in which forensic anthropologists are employed and for which they perform their duties is dangerous. We may attempt to mitigate unchecked bias through standard operating procedures, but it is amiss to not recognize our day-to-day bias. As noble as it is to believe that "the bones speak for themselves," they do not (Keenan 2014). Forensic anthropologists act as translators, rendering a particular narrative of a decedent's identity, life history, and death. Blakey (2001) calls on biological anthropologists to be humanistic and reflexive in their approach to science, considering politics and hidden assumptions embedded in their analyses. Scientific expertise is never practiced in a vacuum, and while we may aspire to "mitigated objectivity," we should never fool ourselves into believing we are not what we study: human.

As a nongovernmental organization, Colibrí's stakeholders are the families of missing migrants: these families share personal, sensitive, and sometimes incriminating information (e.g., names, immigration status, local addresses, etc.) with Colibrí in the hopes of identifying their missing loved one, with the assumption that the information they share is discretionary, will not be provided to enforcement agencies, and will not be used in a manner detrimental to the missing person or his or her family. In addition to family advocacy, one of Colibrí's primary stated objectives is policy reform through activism. Members of Colibrí have been vocal in their opposition to the militarization of the border and view the allocation of government resources for border surveillance and enforcement of immigration policies as contributing to the suffering of migrants and their families. And there is truth to these statements. The migrant humanitarian crisis occurring in southern Arizona during the last 15 years is the direct result of US federal policies that funnel migrants into the most arid, desolate, and dangerous parts of the border (Martínez et al. 2013). Numerous migrant advocacy groups view US Border Patrol and their agents as tools of the State that helped create and continue to perpetuate the migrant humanitarian crisis. Thus, collaborating with US Border Patrol to identify deceased migrants while simultaneously advocating on behalf of undocumented migrants and immigration reform can at times be a difficult line to skirt. Humanitarian organizations, such as Colibrí, must weigh the consequences of collaborating with government enforcers who could both help identify deceased migrants while putting their constituents (i.e., families of the deceased and the missing) in danger of deportation.

US Border Patrol agents who participate in this interagency meeting and in the Missing Migrant Initiative are also in a unique situation, acting simultaneously as enforcers of border security and as first responders for illegal entrants. The Tucson Sector Border Patrol allocates a significant number of resources to rescue migrants in distress, including creating a network of rescue beacons; establishing the Border Patrol Search, Trauma, and Rescue Unit (BORSTAR); employing 250 EMTs; and training over 4,000 agents as first responders (USBP 2015b). While initiating emergency search and rescue teams to assist injured or stranded migrants, border patrol agents are also responsible for apprehending migrants and processing them for deportation out of the United States. Furthermore, the interaction between nongovernmental and governmental organizations can be challenging when proprietary information must be shared. Residing under the US Department of Defense, Border Patrol agents have access to comprehensive biometric data and advanced technological tools to significantly aid in the identification of deceased migrants. To shun their assistance based on ideological disagreements may be unethical when provided the chance to actually identify a decedent and return his or her remains to their family. At the present, the PCOME and Colibrí are navigating their collaboration with Border Patrol cautiously. It is also important to recognize that while Border Patrol translates and enacts federal border enforcement policy, individual agents do not uniformly reproduce state surveillance and punitive forms of control. Some border patrol agents are Latino- or Latina-Americans, who are generally concerned about the lives of migrants and their families. Stated simply, the brutality of Prevention Through Deterrence unfolds alongside individual acts of care and concern for migrants. Like other "street-level bureaucrats" who interact with the public in service of the state (Lipsky 1980), border patrol officers have some discretion in how they go about their work.

One wonders if the identification process can ever truly be neutral, given the State structure in which it is embedded. As anthropologists, we understand the tribulations of this sometimes sticky interagency alliance when the diverse parties have conflicting vested interests. At times, the confluence of agencies with different institutional objectives, different stakeholders, and different approaches may create seemingly impassable obstacles. Conflict does exist among this partnership. But in this particular case, these agencies have managed to overlook their differences and continue coming to the table with the common goal of identifying unknown decedents through shared resources and knowledge. The case of identifying foreign nationals along the US-Mexico border through dialogue across agencies and States is rather unique in the United States. The interagency meeting at PCOME has worked because individuals from diverse agencies are devoted to a common goal. The PCOME's model of bringing together disparate agencies represents an exceptional adaptation to the problem of identification of unknown decedents in domestic medicolegal casework. Other medical examiner and coroner offices in the United States would benefit from adopting this progressive model of incorporating non-forensic agencies into the identification process in order to identify unknown decedents from vulnerable populations, especially when identification is not possible through traditional medicolegal channels.

## References

Anderson, B. E., & Parks, B. O. (2008). Symposium on border crossing deaths: Introduction. *Journal of Forensic Science, 53*(1), 6–7.

Bird, C. E. (2015). *Bodies without representation: Invisible communities and problems of identification in domestic casework*. Presentation at the 2nd disasters, displacement, and human rights conference. Knoxville.

Blakey, M. L. (2001). Beyond European enlightenment: Toward a critical and humanistic human biology. In A. H. Goodman & T. L. Leatherman (Eds.), *Building a new biocultural synthesis: Political economic perspectives on human biology* (2nd ed., pp. 379–405). Ann Arbor: The University of Michigan Press.

Christensen, A. M., Passalacqua, N. V., & Bartelink, E. J. (2014). *Forensic anthropology: Current methods and practice*. San Diego: Academic.

Crossland, Z., & Joyce, R. A. (2015). Anthropological perspectives on disturbing bodies: An introduction. In Z. Crossland & R. A. Joyce (Eds.), *Disturbing bodies: Perspectives on forensic anthropology* (pp. 3–27). Santa Fe: School for Advanced Research Press.

Fondebrider, L. (2015). Forensic anthropology and the investigation of political violence: Notes from the field. In Z. Crossland & R. A. Joyce (Eds.), *Disturbing bodies: Perspectives on forensic anthropology* (pp. 29–40). Santa Fe: School for Advanced Research Press.

Goodman, A. H., & Leatherman, T. L. (2001). Traversing the chasm between biology and culture: An introduction. In A. H. Goodman & T. L. Leatherman (Eds.), *Building a new biocultural synthesis: Political economic perspectives on human biology* (2nd ed., pp. 3–41). Ann Arbor: The University of Michigan Press.

Hernandez, G., & Hess, G. L. (2014). Rehydrating mummified hands: The Pima county experience. *Academic Forensic Pathology, 4*(1), 114–117.

Juhl, K., & Olsen, O. E. (2006). Societal safety, archaeology and the investigation of contemporary mass graves. *Journal of Genocide Research, 8*(4), 411–435.

Keenan, T. (2014). Getting the dead to tell me what happened: Justice, prosopopoeia, and forensic afterlives. In A. Franke & E. Weizman (Eds.), *Forensis: The architecture of public truth* (pp. 35–55). Berlin: Sternberg Press.

Lipsky, M. (1980). Street-level bureaucracy: The critical role of street-level bureaucrats. In P. Hupe & M. Hill (Eds.), *Classics of public administration* (pp. 414–422). New York: Russel Sage Foundation.

Martinez, D. E., Reineke, R., Rubio-Goldsmith, R., Anderson, B. E., Hess, G. L., Parks, B. O. (2013). A continued humanitarian crisis at the border: Undocumented border crosser deaths recorded by the Pima County Office of the Medical Examiner, 1990–2012. Pima County Office of the Medical Examiner. (2015). Annual report. http://webcms.pima.gov/government/medical_examiner/.

Missing Migrant Project. 2006. http://www.colibricenter.org/.

Pima County Office of the Medical Examiner. 2015. Annual Report.

Soler, A., Reineke, R. C., Beatrice, J. S., Anderson, B. E. (2014). *An integrated approach to the identification of human remains: The biocultural profile of undocumented migrants*. Proceedings of the 66th annual scientific meeting of the American Academy of Forensic Sciences, Seattle.

U.S. Border Patrol. 2015a. Along U.S. Borders. https://www.cbp.gov/border-security/along-us-borders.

U.S. Border Patrol. (2015b). *Border patrol agents train to save lives*. https://www.cbp.gov/newsroom/local-media-release/border-patrol-agentstrain-save-lives.

Winburn, A. P. (2015) *Subjective with a capital "S"? Issues of objectivity in forensic anthropology*. Proceedings of the 67th annual scientific meeting of the American Academy of Forensic Sciences, Orlando.

# Chapter 13
# Charting Future Directions

**Krista E. Latham and Alyson J. O'Daniel**

The work of migrant identification and repatriation will continue as a grassroots effort for the foreseeable future. In Texas, there are plans to conduct exhumations in multiple counties, as organized by the Forensic Border Coalition (FBC). The FBC consists of members of the Colibrí Center for Human Rights, the Argentine Forensic Anthropology Team (EAAF), Operation Identification, the South Texas Human Rights Center, and cultural anthropologist Dr. Christine Kovic. Created in 2013, the FBC has undertaken a Cemetery Survey Project with the goal of surveying cemeteries across Texas that are believed to contain the remains of unidentified migrants. This will allow for documentation of where exhumation efforts need to occur, with the first of such concentrated exhumation efforts occurring in 2017 in Starr County. The FBC's formation and work is novel in that it allows multiple stakeholders to explicitly position themselves as advocates within the political, social, and scientific landscapes of migrant identification. They address policy and procedural issues as a collaborative effort. For example, the FBC is currently working toward development of best practices in regard to the migrant identification crisis in the Texas Borderlands. A complicating factor, perhaps, is that the work of migrant identification will continue to rely on extra-local volunteers, like the forensic team from the University of Indianapolis, until funding and additional resources are made available. As a community of scholars, advocates, and humanitarian actors invested in the meanings and practicalities of our work, we eagerly anticipate discussion of the lessons and realities of coalition building in this context.

K.E. Latham (✉)
Biology & Anthropology Departments, University of Indianapolis, Indianapolis, IN, USA
e-mail: lathamke@uindy.edu

A.J. O'Daniel
Anthropology Department, University of Indianapolis, Indianapolis, IN, USA
e-mail: odaniela@uindy.edu

 
K.E. Latham, A.J. O'Daniel (eds.), *Sociopolitics of Migrant Death and Repatriation*, Bioarchaeology and Social Theory,
DOI 10.1007/978-3-319-61866-1_13

As we continue the work to identify and repatriate migrants, we observe the complexities of operating within the current system and are just beginning to unravel the dynamic pathways articulating forensic science, global histories, and processes of culture. We should consider how we might use the lessons of this volume as we move into the future of this work. We must reflect upon what we are to do with an understanding of ourselves as situated within broader processes of global capitalism and local social life. While we know there are no easy answers to these questions, we suggest heightened attention to contingencies of the work.

As we move forward in our varied responses to migrant death in the border region, we must remind ourselves of ways in which historically driven political and economic contexts simultaneously shape, constrain, and enable our work. We are thus not "just" doing our jobs in novel contexts; rather, our jobs are perhaps (re) constructed in historically and culturally specific sets of interacting processes and social relationships. As various chapters in this volume suggest, we must be aware of who various stakeholders in this process might be, including families of the missing (see Chaps. 2, 4, and 5, this volume), Border Patrol (see Chaps. 6 and 12, this volume), local medicolegal authorities and offices (see Chap. 11, this volume), scientific experts (see Chaps. 8, 9, and 10, this volume), and local community members within border counties. The fomentation of these varied stakeholders around key issues of migrant death reflects their operation within the broader historical context of economic globalization, racial division, state sovereignty, and the forms of privilege and disadvantage these processes engender (see Chaps. 3 and 7, this volume). Migrant death and identification is thus in some ways a window onto pressing social issues of our times. As mediators of the identification process, we become actors in politically charged and ethically uncharted terrains. Will the exhumation and identification process bring the families of the missing closure or will it add to an already stressful and painful time? How can we better understand the sociopolitical operations of governmental agencies like Border Patrol and how might that allow us to better understand the ways in which they distribute their resources and efforts? How might we approach the medicolegal resources of a community in a way that allows for greater attention to the unidentified migrants without taking away from their own community members?

We recognize that with this volume, we are just beginning to visualize the ways in which thinking sociopolitically can influence the work of forensic scientists in the borderlands. At this point, we thus have more questions than answers. We propose that such questions can and should be asked as a way to move forward. For example, we must carefully think through what enables volunteer forensic scientists to engage with humanitarian work. How do our respective institutions support and/or constrain our efforts? In what ways do our disciplines, our departments, and our employers recognize this work, and how do the specific forms of recognition granted shape the way we go about our work? Stated otherwise, how can we leverage our professional resources and networks to create/sustain greater methodological and ethical integrity?

We must also be mindful of the impact of media attention. The majority of media attention during the field seasons focuses generally on the local communities and what the work means for local residents. In this sense, the media illuminate a pathway forward. In other words, we need to more carefully look at what migrant death means on the US side of the border. We must consider how our presence, our advocacy, and the attention we draw affect local communities. However, given the paucity of resources at our disposal, we must reflect on ways to utilize media outlets to bring attention to the crisis and potentially garner material support. We must find ways to balance the release of sensitive information that might offend families of the missing, with the release of information that would grab the attention of a national audience. How can we best work with media outlets to bring awareness to this crisis while not exploiting or sensationalizing the deaths? How can we educate the media about the scientific process so they report factual information? Are there ways in which media attention can be used to acquire resources for the work as well as for the local community?

Finally, we must continue to pay sustained attention to how forensic scientists may use their positions of authority to facilitate building of collaborative knowledge that involves multiple positioned stakeholders. The current models in Texas and Arizona both utilize a grassroots effort to mobilize a multifaceted approach to identification. They utilize the strengths of multiple experts and emphasize the need for collaborations to navigate the complexities of migrant identification. However, the Arizona model is inherently different due to the centralized identification efforts of the medical examiner system. The organization of such efforts in Texas, if replication is desired, will take time, patience, and determination. Additionally, we must consider how securing funding from varied sources may reshape what perhaps began as grassroots efforts into perhaps bureaucratized or institutionally minded structures. While funding is essential to the identification process, we must consider the trade-offs that will automatically occur if certain funding bodies were to take initiative in these efforts.

By delving into under-discussed sociopolitical terrains of volunteer forensic science in contexts of migrant death, this volume has expanded the field of vision currently used to make sense of forensic science practiced in the border region. Seeking to interrogate the common filters of humanitarian sentiment, scientific neutrality, and state neglect, contributing authors illuminate the "compassionate response" to migrant death as politically fraught and power laden within global contexts of neoliberal capitalist expansion and the concomitant ascendance of volunteerism as the preferred response to social crises. It is our hope that authors' willingness to engage with the sometimes intellectually destabilizing work of critical analysis will lead to further humanitarian and research innovation. It is through the development of a contextually rich, multifaceted understanding of contemporary forensic scientific practice that we learn to effectively navigate the sociopolitics of migrant death.

# Index





K.E. Latham, A.J. O'Daniel (eds.), *Sociopolitics of Migrant Death and Repatriation*, Bioarchaeology and Social Theory,
DOI 10.1007/978-3-319-61866-1

MIX
Papier aus verantwortungsvollen Quellen
Paper from responsible sources
FSC® C105338

If you have any concerns about our products,
you can contact us on
**ProductSafety@springernature.com**

In case Publisher is established outside the EU,
the EU authorized representative is:
**Springer Nature Customer Service Center GmbH**
**Europaplatz 3, 69115 Heidelberg, Germany**

Printed by Libri Plureos GmbH
in Hamburg, Germany